THE
MARLOW
BRANCH

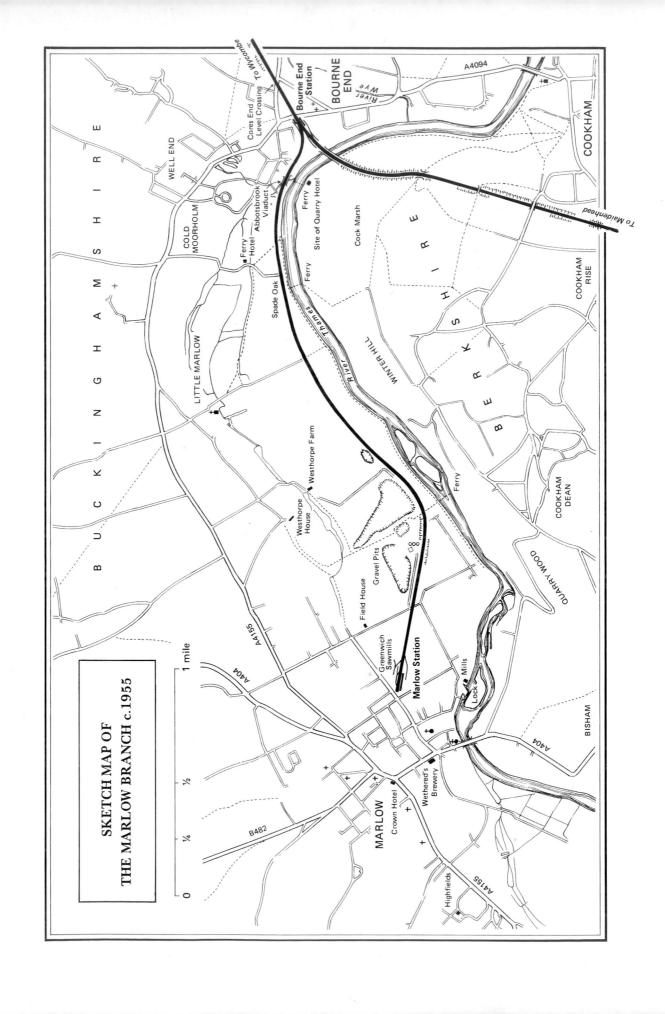

SKETCH MAP OF
THE MARLOW BRANCH c.1955

1 mile   ½   ¼   0

BUCKINGHAMSHIRE

BERKSHIRE

WELL END

COLD
MOORHOLM

LITTLE MARLOW

To Wycombe

Cores End
Level Crossing

Abbotsbrook
Viaduct

Ferry
Hotel

Ferry

Ferry

Spade Oak

River Thames

River Thames

Westhorpe Farm

Westhorpe
House

Field House

Gravel Pits

Greenwich
Sawmills

Marlow Station

MARLOW

Crown Hotel

Wethered's
Brewery

B482

A4155

A404

A4155

Highfields

Lock

Mills

BISHAM

A404

QUARRY WOOD

COOKHAM
DEAN

COOKHAM
RISE

COOKHAM

To Maidenhead

A4094

River Wye

BOURNE
END

Bourne End
Station

Site of Quarry Hotel

Cock Marsh

WINTER HILL

Ferry

THE
MARLOW
BRANCH

PAUL KARAU & CHRIS TURNER

WILD SWAN PUBLICATIONS LTD.

© Wild Swan Publications Ltd. and Paul Karau & Chris Turner
ISBN 0 906867 54 1

FOR
JAMES VENN

Designed by Paul Karau
Typesetting by Berkshire Publishing Services
Printed by Oxford University Press

Published by
WILD SWAN PUBLICATIONS LTD.
1-3 Hagbourne Road, Didcot, Oxon OX11 8DP

CONTENTS

No. 1421 leaving Marlow with the 11.45 a.m. on Sunday, 25th September 1960.

M. F. Yarwood

FOREWORD

Like every community, great or small, Marlow seems always to have had a burning issue. In the 1820s it was the parish church: badly damaged by flood water from the Thames, had it better be raised or razed? (It was razed and rebuilt.) At the present time it is the multi-storey car park: does Marlow really need one? But in the 1860s, while a separate controversy raged over gas rates for street lighting, it was 'Are we to have a railway?'.

Not everyone was in favour. To Mr. and Mrs. S. C. Hall, authors of *The Book of the Thames*, which appeared in 1859, the absence of a railway was a positive advantage. 'Marlow is a quiet town', they wrote, 'and has the recommendation of being not very close to a railroad'. But the majority of the townspeople disagreed. The town was *too* quiet, trade was languishing, a rail link would help restore Marlow's prosperity.

A group of local businessmen, including my great-grandfather Owen Peel Wethered, got together to form a company. Meetings were held, shares issued, and in the spring and summer of 1868 the Great Marlow Railway Bill passed through Parliament and became an Act. That, of course, was only the beginning. Confronting these Victorian gentlemen were a host of problems of which money was but one. There were difficulties over land acquisition, and over relations with the mighty Great Western Railway whose rolling stock would be using the Marlow line. It would be five more years before the first passenger train could huff and puff its way across the green fields on the two-and-a-half-mile journey from Marlow to Bourne End.

The Marlow Donkey, as the line is known, has always been held in great affection by its users. Now its story has been told by two men who are well qualified to write it. Chris Turner admits to being a railway enthusiast: a train-spotter as a boy, he pursued a career in the railways and currently works at St. Pancras Station. His special fondness for branch lines is shared by his co-author, Paul Karau, who is also the publisher of the book. This is their second book together, the first one being *The Wallingford Branch* which was published in 1982. Mr. Karau has written a further book about a third Thames Valley branch line — the neighbouring Henley branch.

I am pleased to contribute a foreword to the story of the Marlow Railway, of which my great-grandfather was the first chairman and which, in a diesel version, is still in service after more than a hundred years. Gone now are the old station buildings, the waiting room with its coal fire, the uniformed staff, and the hissing steam engines and sturdy wooden carriages I remember as a boy. And with them, it must be said, has gone much of the romance of the branch line. I am grateful to Mr. Turner and Mr. Karau for recreating those days through their informative text and a selection of wonderfully evocative pictures. Thanks to them the Marlow Donkey has taken its place in railway history.

Anthony Wethered

GREAT MARLOW c.1900.

CHAPTER ONE

RAILWAY PRELUDE

'Marlow is one of the pleasantest river centres I know of. It is a bustling, lively little town; not very picturesque on the whole, it is true, but there are many quaint nooks and corners to be found in it...'

Jerome K. Jerome

ONCE known as Great Marlow to distinguish it from the neighbouring village of Little Marlow, this ancient market town is situated on the border of the county of Buckinghamshire, on the north bank of the Thames, a little over 30 miles from London.

Daniel Defoe, who visited the town in the mid-1720s, described Marlow as 'a town of great embarkation on the Thames, not so much for goods wrought here (for the trade of the town is chiefly in bone lace) but for the goods from the neighbouring towns, and particularly a very great quantity of malt and meal is brought hither from High Wickham.'At the time of Defoe's visit, Temple Mills at Marlow were being utilized as a copper foundry. Since the days when the Templars obtained their flour from them, the mills had served many purposes including the production of corn, paper and metal. He also mentioned vast quantities of beechwood being brought down from the Buckinghamshire woods for forwarding to London. In fact the trains of pack horses, mules and donkeys carrying goods to the riverside prompted the local people to christen the train on the Great Marlow Railway, the 'Marlow Donkey', a name which survives to this day.

The Thames was bridged here as long ago as the 13th century, the famous suspension bridge, built 1829-32, being the third known structure to connect the borders of Buckinghamshire and Berkshire. When the town was first 'lighted by gas', a few years later in 1848, the principal trades were brewing, malting, chair and paper making.

The river was the main means of transporting bulk supplies or heavy loads to and from the town and for many years barges were hauled by gangs of men or hauliers, horses apparently not replacing them until the mid-18th century. The rapid displacement of the waterways by the new railways caused alarm to trustees of the turnpike, innkeepers and bargemasters alike, and by the mid-19th century the Thames Commissioners were in serious financial trouble. Marlow wharfingers at this unsettling time included George and William Cresswell at Thameside, John Rolls at Marlow wharf and William Sparks at Church Passage. In 1869 George Cresswell was described as a farmer, barge owner and coal director of St. Peter's Street. Thomas Gibbons was also a coal merchant there at this time and undoubtedly both he and Cresswell received supplies by barge. In 1853 John Rolls and Sons at Marlow wharf were described as coal and timber merchants and rope manufacturers. The wharf referred to was almost certainly at St. Peter's Street.

The railways not only offered greater mobility and speed over the waterways but the state of the roads had left much to be desired. Their upkeep had been carried out most unsatisfactorily, each parish maintaining its own roads with the inevitable inequality of standards. It was apparently regarded as a public duty for every man to contribute towards the cost of maintenance or provide his labour for six days in the year. Enforcement fell to the lot of the church wardens or petty constables and this was doubtless an unpopular and difficult task to effect.

The condition of the roads was not the only peril as highwaymen and 'footpads' abounded, particularly in Maidenhead Thicket, a notorious haunt in the neighbourhood. It seems that farmers returning from market after selling their stock were a favourite target and perhaps easy prey after a few celebratory drinks.

Despite all these problems, by the late 18th and the early years of the 19th century, Marlow was well served by coaches and carriers. In 1792 a stage coach set out for London from the Upper Crown at 5 a.m. and returned the same day. Another coach left from the Lower Crown three times a week. Two stage wagons set off on Monday morning, and returned on Wednesday. In the 1820s a coach left 'The Crown', Market Place, daily at 6.30 a.m. (5 a.m. on Monday) for the New Inn, Old Bailey, and by the 1830s 'The Industry' ran between Wycombe and Reading via Marlow and Henley-on-Thames.

With the opening of the GWR to Maidenhead, in addition to a coach serving London, one ran three times a day 'to and from the railroad'. In 1844 this service was known as 'The Wonder' but only ran twice a day, from 'The Crown' at 8.30 a.m. and 3.30 p.m. The Wycombe and Henley services were run by Samuel Loftin from 'The Three Tuns', West Street, and 'The Greyhound', Spittal Street. The latter service was 'Farley's Van' by the early 1850s and ran twice a week.

The 1850s saw the introduction of another railway 'feeder' service, this time to Windsor, 'to meet the trains of the South Western Railway', an omnibus leaving 'The Greyhound' every morning, except Sunday, at 6.45.

By the late 1850s further railway developments in the area meant the days of the long distance coach services were numbered and it appears that only Marlow Road station on the Maidenhead to Wycombe line was being served.

Carrier services were run mainly by the Wyatt family. In 1823 William Wyatt's Waggon ran to the 'King's Arms', Holborn Bridge, on Monday and Friday and by 1830 Thomas Wyatt was running via Maidenhead, Salthill, Slough and Colnbrook from 'The Horns', Chapel Street. Services to Wycombe and Thame, both by James Druce, and to Wycombe, Henley and Reading by Thomas Hall, also conveying passengers, were running by this time, Reading also being served by T. Platts in the late 1830s.

George Wyatt offered a carrier service to London in 1844 as did Richard Robinson who operated from 'The Crown'. By 1853 Charles Wyatt was serving London, and it appears Robinson was also serving Maidenhead

Railway station. Luke Maskell, a ginger beer manufacturer and carrier of West Street, ran to Reading in the early 1850s and a Mr. Cook also ran to Henley. Messrs. Blackwell and Hall appear to have taken over the Henley, Wycombe and Reading services by 1863, the Wyatt family apparently becoming the only carriers to London, leaving 'The Horns' every Monday and Thursday to 'The New Inn', Old Bailey, returning every Wednesday and Saturday.

By 1869 James Johnson was 'a Carrier for the G.W. Company' serving Marlow Road station from his home in Chapel Street. At this time Edward Tracey Wyatt ran to London and John Palmer served Wycombe and Reading.

William Wickens appears to have taken over Wyatt's business in the 1870s and by 1877 was running from 'The Horns' to London, with Palmer still providing the 'country' service. Incredibly, even at this time, another London service was being operated by a John Bray of Beech House, Station Road. The London services appear to have ended around 1890 but the Reading and Wycombe services survived under various operators, even into the 1920s, when they were run by George Hearn, a motor carrier of Oaken Grove.

Whilst some local coach and carrier services worked with the railway, others were put out of business or had to move elsewhere. The *Bucks Herald* in early 1872 stated that Fred Wyatt had been deprived of his livelihood by the establishment of the railroad and had been compelled to take to a London cab, but 'a most inefficient means it proved — giving a very scanty subsistence'.

In mentioning a scheme to bring a railway to Marlow, the *Bucks Herald* of 8th December 1855 said 'A railway to this town has long been desired, and the Great Western Railway Company, with a promptitude and spirit which does them great credit, are at once willing to execute this valuable project and we are led to believe that no important opposition will be offered against the enterprise.'

The Wycombe Railway Company, incorporated in 1846 and leased to the GWR under Section 45 of that Act, was promoting the branch, the scheme undoubtedly being prompted by the opening of the Maidenhead to Wycombe line in 1854. It was to have taken an almost identical course to the final line, except that it was to terminate 'near to the end of St. Peter's Street'.

The scheme was discussed by the Wycombe Railway Directors at their meeting of 9th November the same year, plans having been prepared by I. K. Brunel. It was anticipated that a satisfactory arrangement could be made with the GWR for the working and leasing of the line and the customary notice appeared in the *Bucks Herald* on 17th November. It appears, however, that despite the newspaper's optimism, the local people were not enthusiastic. In a later reference the *South Bucks Herald* said the scheme had been 'abandoned from a conviction that the inhabitants thought it adverse to the interests of Marlow'.

'Local parties' had made an application for the railway but their identity is not clear. It is believed that Peter Borgnis, later to become a director of the Great Marlow Railway, was opposed to the scheme, believing it to represent part of a through route threatening the beauty of the Thames Valley.

The proposal was not presented to Parliament and no further reference appears in the Wycombe Railway minutes at this period, the directors turning their attention to extending their line through to Oxford.

The people of Marlow had about nine years to wait before a railway to their town was seriously discussed again, and almost 18 years before it became a reality, and it was their own enterprise, in particular the spirit and energy of certain individuals, which won through and provided the still valued link.

CHAPTER TWO

THE GREAT MARLOW RAILWAY

THE district was first served by rail when the Wycombe Railway (opened on 1st August 1854) provided a station at Bourne End, and with customary optimism named it 'Marlow Road'. Ten years later a Bill was lodged for the 1865 session of Parliament to extend the Wycombe Railway to Uxbridge and Great Marlow.

The submission of the Parliamentary notice had been reported at the Wycombe Railway meeting of 22nd November 1864, when it was agreed 'that the Chairman, Mr. Barlow, be requested to act as he may think proper and most conducive to the interests of this company in reference to the proposed scheme, and more especially to see that no liability is incurred by this company in respect of the existing capital with apportionate security and further that the Bill be allowed to be undertaken only upon the understanding that neither the Parliamentary Agent, Solicitors or the Engineer look to this company for payment of any expenses.'

The scheme was brought to the notice of the people of Marlow through a public meeting held in the Town Hall on the evening of Monday, 19th December the same year, to ascertain support for the Marlow extension. It was attended by most of the principal gentry and tradesmen of the town and neighbourhood, and chaired by Col. Brownlow Knox, MP for the borough. He was supported by several local dignitaries, some of whom were later to become directors of the Great Marlow Railway Co., and representatives of the Great Western and Wycombe Railway Companies were also in attendance.

In opening the meeting, Knox said 'there could be no doubt but that a railway into Marlow would be most beneficial, and improve the town'. According to the *South Bucks Free Press:*

Mr. H. Rose [Solicitor for the Wycombe Railway] said he attended on behalf of the Company, having received a handbill on the previous day, in which it was announced that a deputation from the Company would attend. Neither the Chairman nor Engineer of the Wycombe Company were able to be present, but he believed that the course of the present line was almost identical with that projected by the late Mr. Brunel, and which was abandoned from a conviction that the inhabitants thought it adverse to the interests of Marlow. The line ran from the common fields near Suffolk Lodge, and the only difference between this and the former scheme was that it had a double fork at Marlow Road station — one towards London and the other towards Wycombe.* The cost of the line had been estimated at from £30,000 to £35,000, one of the items being £7,000 for a station, engine-house, &c, at Marlow. This might appear large, but was necessary because the Great Western Company, who would have to work the line, required such commodious buildings. If they could be satisfied with less, the company would gladly manage. The cost of land, too, in this estimate had been put high, as it traversed some ornamental and residential property. As the Great Western Railway Company were tied by a resolution of their shareholders from

directly promoting any branch lines, all new branches must be mainly carried out independently of their help. Under ordinary circumstances, when a line was made to a town like Marlow, the undertaking originated with the inhabitants. In the ensuing year the Company was going to Parliament about a line from Loudwater to Uxbridge, as being a connecting link with the Wycombe system, which was now of much importance, as it extended over a distance of 42 miles, although originating in the short line from Maidenhead to Wycombe, and it was thought as they were in Parliament for the line to Uxbridge, and the plans of the Marlow branch were all prepared, that there would be little difficulty and no additional expense in putting these plans into operation at the same time, if the feelings of the Marlow people were such as to warrant the undertaking. He knew nothing yet of their wishes upon the subject. Their Chairman, Colonel Knox, had expressed his own desire to see the line formed, and if the inhabitants of the town present were convinced of the importance of the project he need say nothing upon that point; but if they were doubtful he would just take one item — coal. The river navigation was very expensive, the locks were going to pieces, and much injuring even the present traffic, but by a railway these difficulties would be obviated and great advantages conferred. When coal came from Oxford round by Didcot, Maidenhead, and that way to Wycombe, coal was selling at 21s. a ton. Now he believed the reduction (without speaking from an exact knowledge) by the coal coming direct from Oxford to Wycombe, was something like, or if not it would be, 1s. 6d. a ton cheaper. It was now therefore from 18s. 6d. to 19s. 6d. a ton. (A voice: The average, I suppose.) He was speaking of the best coal, and now in Marlow the price was — (A voice: 35s.); and rating the people in Marlow 7,000 — (No, no), 5,000 then, and taking the coal at 5s. per head, they would have a reduction of 10s. per ton.

Mr. Gibbons asked to be allowed to state that the reduction of 10s. would be on sea coal; the price of inland coal at Marlow was 25s. per ton.

Mr. H. Rose continued: Taking it at 25s. there would be a saving of 5s. per ton on about 7,500 tons of coal a year, and of course the reduction of inland coal must necessarily from competition lower the price of sea coal. Taking these figures there would be a saving to the people of Marlow of about £1,250 a year from this item alone. The proposal which he made on behalf of the Wycombe Railway Company was this, either that they should find one-third of the capital, or that they should undertake to supply the land for the Company — either of which would enable them to make the line, provided the Directors consented to the project. One-third of the money would be £10,000 or £12,000. Many persons would think that the Great Western Railway Company might in their own interest make the line to Marlow, thinking that the South Western Railway would be likely to bring a railway there. Now the South Western Railway were under a binding agreement with the Great Western Company from promoting any extension in the Great Western district. Therefore for ten years there was no chance of such a line being carried out, and they must remember that if this project was carried the line must stop at Marlow, for no railway could be carried on from Marlow to Henley, as it would have to go through Scott Murray's and other very expensive properties, and he very much questioned whether when those ten years should have elapsed, it would be thought worthwhile for the South Western Railway or any other company to bring a line on to Marlow merely as a

* There is no evidence on the deposited plans of a double fork.

terminus. The Great Western Railway then were willing to promote the line if the Marlow people would find one-third of the money, and it should pay a fair working rental, otherwise they would abandon the scheme, and if the Great Western Company were ever compelled to make the line in self-defence, they would construct it on the other side of the river from Cockmarsh Common, skirting Quarry Woods.

The *Bucks Herald* reported that some £10,000 was taken up in shares at the meeting within a few hours. The GW and Wycombe companies undertook to find the remaining amount.

The scheme was discussed by the board of the Great Western a few days later on 22nd December, but Rose wrote to the GWR on 2nd February the following year enclosing a resolution of the Wycombe company to the effect 'that unless provision is made in the Uxbridge and Loudwater Bill of this session for the protection of the Wycombe Company in respect of the traffic receipts of the Thame Extension Line and an undertaking given to serve such provision a petition will be presented against the Bill.'

Apart from the Wycombe company's unrest, Mr. Hargreaves, a resident landowner, had expressed his intention to oppose the Bill and on 16th February 1865 the GW directors decided to withdraw it.

The Bill had first been read to the House of Commons on 10th February and was ordered to be withdrawn on the 23rd.

The idea of promoting the scheme was kept alive as another Bill was lodged for the 1866 session of Parliament. However, this was also withdrawn according to the *Bucks Herald* for 27th January 1866 because of 'threatened opposition of Mr. Way, of Denham, and the want of active support on the part of the Great Western Railway Company'. Way was one of the principal landowners.

In the meantime, however, Knox had reservations about the scheme which he expressed at his re-election speech on Tuesday, 11th July, reported in the *Bucks Herald*:

With regard to your local interests, I have always been ready to do my utmost to promote them. I know it has been represented that I opposed your having a railway. The very contrary of this is the fact. I exerted myself in its favour, and induced Messrs. Baxter, Rose, and Norton to come down to you; but when I found that the Great Western Railway had formed a compact with the Wycombe branch to make you pay an exorbitant sum, I exerted myself to obtain the overthrow of the Bill. You were told the cost of your branch would be £36,000. I went to the expense of ascertaining from a competent person what the cost really ought to be, and I found it was only from £9,000 to £12,000, instead of £36,000 demanded from you. (Cheers.) The gallant Colonel then went on to detail the exertions he had made to obtain the improvement of the Thames navigation. The measures in prospect would increase the traffic, and benefit the towns on its banks. He concluded by observing, I have been your representative for 18 years, I have always acted up to the principles upon which you have returned me, and shall continue to do so in the ensuing Parliament. (Cheers.)

On the proposition of Colonel Williams, seconded by Colonel Knox, a vote of thanks was passed to the returning officer; the crowd soon dispersed, and the town resumed its ordinary quiet.

On 1st February 1867 the Wycombe Railway had amalgamated with the GWR under powers granted by the Great Western Railway (Wycombe Transfer) Act of 23rd July 1866.

It was not until 29th August 1867 that the inhabitants of Great Marlow attended a meeting to consider another proposal which eventually became the Great Marlow Railway. It was held at the Crown Inn and chaired by Col. Peers Williams, MP. The engineer for the scheme was a Mr. Wilkinson of Messrs. Lucas and Wilkinson, 31 Duke Street, Westminster, who attended and stated that:

. . . a company would be formed with a capital of £15,000 in £10 shares. The line could be constructed for £12,000, and if the Marlow people would subscribe £6,000 in shares the firm would guarantee the construction of the line and would pledge themselves not to call up a single farthing of the money until the line was actually commenced. O. P. Wethered, Esq., supported the proposition, and the meeting was strongly in his favour. Ultimately, on the proposition of W. L. Ward, Esq., the following resolution was unanimously agreed to, 'That it is desirable to form a railway into Marlow.' The following gentlemen were elected a committee to carry out the plan: — Sir W. R. Clayton, Bart., T. S. Cocks, T. O. Wethered, J. Carson, O. P. Wethered, P. Borgnis, W. H. Cripps, W. L. Ward, J. Rose, C. Forjett, and W. J. Shone, Esqrs.; Messrs. J. W. Morgan, T. Wright, R. Foottit, E. Hewett, T. Corby, and C. Carter.

Further meetings were held on 31st October, to decide on the practicability of the scheme, and another on the 8th November when it was resolved to proceed with the railway independently. At a special meeting of the shareholders on 15th November, whilst agreement to proceed was ratified, the contractor's proposals (which are unclear) were rejected and a provisional committee was authorised to negotiate with a Mr. Moreton over the terms on which they were willing to award him the contract. They were also empowered to make a call of 10% on the subscriptions if needed to carry the Bill through Parliament indpendent of a contractor, Messrs. Lucas & Wilkinson subsequently agreeing to do all the necessary engineering work up to the passing of the Act, for the sum of £50.

The *South Bucks Free Press* reporting on the meeting of 8th November said:

PROPOSED RAILWAY

If any were so foolish or so sceptical as to doubt whether the tradesmen and the inhabitants of Marlow were indifferent upon the subject of the proposed railway, recent events must have dispelled the illusion. In every circle during the past week or two the all-absorbing subject of discussion has been — Are we to have a railway? The fact that some in high places, from whom better things were looked for, turned a deaf ear to the earnest wishes of the inhabitants, is commented on in no measured or complimentary terms. Election addresses had frequently told us in large capital letters how that one of the proudest and most pleasant duties of our representatives would be at all times and in every possible way to promote the local welfare of their constituents; how they have redeemed these pledges in the past, and how they have fulfilled them in the present the popular voice will answer emphatically. The trade of our town is languishing; on all sides people are complaining that it is getting from bad to worse. It is believed that a railway would be a great means to ameliorate this retrograde, or at best, stagnant position; an opportunity offers to obtain

The lower end of Marlow High Street c.1900.

Collection C. E. Turner

this boon, and then, instead of helping the scheme forward, pledges are evaded or forgotten, and for ought some care, we may dwindle into nothingness. Doubtless all this neglect and indifference will rise up in judgment against these individuals at some future day.

Finding so many difficulties in the way, and the indisposition of some of the leading gentry to assist, the tradesmen aroused themselves to greater earnestness and determination. The adjourned meeting was held at the Magistrates' Room on the evening of Friday, the 8th inst, and the room was soon crowded by townspeople all eager for the success of the undertaking.

O. P. Wethered, Esq., was moved to the chair, and opened the proceedings by observing that this meeting was convened in order to afford the inhabitants a final opportunity of deciding the question of a railway to Marlow. He did not believe they would ever again have the chance of getting a line upon anything like such favourable terms as those now offered. He then went on to state that he had received letters from Col. Williams, M.P., and Sir William Clayton, both declining to support the railway, — the former basing his refusal upon the ground that the scheme was objectionable to Mr. Ellames, and the latter was guided by his solicitor, a Mr. Bonner, who gave it as his opinion that calls would be made on the shares, and that a railroad would be detrimental rather than advantageous to the Harleyford estate. The chairman concluded by asserting that each member of his firm was equally desirous with himself for the successful establishment of the railway.

Mr. E. Hewett said some persons hesitated to come forward because last year they had to pay a large sum of money, although the scheme fell through.

Mr. Wilkinson said that could not be the case this year, the promoters had undertaken not to ask anyone for a single farthing unless the bill passed and the line was commenced; and in reply to questions by Mr. T. O. Wethered and others, Mr. Wilkinson said he estimated that the line would require about eight acres of land, at an estimated cost of £300 per acre. The amount call on the shares would be gradual as the work progressed and was certified by the engineer; the shares taken by the contractors contributing *pro rata* with the others. The capital of the company was fixed at £15,000, although, perhaps, the whole of that amount might not be required. He had spoken upon the subject to some of the leading men on the Great Western, and had no doubt that the Company would work this branch.

The Chairman said Mr. Borgnis had called his attention to the fact that many persons expressed an opinion that the shareholders would get no dividend. He (the Chairman) could not hold out any hope of a 5 per cent or of even perhaps a 3 or 4 per cent dividend; but his belief was that the shareholders would receive an ample return for their outlay in an indirect manner by the many advantages they would derive from railway communication. The capital £15,000 would be sufficient to complete the line.

A desultory conversaton here took place. Close upon 300 shares were required to raise the stipulated amount of £6,000, and only a few additional shares had as yet been taken.

Mr. T. O. Wethered said there really seemed no prospect of the shares being taken up. He suggested that the matter should not be allowed to drop entirely, but that the share list should be kept open, and probably by another year a sufficient number would have been taken to enable them to proceed.

The wooden viaduct carrying the Wycombe Railway over the Thames at Bourne End.

Mr. Wilkinson said they could keep the list open for another year if they chose; but he gave them distinctly to understand that he should in that case withdraw entirely from it. If the district really desired a railway, he could not imagine they would find much difficulty in raising the small amount now required. It would not be worth their while to come down another year and take all that trouble over again for so small an affair. It must therefore be distinctly understood that if the matter were postponed to another year his firm would have nothing to do with it in any shape.

The Chairman: Postponement then will amount to giving it up altogether.

Mr. Croxon: If we are to have no railway you may as well put Marlow into the Thames and swim it away altogether.

Another conversation ensued: shares were not taken, and the abandonment of the scheme seemed inevitable.

Mr. O. Wright pleaded hard for an adjournment for a few days, expressing a strong opinion that if this were acceded to, the necessary number of shares would be taken now that people knew how much depended upon them.

Mr. Toogood, the parliamentary agent, said they might manage if they knew by Monday morning.

Then more hopeful signs set in. Mr. J. Langley said he would double his shares if the Messrs. Wethered would theirs. After some consideration, the Chairman said the Messrs. Wethered would take another 100 shares upon condition that a sufficient number, including this additional 100, was taken to raise the necessary amount. Loud applause greeted this announcement, and a new spirit came over the scene. The Rev. B. Smith, Mr. Borgnis, and others present consented to increase the number of shares they had taken. This went on until only 100 more shares were required. It was then arranged that the following should form a sub-committee to wait upon the inhabitants on the following day and solicit support – O. P. Wethered, Esq., T. O. Wethered, Esq., and W. L. Ward, Esq.; Messrs. Foottit, E. Hewett, J. Roberts, W. H. Brown, O. Wright, and R. Carter.

The meeting terminated with a vote of thanks to the Chairman.

On the following day the Committee mentioned above commenced a vigorous canvas. They met with such support that ere the termination of their labours the necessary number of shares had been subscribed. In all directions our townspeople were congratulating themselves upon having at length arrived at a point from which they could look forward with much confidence to the accomplishment of a work for which they had so long hoped and yearned in vain.

Much of this success was due to the great liberality of the Messrs. Wethered in subscribing for 200 shares. Mr. O. P. Wethered also laboured hard to get the other shares taken up. He laboured nobly and zealously in the good cause, and it needs no words of ours to assure him that the town appreciates and thanks him for his exertions on its behalf.

On Tuesday last, Mr. T. O. Wethered, Mr. O. P. Wethered, Mr. Borgnis, and Mr. Ward, held a conference with the promoters of the railway at the office of Mr. Toogood, in London. The information gleaned at that interview was of sufficient importance to induce the above gentleman to convene a meeting of the shareholders at the Crown Hotel this (Friday) evening. We hope after overcoming so many difficulties that nothing will now arise to jeopardise the prosecution of the project.

In appalling metaphors the *South Bucks Free Press* for Friday, 29th November was at last able to proclaim:

This project seems now to be fairly launched into deep water, and with fair winds there is every reason to hope it will reach port in safety. The Provisional Committee are navigating the vessel with skill and caution, and everything looks propitious. The letter from Sir William Clayton announcing his adhesion to the scheme and his intention to give it all the support in his power, has been received with general satisfaction.

The scheme was initially opposed by the Great Western Railway, although they were hastily appeased by the insertion of certain unspecified clauses in the Bill. However, Mr. J. P. Ellames, Lord of the Manor of Little Marlow, also objected. He owned the largest portion of the land required for the railway and had tried for high rates of compensation to which the company would not concede. A draft agreement was, however, drawn up embodying terms on which he was willing to withdraw his opposition and the Bill was passed.

The Great Marlow Railway Act was given Royal Assent on 13th July 1868, having been brought into the Commons on 17th February the same year and read for the first time the following day. It incorporated the Great Marlow Railway Company and gave it powers to construct a railway from the Wycombe branch of the GWR to Great Marlow. The authorised capital was £18,000 in 1800 £10 shares, with powers to borrow an additional £6,000. The Act stated that the railway could be made and maintained on the broad or narrow gauge, or both, as the company thought fit, but did not indicate that the GWR were to work the line, although negotiations between the two companies were already in hand.

The directors of the company were initially all from the locality. Owen Peel Wethered, the chairman, was a brewer and maltster with premises in the High Street and Peter Borgnis, the vice chairman, was a gentleman living at 'Highfields'.

The other directors were James Carson, a magistrate of 'Spinfields', Thomas Owen Wethered, another member of the brewery family and MP for Great Marlow, James Rolls of Palmer House, Thomas Rolls, a wine and spirit merchant in the High Street and Robert Foottit, a chemist and druggist, again in the High Street.

The engineers were Messrs. Lucas & Wilkinson with Edwin Clark CE as consulting engineer; the bankers were Messrs. Cocks, Biddulph and Company, the Parliamentary agent William Toogood, and the Secretary William Larkin Ward, solicitor and clerk to the magistrates, and to the Commissioners of Property, Land and Income Tax who had an office in the High Street.

Edwin Clark was a local man renowned for his engineering achievements. He was born the son of a pillow lace manufacturer in Marlow in 1814 and sent to London to become a solicitor. However, he preferred to study the sciences and after only two years, to the great disappointment of his parents, returned home and led an idle life for four years, apparently being regarded by his friends as a 'ne'er-do-well'. He was certainly misjudged as through private study and experiment he pursued his scientific interests, observed the reconstruction of the old Marlow lock on the Thames, and work in progress on the Marlow suspension bridge and the Great Western Railway.

He eventually became a teacher in his old school at Marlow but, wishing to pursue something higher, subsequently went to Cambridge University to study the classics. Afterwards he toured the continent and on his return obtained mathematical masterships.

His story would prove too much of a diversion in these pages but, in short, in 1846, during the 'railway mania', he gained an introduction to the great Robert Stephenson, who offered him a few days' work drawing on his mathematical knowledge with regard to the strains on the Britannia Bridge tubes. Stephenson was so impressed with his criticisms that he appointed Clark resident engineer of what was then the greatest and boldest engineering work in the world.

His interest in electricity led him to be appointed engineer in chief to the Electric and International Telegraph Company. His work for the London & North Western Railway led to the invention and introduction of the 'block telegraph system' of train regulation.

Altogether he was much celebrated and went on to engineer works of great magnitude both at home and abroad including numerous railways in a remarkable career. Yet it was this great man who agreed to be consulting engineer of the humble branch line to his home town.

Following authorisation, a public meeting of landowners, inhabitants and others interested was held on Thursday, 6th August 1868 and reported in the *South Bucks Free Press*. James Carson said:

> Now gentlemen, when we last held a meeting upon this subject there were a great many difficulties, and much more opposition staring us in the face. However, on that occasion, we determined to push forward the Bill in Parliament on our own account. It was then anticipated that the bill would be strenuously opposed by Mr. Ellames, and some influential gentlemen in the neighbourhood upon whose assistance we had calculated withheld their support because they were unwilling to take part in anything calculated to annoy or injure a neighbour, or that would interfere with the privacy of his property. Happily all these fears and surmises have been dispelled. We have to congratulate Mr. Ellames upon the kind and courteous feelings with which he has treated us; he was with perfect unanimity with us, only laying down a just and fair compensation for the land we required from him. Their acknowledgments were certainly due to Mr. Ellames for the fine gentlemanly feeling he had displayed in the negotiation of the subject. The bill passed unopposed through all its stages, and received the royal assent on the 13th July. You will be gratified at this because a railway must have the effect of benefiting the trade and increasing the value of property in the neighbourhood. I am glad to see some gentlemen here today who have already largely benefited from the mere announcement of the scheme, and that, gentlemen, is only a very small instalment of the advantages that must be ultimately derived from a railway. In consequence of our meeting with no opposition we have arrived at this stage at much less cost than we anticipated. We are yet very far short of the number of shares actually required to be taken up to enable us to carry out the scheme to a successful and economic conclusion. We do not want to put ourselves in the hands of contractors, and be compelled to pay them in shares at a large discount, and overpay them in other ways; 551 shares have been taken up and the calls paid upon them. We still require another 600 shares to be taken before we can exercise our borrowing powers. We have fixed our capital at £18,000, a much larger sum than we shall want, but we shall certainly require the number of shares I have mentioned to be subscribed for, and if the people will now come forward and take the necessary number of shares, we shall be able to carry out this undertaking at a very much less cost than we originally anticipated, and there is no doubt that any person investing his capital in our shares will be handsomely paid. We are convinced that they will receive a much higher dividend than they can obtain from investments offering equal certainty and security.

O. P. Wethered explained that the subscribed capital of £5,510 would probably cover the preliminary expenses, the passing of the Bill and purchase of the land, but more shares had to be taken up to provide ready money for the line's construction. He went on to say:

> . . . more money is absolutely necessary, and unless the people are prepared to find it the project must, at least for the present, stand still, for it will be quite useless our incurring further expense. At first people were frightened to join us because we were threatened with opposition, but Mr. Ellames withdrew his objection, and we are now in a far better position than we were before, and we now confidently appeal to those who hung back on these grounds, or from a dislike to annoy a neighbour — these objections are dispelled, and we now appeal to those gentlemen for their support, and unless they give it us the project must drop through. If they come forward and give us their assistance and do so liberally, I see no reason why by this time next year we should not have our railway into Marlow. From Mr. Edwin Clark, our eminent townsman, and of whom we are all so justly proud, we have received much valuable advice and assistance, and he will, perhaps, give you some information, and tell you what he thinks of our project.

Clark said he was only interested in this subject as a townsman and anxious for its prosperity and welfare:

> . . . So far as this undertaking is concerned, it really appears to me that the townspeople have not yet taken it in hand — only a very few individuals have taken shares. If you do not get a railway to keep up your position, you will be left out in the cold, and dwindle down into perfect insignificance. Everybody must benefit by a railway, and I think a feeling of patriotism ought to induce the people to come readily forward in support of this scheme. It is not of small importance to get the name of our town inserted in 'Bradshaw'. Many gentlemen in London do not know there is such a place as Marlow, and 'Bradshaw' would make its existence known everywhere; and it would no doubt be the means of bringing many amongst us to enjoy our charming scenery. Now just admit it possible, that you did not get a farthing return upon the capital of this railway, it would only be a loss of £100 a year which would be returned to you with considerable additions, in the material improvement of the town and in its largely increased trade and prosperity, but when it is not only possible but more than probable that in little time you will get a good return for your capital in the shape of dividends. I do not see that there ought to be any difficulty or hesitation in the matter. I do not consider that a local undertaking like this ought to be thrown upon two or three individuals. I contend that it is the duty of every townsman to assist by taking shares according to his means, in the firm assurance that if by any remote possibility the money should be lost to him as an investment, that he will have taken part in conferring an incalculable benefit upon the town. In fact the man who does not assist ought henceforth to be pointed at with the finger of scorn, as the man who did not take a share in our railway.

T. O. Wethered said:

> After the satisfactory statement of the Chairman, and the decision of the Directors not to purchase a single piece of land until a distinct and binding agreement had been entered into

A well-known early view of Marlow Road station c.1869 as a simple wayside station with only one platform. Beyond the platform, adjacent to the level crossing is the disc and crossbar signal protecting the gates. Cores End crossing was protected by a similar signal (see the drawing on p. 198). The GWR used different shapes on its crossbar signals to denote usage. Down line signals had downward pointing extensions at the outer ends of the crossbar. Level crossing signals (almost invariably applying to traffic in both directions) had extensions pointing both up and downwards, as seen here.

with the Great Western Company, he thought they might confidently rely upon the Directors properly protecting the interest of the shareholders, and it was now necessary for all to put their shoulders to the wheel to ensure the success of the project, and with that view he would propose, that a committee be formed to make a house-to-house canvas to solicit people to take shares.

Although the scheme was finally underway, by 12th July the following year at the first ordinary and general meeting of the Great Marlow Railway, held at the Crown Hotel, the directors had to report that they regretted the progress made during the past year in increasing the number of shareholders was 'not more satisfactory'. However, since the Wycombe line had been taken over by the GWR from 1st February 1867, it had been decided to convert it to standard gauge. The consequent adoption of the narrower gauge would thus lessen the cost and, the directors hoped, compensate for the delay that had arisen. They also expressed the hope that in their financial circumstances a contractor might be found who would take part payment in shares and complete the line on the present subscription. Although this was not to be, they did, however, state that they were 'extremely averse to recommending such a contract from the great sacrifice it would entail'.

By September a further £910 had been received and it was decided that the line should be staked out. A prospectus for 17th October 1868 stated 'owing to the extreme levelness of the route chosen and avoidance of public roads, the expense of the formation will be unusually small. Highly respectable and responsible contractors have offered to construct it for £10,000 cash which includes the necessary station works, and all other expenses, except the land required for the line and goods station, which probably will not exceed twelve acres.'

Clark prepared plans and sections which were laid before a directors meeting on 1st October 1869. It was agreed that he would superintend the construction of the line at 'a commission of 5% on capital expended, payable in fully paid up shares and also take 50 additional shares in the company in accordance with his letters'.

At the same meeting Clark expressed his wish to consult with the GW engineer over the junction and within a few days the meeting was arranged, although Clark did not attend himself; instead a Mr. McKeen, on his behalf, met Messrs. Henry Voss, divisional engineer, Reading, and F. G. Stephens, chief clerk of the GWR at Marlow Road. They were unanimous in the need to move the existing Great Western 'sidings and sheds' to the opposite side 'into Mr. Du Pré's field, the cost of which would not exceed £800'.

In July 1869 Wethered's brewery had offered to subscribe an additional £1,000 on condition that the general shareholders subscribed an extra £2,000 beyond their previous subscription. Although several of the larger shareholders had agreed to increase their holding, in the event this appeal was not fully responded to and the condition was waived. Wethered's had now increased their holding to £3,000 whilst those of the general shareholders had been raised from £4,450 to £5,310, bringing the total subscription to £8,310.

In the same month James Grierson, general manager of the GWR met Owen Peel Wethered and a Mr. Currie, another of Clark's representatives, at Marlow Road to discuss the junction and terms for working the line, but by September the directors were still unable to announce much progress, particularly as negotiations for land were becoming prolonged.

In November 1870 the tender of a local builder, John Smith, for 'fences, gates &c.' was accepted but still no

Another glimpse of Marlow Road station before the construction of the Marlow branch. So far this is the only view to feature the original goods shed which was removed to accommodate the Marlow branch bay and train shed. The roof of the building can be seen behind the station building.

Bourne End Residents Association Collection, courtesy F. Lunnon

contractor had been found for the construction of the line. The following February the company wrote to Mr. Moreton, who in 1867 had offered to construct the line. However, he had since died. By the end of March they were in communication with various contractors with a view to completing the line in the ensuing summer but evidently none was interested in a contract which would have depended so largely on the line's success for much of their payment. In short, the company was under-subscribed and the promoters were unable to find the capital necessary to complete the line. It was therefore finally decided on 15th August 1871 to approach the GWR for the balance required.

The Great Western had previously agreed to provide stock for working the line, viz., 'an engine, certain carriage and wagon stock with the drivers and firemen (but not guards) for £1,090 per annum'. The Marlow company were to provide station staff and maintain the line. They were also to be required to pay £100 p.a. for the use of the junction at Marlow Road when 3% was earned on their ordinary share capital.

In a letter of 28th August, Owen Peel Wethered asked whether the Great Western would assist the Great Marlow Railway in the construction of their line by taking shares in the undertaking, apparently pointing out that this was 'no contractors' speculation' but a bonafide endeavour on the part of the local shareholders to provide more direct railway communication with the Great Western to whom it could not fail 'to be of great advantage'. The Great Western Board were unable to come to any immediate decision on the information before them, but Grierson and the GWR's chief engineer, W. G. Owen, were instructed to investigate and report on the condition and prospects of the undertaking.

In the meantime, the *Bucks Herald* for 2nd September was able to report that land purchases had been settled and 'exhorbitant demands made in some instances are very largely reduced'. The newspaper also went on to state that there was ground for hope that the expectation of the directors that the construction of the line would commence 'during the present summer' might be realized. The gross amount to be paid for land was £5,784 which, together with legal costs, was far in excess of the original estimate. Considerable difficulty thus resulted in the way of letting a contract for construction. The land would nearly absorb the whole of the present capital and before they could exercise their borrowing powers the company had to have a fully subscribed capital of £12,000. Furthermore, just to add to their anxieties, a large amount was overdue on calls made on the existing subscribers and the local press announced that the directors would have no alternative but to take legal proceedings. The amount concerned, £2,075, was urgently required to complete various land purchases.

Despite these difficulties and still without a contractor, a ceremony took place for the turning of the first sod on 22nd November 1871. The sod was turned by Mrs. Owen Peel Wethered and, whilst no press report of the event has been discovered, there appears to have been the usual arrangements on such occasions, the company hiring tents,

tables and chairs, ropes and stakes. Curiously, it was not until January 1873 that Mrs. Wethered was presented with a suitably inscribed 'handsome silver salver'.

By March 1872 £1,999 of calls were still in arrears (from 1st January) and the directors had overdrawn upwards of £1,000 which five of them pesonally guaranteed while they took legal proceedings to recover the calls. Messrs. Wethered were sympathetic to the situation and agreed to require only half of the amount for their land in cash.

Grierson's report was first read to the officers of the GWR at a meeting on 20th March, but, because of other business, it was postponed until the following meeting on 4th April. It contained 'estimates of the probable receipts and expense of the line'. He estimated the cost of construction at about £15,000. £8,310 had been subscribed, of which £3,757 had been paid up and £5,913. 18s. 2d. expended! He said 'The population of Marlow is 6,619, and being so near London and a place which might be more resorted to if there were railway communication, I think it is quite possible that £2,260 per annum may be earned on the line'.

After discussion the GWR resolved that if the Marlow Company put up £8,000 in their ordinary stock, they would arrange to provide the balance on the condition that they received a preference dividend of 5% on the contribution. The Marlow company gratefully accepted and two separate agreements between the companies were prepared, one for raising the money for the construction and one for working the line. The profits from the line were therefore to be paid in the following priority.

1. Working expense
2. New shareholders (GWR) to be paid 5%
3. Present shareholders to be paid 5%
4. Remainder of profits to be divided amongst the whole shareholders

The Marlow company's seal was affixed to the agreements at a meeting on 12th September.

The company's position was stated at the half yearly meeting on 27th September when it was declared 'it now only remains to settle finally the question of a contractor and your directors have every reason to hope that at the date of the next half yearly report the line will be — if not then actually open for traffic — at any rate very far advanced towards completion'.

In accordance with their investment, the GWR took three seats on the Board. James Carson had died during the summer and at a meeting on 5th November 1872, T. O. Wethered and Joseph Wright Morgan, who had taken his seat on the board from July 1869 following Thomas Rolls' resignation, resigned to make room for the Great Western representatives. They were W. C. King of Warfield Hall, Bracknell, Berks, Edward Wanklyn of Warwick Road, Paddington, and Captain Thomas Bulkeley of Clewer Lodge, Windsor, the Marlow company still holding a majority of four seats at this time. In 1869 Wanklyn and Bulkeley represented the GWR on the board of the West London Extension Railway and Bulkeley on the Birkenhead, Bristol & North Somerset Railways

Unfortunately, the details are now obscure, but it seems that in the absence of any contractor, Edwin Clark may have persuaded William Henry Punchard and Matthew Cury to join him in forming a company to undertake the construction of the line, all three trading as Clark, Punchard and Co. of '5 & 6 Westminster Chambers, Victoria St. in the County of Middlesex'. The engineer in chief of the railway was the Great Western's eminent William George Owen.

The Great Western engineer agreed the specification of works with Clark, Punchard & Co., whose estimate for construction amounted to £15,698. 10s. 0d., excluding the junction at Marlow Road, for which the Marlow company was to contribute £2,500. The total cost of completion exceeded the authorised capital by £3,272 10s. 0d., and, after a meeting in November with the GWR at Paddington, Wethered and Borgnis agreed to find the additional money required on condition that they maintained the majority on the Board and the further amount would be placed in a similar position to the GWR preference shares as regards dividends.

However, at a meeting on 5th November 1872, Thomas King of Widmere, the returning officer of the borough, who had replaced James Rolls on the board in November 1869, and Charles Foottit, who had become a director in September 1870 following the death of his father, resigned and the number of directors was reduced from seven to five, leaving the GWR with the majority. At the same meeting Clark's tender was accepted subject to his making a reduction of £600 'in consequence of the recent fall in iron'. However, Clark held his ground and claimed that everything in his estimate was at cost and that he could not make the required reduction in the price of rails. This was agreed, but subject to the condition that the GW provided the rails if they were able to do so at a cheaper rate.

Much to the relief of all concerned, in their half-yearly report for the end of March 1873, the directors were able to report that work had commenced and, considering the continued wet weather and floods, the contractors had made good progress, 'the remainder of the share capital £9,240 has been subscribed for and the balance due for the land &c. have been paid, and a balance now stands at the bank'.

The GWR carried out the alterations at Marlow Road which, besides the track alterations, provision of 'a proper signal box', platforms etc., included the removal or re-erection of the goods shed and construction of a new waiting room. The total cost of the work, together with the locking arrangements was estimated at £4,278 15s. 0d. including the Marlow company's contribution.

At the end of April the GW engineer, Owen, issued a certificate for £5,363 for Clark, Punchard & Co. against their contract, 'but only £53 12s. 6d. instead of £186 6s. or 10% from certified amount of work done, viz., £1,863 exclusive of £3,500 for rails.' According to the agreement, the contractors would receive the first payment in cash and the remaining instalments half in cash and half in Lloyd's bonds of the company 'bearing interest after the rate of 5%'. Each payment was subject to a 10% retention, one half of which was to be paid when the line was open and the balance after one year during which time the contractor was responsible for the maintenance of the line.

The *Reading Mercury* for 10th May reported the works for this short line were 'progressing most satisfactorily. The station, goods shed, and other buildings are fast advancing towards completion. The greater length of the

Cty. C H. C. Borgnis

permanent way has been laid, and a transit by rail through some of the most picturesque scenery of the Thames Valley will soon be available'. As is so often the case, details of the construction are sparse but it seems that ballast was obtained from a pit adjoining the line apparently leased from a Mr. Atkinson.

The company was anxious to open the line in time for the Maidenhead and Marlow Regatta to be held on 28th June, so in the inevitable haste the contractor was urged to proceed with all speed. In the meantime it seems that the junction at Marlow Road was not constructed according to the plans approved. Although the chairman and vice chairman expressed their concern as they did not think the accommodation would be sufficient, the matter was deferred. In any case they were hardly in a position to do anything about it and probably did not consider it worthwhile jeopardizing the good relationship between the two companies.

Owen inspected the line on 17th June prior to giving the second notice to the Board of Trade, and on Tuesday, 24th, the day before the official inspection, Borgnis travelled on the engine to Marlow, the journey being performed in just five minutes on a '517' class 0—4—2T No. 522, driven by a Mr. Thomas, a GWR employee. This particular engine appears to have remained in use on the branch for some time afterwards.

Colonel Yolland carried out the official inspection of the line on 25th June. He was certainly afforded every courtesy, being met at Maidenhead by the chairman and his wife, who travelled with him from there on the engine and laid on lunch for him and the rest of the party at their house afterwards.

They travelled 'on a heavy goods engine' which had been selected to test the line. At Marlow Road, according to the company's minute book, they were joined on the engine by a formidable party which included the company secretary, Clark the contractor, Owen the GWR engineer, Higgins the superintendent of the GWR, and Messrs. Benyon, Cambridge, Thompson, Currie and Batting. Contemporary accounts make no mention of any carriage, but this must surely be an oversight, for one can hardly imagine there was room for them all to board the engine. Later, in September, a GW official visited the line and ordered that no person be allowed to ride on the engine and J. Saunders was fined 2s. for having taken the chairman!

The company minutes record 'the Colonel expressed himself (with one or two trifling exceptions) satisfied that the line might be opened at once'. His report was as follows:

Leamington 25th June 1873

Sir,

I have the honour to report for the information of the Board of Trade in compliance with the instructions contained in your Minute of the 18th Inst., that I have inspected the Great Marlow Railway commencing at Marlow Road Station of the Great Western Railway and terminating at Great Marlow, a length of 2 miles and 58.66 chains.

This line is single throughout and almost entirely on the surface, the land having only been bought and the works constructed for a single line, with sidings at Marlow Road and Great Marlow Stations.

The width of the line at formation level is 18 feet for cuttings and 17 feet for Embankments. The gauge is 4 ft 8½ inches.

The permanent way consists of a flat bottomed rail weighing 70 lbs per yard in average lengths of 22 feet, laid on cross sleepers of Baltic Timber creosoted, 9 feet long by 10″ x 5″ rectangular placed 2 ft. 9 in. and 3 ft. 2 in. centre to centre apart except at the joints where the distance is 2 feet.

The rails are fastened with fang bolts on curves and dog spikes on the straight positions, the joints of the rails are fished.

The Ballast is of gravel and stated to be 1 foot deep below the under side of the sleepers.

The fencing is of post and rail, posts 9 feet apart and with centre stays and rail 4 feet high.

The steepest gradient is 1 in 132 and the sharpest curve has a radius of 9 chains.

The Marlow Road Station of the Great Western Railway is made use of as an exchange Station; and the only station on the Line is at Great Marlow. There are no bridges over or under the Line, but there is a wooden viaduct 55 yards in length, with small openings of 11 and 12 feet on the square, and in one instance 19 feet on the skew.

There are no unauthorized Level Crossings of Public Roads on the line.

The Line is well ballasted and in fair order throughout, and the points and signals at the Stations are properly connected and interlocked with each other with one or two exceptions at the Marlow Road Station, where Levers 4 and 3 should interlock Nos. 15 and 16, with No. 17 and 15 & 16 also to lock No. 12, so as to stand with the points open for line west of platform instead of for Great Western line. These alterations will be made tomorrow. At Great Marlow Station, a signal Box is to be placed over the Levers.

A name Board has to be put up at this Station and a clock to face the platform. The Station Building is in an unfinished state. I pointed out the desirability of providing some additional shelter at the Great Western Exchange Station at Marlow Road Station and that the 9 chain curve should have a check rail throughout its length of 12 chains, and the Company's Engineer Mr. Owen promised that this should be done. On the understanding that these matters are forthwith attended to, I am of opinion that the Board of Trade may authorise the opening of this Short Line for traffic as the undertaking, which I herewith forward, to work with one Engine only is satisfactory.

The line, costing about £23,500, was formally opened for passenger traffic on 27th June. A Mr. Patterson of the GWR was also in attendance and handed over a book of rates to be charged for goods.

The *Reading Mercury* for 12th July expressed the opinion that the line 'bids fair to become a great success, the trains being most liberally patronised. On Sunday evening last, the carriages of the Marlow train were literally besieged, some 150 passengers packing themselves into four carriages'.

The first timetable offered 10 trains each way and a through carriage was run on the 10.10 a.m. from Marlow, with a return carriage on the 5 p.m. from Paddington. Goods traffic commenced during the week ending 5th July and it was reported that 'close upon 100 tons of goods passed over it' between Wednesday and Friday, 9th-11th July.

Sadly, no photographs have been found showing the construction or opening of the branch. However, this well-known classic has survived and does give a hazy window on the early years. It was probably taken soon after the line had opened in 1873 and shows the locomotive, a '517' class 0—4—2T No. 522, at Marlow with a train of 4-wheeled stock all hired from the GWR.

CHAPTER THREE

"QUASI INDEPENDENT MANAGEMENT"
1873—1896

Marlow is said to be advancing by leaps and bounds . . . If there is such a being as an old and discontented inhabitant of the town, who is sighing with regret over the past, talks about the good old coaching days, and the departed glories of his native place, even he would be obliged to admit that much has been done of late years to improve the condition of our town and neighbourhood, and now we could point with just pride to our latest and crowning effort, by which, in the face of much discouragement, by the indefatigable exertions of my brother and good friend, Mr. Borgnis, a railway has been brought to our very doors, thereby opening out to us a new era of prosperity and we are beginning to see the first fruits of it. Mills have been reopened which have been for many years lying idle, a new trade has been established which will probably prove eminently successful; labour is well employed; the houses are filled to overflowing; new houses of a better class are springing up, all contributaries to the same stream, all contributing to the wealth and prosperity of the town.

T. O. Wethered MP

IN their original condition the stations were very much simpler than the arrangements which later evolved. At Marlow Road the line simply ran into a bay along the back of the existing single platform and there was neither a direct connection with the Wycombe line nor a conventional run-round loop for the locomotive to run to the other end of its train. Traffic on and off the branch had to undergo two reversals with the short bay line acting as a headshunt. The arrangements are not at all clear, but it appears that the coaches were backed into a siding provided for the purpose and presumably chain shunted out again or run back to the bay by gravity.

Apart from the necessary removal of the goods yard to the opposite side of the running line and the minimal junction arrangements, passenger facilities do not seem to have undergone any enlargement. The Great Marlow directors had already expressed their concern over the facilities and the inspecting officer had pointed out 'the desirability of providing some additional shelter'. Again details are obscure, but certainly an 1879 survey shows the short passenger train shed in position over the bay line and platform, presumably built subsequently to meet the recommendation. In the absence of any photographs, we can only try to imagine the line's virginal appearance, the light flat-bottomed rails stretching across the Thames flood plain, its fresh earthworks lined with the post and rail fencing, including occupation crossing gates erected by John Smith independently of the main contract. In later years there is little evidence of the hedging stipulated — 'the contractors to plant quick set on mound the quick to be of three years growth and to be not greater than 6 inches apart in double rows'. Six feet long mileposts buried 3 feet deep and painted white with black figures are also recorded but there is no record of the makers of 'necessary station signals, electric telegraph and locking apparatus', all of which was supplied by the contractor. It seems likely, but by no means certain, that the signalling at least was purchased from the GWR. The contractor was also responsible for the provision of 'lamp posts, gas pipes and burners, nameboards, clock, office fittings, shelves, counter, drawers and other fixtures'.

At Great Marlow the layout was again minimal as shown on the first edition 25 inch Ordnance Survey map, but there is no evidence of the 32 ft diameter turntable included in the contract, nor any mention of it in the inspecting officer's report. It seems likely that it may have

been intended to install the turntable at the end of the running line, perhaps doubling as a loco release as at some other termini. The arrangement of the platform, headshunt, etc. certainly appears to allow for this. The compact layout was provided with a brick-built station building, goods shed and engine shed and, according to the Board of Trade recommendations, a small, perhaps timber-built, cabin to house the lever frame. The station building was a handsome structure built to a GWR design similar to that employed at Taplow and Hungerford. The goods shed also had a Great Western flavour but the engine shed appears to have been quite unique.

Under an agreement of 26th August 1872, confirmed by GWR Act of 21st July 1873, the following locomotives and stock were provided by the Great Western for £1,090 per year: '1 engine, 1 van, 1 long 1st, 2nd & 3rd compo, 1 second; 1 extra compo, horsebox and carriage truck if required and 12 goods trucks'.

The GWR were to run a service of five trains each way on weekdays (not Sundays) but from the outset they provided more.

Fares charged for the journey between Great Marlow and Marlow Road were as follows:

1st class single	9d.	return	1/2d.
2nd class single	6d.	return	9d.
3rd class single	3d.		
Parliamentary	3d.		

In order to comply with the Cheap Trains Act, fares on the 12.05 p.m. ex-Great Marlow and the 8.6 p.m. ex-Marlow Road were reduced to 2½d. at the end of 1873. During the following August it was also decided to offer 4d. return fares on Saturdays for the poor in the Bourne End district.

With the inevitable confusion between the names of the two stations, Wethered and 'other persons in the neighbourhood' succeeded in persuading the GW to rename Marlow Road station, and from 1st January 1874 it became 'Bourne End'.

The line was heralded as a great success and far exceeded 'the most sanguine expectations of the directors and shareholders'. At the half-yearly meeting of the Great Marlow Railway held at the Crown Hotel on 30th September, directors proudly declared they had every reason to look forward with satisfaction and confidence to the future of the company. The 'cordial assistance' given to them by the Great Western officials was also warmly acknowledged and it was reported that up to that day 13,292 passengers had been booked from Marlow alone.

The contractors were evidently still hard at work during this euphoria, 'the station buildings, yard and other matters connected with the development of the traffic' still undergoing completion.

Although the 1872 agreement with the GWR provided that the line should be maintained and staffed by the Marlow Company 'not having proper men at their disposal', it was arranged that the GW should send men of their own, the Marlow Company paying the staff, except the driver, fireman and guard.

The first station master at Great Marlow was William Porter, formerly employed in the same post at Marlow Road. He had previously also applied not only for the small parcels delivery agency but also for a coal wharf tenancy at the new terminus. The Crown Hotel had also applied for the parcels agency and, under the new and enterprising management of Samuel Hill, operated an omnibus service to the station. He successfully contended that the public were complaining about having to send parcels to the station instead of 'The Crown' as before and the chairman awarded the agency to him for 6 months at one penny per parcel. Goods deliveries were handled by the existing agent, James Johnson, at 1s. 6d. per ton, also W. Porter according to a local directory.

Porter's term of office as station master only lasted until the end of the year. It seems that besides his coal business, for which he had been granted a wharf, he also owned or managed a hotel and certainly by 1875 was operating a cab service from the station forecourt. The minute books simply record that he was unable to continue his station master's duties satisfactorily owing to his other businesses. The next station master, a Mr. Arnold, did not hold the post for long either as he died in July 1875. In October the Marlow company asked the Great Western to nominate an official to take charge of their station at Great Marlow and in response John George Smyth, a booking clerk at Windsor, was appointed at a salary of £100 per annum which was paid by the independent company.

The loco crew, indirectly paid by the Marlow company, were nevertheless under GWR supervision, circumstances which presented Wethered with an embarrassing situation. The incident previously referred to of the driver, J. Saunders, being fined 2/- for carrying him on the engine highlights the situation. Under instructions from J. Armstrong, locomotive superintendent of the GWR, a Mr. Thompson from 'Oxford station Loco dept.' ordered the driver not to allow anyone on the engine and Wethered wrote to Grierson complaining:

I suppose that Mr. Thompson is under the impression that our line is a part of your system, and as I have no intention of entering into a discussion on this point with Mr. Thompson or any other subordinate officer, I shall feel obliged if you will undeceive him. I consider that no one has a right to be on our engine without my express permission and if I am not to be trusted to this extent, I am certainly not fit to be Chairman of this Co. As a matter of fact I usually go on the engine for the express purpose of seeing how the road is settling down with a view to having any faults put right.

When the letter was forwarded to Armstrong for his comment he replied:

One of our directors Captain Bulkeley complained to me that a few weeks ago one driver on the Marlow branch, with Mr. Wethered on his engine, had run past signals and nearly caused an accident. On investigation I find that the Great Marlow Chairman had been on the engine and the driver, of course, was fined according to rule, for allowing any person on his engine without an order. After this I believe Mr. Wethered again got on the engine, and still he insisted to ride on it whether the driver would go or not.

The driver of course could not dispute any further and allowed Mr. Wethered to ride but I intend bringing the matter before the next Board in order, if possible, to put a stop to such proceedings on the part of Mr. Wethered. If the line belongs to them the engine certainly does not, and I do not see that Wethered has any rights to ride on the engine without a proper pass, and I must ask you to kindly put this matter right with him.

Wethered replied:

Sir,

Great Marlow Railway

I am in receipt of your letter of yesterday's date. You appear to me to misunderstand the position of this Company and my object in writing my letter to Mr. Grierson of the 16th inst. As a matter of fact I care nothing whatever about riding on the Engine, but as a matter of principle, I care a great deal about my right to do so. So long as this Company remains an independent Company, it is my duty as its Chairman, to see that its independence is maintained:

I admit, as readily as yourself, the necessity for stringent precautions of the kind in question: the only question between us is, as to who is to enforce these precautions on the Great Marlow Line, and who is to have any discretion at all in the matter.

At the present moment, my Company pays your Company a fixed Annual Rent for your Engine, Carriages &c. and there the matter ends, subject to certain provisions as to the number of trains to be run &c. &c. So long as this arrangement continues in force, and until — as will probably some day be the case — this Company is absorbed into the Great Western Company, I decline to admit that any Rules and Regulations in force on the Great Western, Great Northern or any other foreign line, have any validity whatever on the Great Marlow Line, unless they have been adopted by the Board of Directors of the Great Marlow Company, or are compulsory Regulations of the Board of Trade.

I am not prepared to admit that a Pass signed by you, or by anyone else excepting myself, has any validity on our Line; for were I to do so, I should thereby be sacrificing the independence of this Company, which I have no intention of doing.

You recommend me to apply to the Directors of the Great Western Company for an order: why should I do this? holding as I do, that the Directors of the Great Marlow Company, through me, as their Chairman, are the only competent authority on our Line, until they divest themselves of that authority by a formal Resolution to that effect.

You will, I am sure, readily understand that I write with no personal feeling whatever, but simply to vindicate the independence of this Company, whose interests have been entrusted to my keeping.

Relations between the two companies were otherwise excellent by all accounts and when Owen was paid 100 guineas for his services as engineer during the construction the Marlow company acknowledged his assistance which they felt was 'so cheerfully rendered'. The line's performance during the first 7 months looked encouraging as summarized in this extract from Grierson's report of 8th April 1874.

With the view of ascertaining how far the opening of the Marlow Railway has brought any increased revenue to this Company I have made a comparison of the gross receipts from Passengers booked at Marlow Road during the 7 months ending 31st January 1873 and the receipts at that Station, and at the Great Marlow Station for the 7 months ending 31st January 1874 and also from Goods Traffic sent to and received from those Stations during the same period, and the result is as follows:-

7 months ending January 1873

	Passengers	Parcels	Goods	Total
Marlow Rd.	£1444. 6.10.	£312.11. 4.	£4822.14. 4.	£6579.12. 6.

7 months ending January 1874

	Passengers	Parcels	Goods	Total
Marlow Rd.	789. 7. 7.	184.17. 8.	3461. 8. 3.	4435.13. 6.
Gt. Marlow	1998.11. 6.	267.12.10.	2145. 6. 0.	4411. 0. 4.
	2787.19. 1	452.10. 6.	5606.14. 3.	8846.13.10.
Increase	£1343.12. 3.	£139.19. 2.	£ 783.19.11.	£2267. 1. 4.

From these figures it appears that after deducting the receipts of the Great Marlow Railway this Company's proportion of the receipts on Traffic to and from Marlow Road and Great Marlow increased in the seven months by £632 in Passenger, £102 in Parcels, and £318 in Goods traffic, being an increase of £1052, which may be considered satisfactory.

In as much however as these figures do not include the receipts from Passengers booked from London and other Stations on this Company's Line to Marlow Road or Great Marlow I have had other statements prepared to show the effect which the opening of the Marlow Line had had upon the receipts on Passenger Traffic to as well as from, those places.

The number of Train miles run was 9317 showing an average receipt of 2/6½ per Train mile.

The payment to this Company for Locomotive and Rolling Stock amounted to £556.19.0. showing an average receipt of 1/2½ per Train mile.

In addition to the £9720 agreed to be subscribed by this Company we have temporarily advanced the sum of £2500 the cost of construction of the Junction at Marlow Road and other works, and interest at the rate of 5 per cent will be paid upon this sum until the amount is repaid.

By the Agreement before referred to it is provided that the £9720 subscribed by this Company shall bear a preference dividend up to 5 per cent per annum, the holders of the balance of the Capital having agreed to allow their Dividends to stand over until 5 per cent had been paid upon the amount advanced by this Company.

The result of the seven months working is as under:

The Gross receipts (as has already been stated) were £1215.7.9.

Deducting the cost of Locomotive power paid to this Company (£536.19.0) and other incidental expenses amounting in the aggregate to £799.11.7.

There remains a balance of £415.16.2 as the profit upon the working for the seven months.

After paying interest upon the £2,500 and interest upon Debentures and Loans at 5 per cent there remained a balance of £280.3.8. which admitted of a Dividend at the rate of 4 per cent per annum upon the £9720 advanced by this Company, but no expense has been incurred for maintaining the Line (the Contractor having undertaken to maintain it for 12 months after its completion) it is to be hoped that the Traffic will increase so that at least this rate may be maintained in the current half year. The cost of maintaining the Line is estimated by Mr. Owen at £330 per annum including renewals, and this sum will have to be deducted from the earnings before any part of them can be made available for Dividend.

	From Marlow Road to London Stations		From London Stations to Marlow Road		From Great Marlow to London Stations		From London Stations to Great Marlow	
	No.	Amount £ s d	No.	Amount £ s d	No.	Amount £ s d	No.	Amount £ s d
7 months ended 31st January 1873		921 16 —	5,882	1,081 7 9				
7 months ended 31st January 1874	2,193	384 3 11	3,514	583 4 6	4,639	1,103 7 11	5,210	1,117 7 9
	7,125	1,305 19 11	9,396	1,664 12 3	4,639	1,103 7 11	5,210	1,117 7 9

From these figures it will be seen that in the 7 months there was an increase of 1900 Passengers booked from Marlow Road and Great Marlow Stations to London Stations and an increase of 2842 Passengers booked from London Stations to Marlow Road and Great Marlow, yielding an increase of £1185.

Neither of these statements show the whole effect of the opening of the Line upon this Company's Traffic, nor could this be done without taking out the Bookings from all the Stations which would be a tedious and troublesome matter, but I think the Board will be sufficiently satisfied from these statements that the opening of the Line has increased and is likely to increase the general receipts of this Company particularly the London and Marlow Passenger Traffic.

I may mention that the receipts upon the Marlow Line proper during the six months amounted to

Passengers	Parcels	Goods	Total
£677.11.7.	£37.14.7.	£466.2.8.	£1181.8.10.

It will thus be seen that while the opening of the line has resulted in an increase in the traffic to the extent of £2267 in the seven months equal to £3886 per annum which would probably afford a net gain of £1800 to this Company, the Earnings of the line itself are sufficient even now to pay the whole of the working expenses including maintenance, and the interest on the debentures, and there is ground for the assumption that in a comparatively short period some dividend will be paid upon the ordinary stock.

I am, Gentlemen,
Your obedient Servant
J. Grierson

To The Chairman & Directors
of the Great Western Railway Company.

The contractor was held responsible for the maintenance of the line during the first twelve months for which part of their payment had been withheld. In the event, of £1,000 owing to him he accepted a £500 debenture and in July it was arranged for the GW to take over the maintenance of the line 'at a cost price including a reasonable charge for superintendence'. This had been estimated by Owen at about £330 per annum including renewals. The Great Western were held free from all liabilities 'in respect of accidents or otherwise'.

Sadly, a fatal accident occurred on the Great Marlow Railway on Friday, the 13th of the following month and involved 64 year old Lydia Price, the landlady of the 'Traveller's Friend', Dean Street, Great Marlow. She had travelled on the 12.05 p.m. from Marlow but, on leaving the train at Bourne End, discovered that she had left a 'bundle' in the train. According to the press, she rushed to retrieve it while the train was being set back, presumably prior to running round, but fell between the carriage and the platform. She died later that day.

The Marlow Company owed much to Owen Wethered who, having previously expressed his wish to stand down from the chair, formally resigned at a shareholders meeting on 21st August. Bulkeley testified that without him the line would not have been completed and the meeting voted thanks to him and the directors and said 'the town owed them an everlasting debt of gratitude for what they had done'. Wethered was succeeded by Borgnis as chairman, with Capt. Bulkeley as vice-chairman.

The limitations of the original facilities at the terminus soon became evident with the increasing traffic but in August 1874 the question of altering and extending the sidings in the yard was deferred. In December it was decided that the 'necessary additional siding from the wharves to the main line' should be constructed by the company's ganger and staff, the rods and locking gear and sleepers being supplied by the GWR. This was probably the 'back' siding but it is not clear whether the work was actually carried out as in September 1875 'new sidings' were again deferred, 'except the one by the goods shed'. This may have been in addition to the 1874 one and would appear to have been laid as in September 1876 it was reported that the platform, which was also considered too short, had been lengthened and a new siding provided 'near the goods shed'. Two cattle pens had also been erected (perhaps on the site previously allowed for a turntable?), the works being carried out mainly by ganger John Plumridge and the men under him. The cash book mentions payment to J. S. Carter for 'making road to coal wharf and extending goods siding'. This must have been a John Samuel Carter, a builder in Chapel Street.

Further enlargements were later carried out at the beginning of 1879 when the short loop on the south side of the running line was extended. Whilst this could have been used for running round goods trains, it seems to have been extended in order to increase accommodation in the goods yard. At this period the railways were at pains to avoid unnecessary facing points on running lines and extending the loop provided a means of extending the 'back' siding in the yard and allowed for future extension, simply by moving an existing facing connection already approved by the Board of Trade.

The alterations were inspected by Col. F. H. Rich on 28th March 1879. He stated that whilst the facing points leading to the loop line (approx. 150 ft from the cabin) were fitted with a lifting bar, they required 'a locking bolt, which should be worked from the cabin'. He also pointed out that the station was opened for passenger traffic 'prior to locking bolts and lifting bars being required by the Board of Trade and there are two other facing points at the station which it would be desirable to secure with bolts and bars'. He also recommended that clocks should be provided 'in the signal cabin and outside the station', from which it would seem that similar advice given when the line was opened was not heeded. On the same visit, Col. Rich also inspected new works at Bourne End where the GWR had converted an existing siding into a short loop alongside the branch curve for running round passenger trains. The new works were approved but the Colonel again recommended locking for all the facing points, and the provision of clocks. He also said that the platform was too short, but this does not appear to have been attended to. Indeed it is difficult to see how this could have been achieved with the limited space available.

Passenger receipts had also continued to rise, the total number of passengers conveyed to the end of 1876 being as follows:

From	26/6/73	to	30/6/73	1,981
	30/6/73	to	31/12/73	41,902
	31/12/73	to	31/12/74	78,461
	31/12/74	to	31/12/75	81,368
	31/12/75	to	31/12/76	87,625
			Total	291,337*

*exclusive of 57 season tickets issued.

On Friday, 13th July 1877, another accident occurred at Bourne End, when a passenger train from Great Marlow came into the station at too great a speed and hit the buffer stops at the end of the bay platform. The official Board of Trade report was as follows:

Board of Trade,
(Railway Department,)
13, Downing Street, 30th July 1877.

Sir,
     In compliance with the instructions contained in the Order of the 20th instant, I have the honour to report, for the information of the Board of Trade, the result of my inquiry into the circumstances connected with the accident that occurred on the 13th instant, at the Bourne End station, on the Great Western Railway.

     A passenger-train from Great Marlow came into the station at too great a speed, and ran against the stop-buffers at the end of the dock-platform siding. Six passengers and the guard of the train were hurt, but their injuries are reported to be slight.

     On the day in question, the passenger-train which is due to leave Great Marlow at 7.46 p.m. left that station five minutes late. It consisted of a tank-engine, running with the coal-bunk in front, three passenger-carriages, a break-van with a guard, ten loaded, five empty waggons, and two waggons loaded with chairs. The vehicles were coupled together in the order in which they are given. The train reached Bourne End at 7.56, which was four minutes beyond its proper time, so that it gained about one minute in running the distance of 2¾ miles between Great Marlow and Bourne End stations. The train is allowed six minutes for running the distance in question, which would give a speed of about 30 miles an hour, allowing for the small delay of starting and pulling up.

The engine-driver stated that he approached Bourne End distant-signal at a speed of about 19 to 20 miles an hour, and that he shut off steam before he reached the distant-signal, which is nearly half a mile from the station. As he approached the station home-signal, which is about 170 yards from the end of the station-platform, he thought that his train was running too fast, so he desired the fireman to put on the break which was screwed hard on as the train passed the signal. The train was then reported to be running at a speed of about six miles an hour. After passing the home-signal, the driver reversed his engine and sanded the rails, but he could not stop his train before he ran into the buffers at the end of the station dock-siding at a speed of about four or five miles an hour.

Three loaded waggons were thrown off the rails, and one other waggon had two wheels thrown off the rails. The cast-iron buffers of the engine were cracked, but very slight damage was done to the buffer-stops and rolling-stock.

The acting-guard of the train stated that he thought his train was going rather faster than usual as it approached the Bourne End distant-signal, and that he put the break on slightly, and screwed it hard on as he reached a bridge over a river just outside the home-signal. This man was knocked down by the collision.

The engine-driver had previously acted as fireman for about seven years. The accident happened about a fortnight after he had been employed as driver, and on the fifth day that he drove the 7.46 p.m. train into Bourne End station. The only reason that he could assign for the accident was that the train was heavier than he had ever driven before, and that he misjudged the power at his disposal for stopping it. He appeared to be a steady man, and bears an excellent character. I think he was mistaken in the speed of his train at the time that he approached the Bourne End distant-signal, as, if he had only been running 19 or 20 miles an hour and had shut off steam as he stated that he did at that time, the train would hardly have reached Bourne End station, which was fully half a mile beyond the point at which he stated he had shut off steam. The line from the place where he shut off steam is level to within about 740 yards of the station, it then rises 1 in 165 for a distance of about 240 yards, and is level thence to the end of the dock, a distance of about 500 yards.

The accident was caused by carelessness or want of experience on the part of the engine-driver.

Although the signals at Bourne End station had nothing to do with causing the present accident, the approach to the home-signal is very much blinded by trees, and I would recommend that this signal should be improved.

I have, &c.,
F. H. RICH,
Colonel, R.E.

The Secretary,
(Railway Department),
Board of Trade.

According to the *Bucks Herald*, the wood and earth buffer stop was broken, one of the goods trucks smashed, its contents strewed the line, the guard was bruised, but the passengers, who were taken to Maidenhead or Marlow in flies, escaped with only a shaking.

A few years later, on Sunday, 26th April 1883, the 10.08 a.m. Bourne End to Marlow train overran the platform at Marlow and 'came into a slight collision with the stop blocks'. However, whilst the passengers were 'somewhat alarmed and shaken', none was hurt nor was the rolling stock damaged. According to the *Bucks Herald*,

this had been the only accident to occur at Marlow since the opening of the line.

The branch also made the news at the end of 1877 when a 'robbery' took place at Marlow station. It occurred between 6 and 7 o'clock on the evening of 30th November. Shortly after the arrival of the London train, Mr. Smyth, the station master went home as usual to tea, locking the till and office door before he left. James, a guard, who was in the adjoining parcels office, disturbed the burglar and an accomplice, who ran off with 30 shillings from the till. It seems that in their haste they had overlooked £4 at the back of the till, and in any case the bulk of the cash had been locked in the safe. It seems that money had also been stolen from a drawer in the parcels office about a year earlier.

The directors subsequently decided that the robbery loss 'should fall on Mr. Smyth the stationmaster, as he ought on leaving the office to have put the money into his safe instead of leaving it in the till'.

Porter Wright also blotted his copybook about this time and an expected rise in income 'was decided to be deferred in consequence of the late mishap of trucks getting off the siding at Marlow'. It was not until 1880 that his wage was raised from 18 shillings to 19 shillings per week. Porter Plumridge's wages were raised to 6 shillings and station master George Thomas Broad's salary was increased from £100 to £110 per annum.

Being so close to the river, the line was subject to flooding. In 1877 the trackbed was raised by 'another 5 inches, thus making altogether since its formation a rise of 15 inches for a considerable distance along its lowest part most affected by floods'. This also altered the gradient 'so that the ascent from the gate lodge could now be managed by goods trains, when being shunted, without difficulty'. In the same context, the chairman reported that he had the ground prepared some distance for a quick hedge, but couldn't get the plants at the price he wished.

Increasing goods traffic brought about the provision of a loading gauge, new wharves and an additional goods siding at Marlow, the latter being completed early in 1879. In the same year the gravel pit, believed to have been used in the construction of the line, was levelled, the fence removed 'and the pit given up in good order'.

In a report to the GW directors in July 1878 analysing the traffic loss at Bourne End since the opening of the Great Marlow Railway, Grierson assessed the financial effects as follows:

> Prior to the opening of the Marlow Railway the whole of the Marlow traffic was dealt with at the Marlow Road, now the Bourne End Station, and the natural result of the opening of a railway into the town of Marlow was to abstract a large part of the traffic which up to that time has been conducted at that station. In the year ending June 1872 a complete year prior to the opening of the Marlow line, this traffic amounted in value to £13,061, but in the following year (during half of which the line was open) it fell to £7,871 and the receipts for each year since that time up to June 1877 have been respectively £8,234, £8,286 and £7,804.
>
> Taking the last year as a basis the traffic diverted from the Bourne End station by the opening of the line to Marlow amounts in value to (say) £5,200 a year, taking no account of the natural increase which, had the through line not been opened, would have been considerable.

605 MARLOW. — *High Street and Crown Hotel.*

Collection C. E. Turner

Marlow High Street c.1900 featuring the Crown Hotel where the GMR board meetings were held.

On the other hand the receipts at the Great Marlow Station have been for the same periods as under

Year ending June 1874			£10,985
,,	,,	,, 1875	12,620
,,	,,	,, 1876	13,512
,,	,,	,, 1877	14,221

and as the Marlow Company's proportion of these receipts amounted only to the undermentioned sums, viz:-

Year ending June 1874			£ 2,363
,,	,,	,, 1875	2,530
,,	,,	,, 1876	2,773
,,	,,	,, 1877	2,803

it follows the real gain to the Great Western Company by the opening of the line, leaving out of the question the natural increase in the traffic which would no doubt have taken place even if the line into Marlow had not been made, has been as under:-

	G.W. Proportion of Marlow traffic	Less decrease at Bourne End	Nett Gain
	£	£	£
Year ending June 1874	8,625	5,190	3,435
,, ,, ,, 1875	10,093	4,827	5,266
,, ,, ,, 1876	10,709	4,775	5,964
,, ,, ,, 1877	11,418	5,257	6,161

a result which the Board will no doubt consider satisfactory.

It has been mentioned above that the Great Western find engines and carriages and pay all running expenses for the sum of £1,090 per annum. On the mileage of 1877 this sum gives us a little over 1/1 per mile and may be said therefore to cover the actual expenses incurred.

The receipts of the Marlow Company have from the first been sufficient to meet all their engagements, to maintain the line in good order, (on which their actual outlay is about the sum which Mr. Owen estimated in 1874 that it would cost) to pay the full amount of interest on their Debentures, and to pay a small Dividend upon our invested capital of £9,720 which, as before stated, has a priority over the remainder of the ordinary stock.

The Dividends have been as under:

½ year ended December 1873 at the rate of 4%		per annum
For the whole year 1874	2½%	,,	,,
,, ,, ,, ,, 1875	2½%	,,	,,
,, ,, ,, ,, 1876	4%	,,	,,
,, ,, ,, ,, 1877	3¾%	,,	,,

or an average of over 3¼ per cent for the whole period.

There can be no doubt that the traffic will contine to improve and that we shall receive a higher if not the full dividend in the future.

The quasi-independent management of the line is to some extent an anomaly, and I have no doubt that we shall sooner or later be asked either to work or take over the line altogether.

The line, however, appears to be very economically managed, and I do not anticipate that if we worked it ourselves any saving could be effected, hence so long as matters go on as smoothly as they have hitherto done there would appear to be no reason why any change should be made especially as the other shareholders would be almost certain to get some provision inserted into any arrangement that might be entered into either for working or purchase, which would secure to them some return if small, upon their capital, and thereby extinguish or prejudicially affect the prior rights which we at present possess.

CAPTAIN BULKELEY

By 1880 the original rails were becoming worn and a start was made on installing steel replacements, a long task which lasted until at least the end of 1889. However, despite expenditure on a stock of new rails, June marked the end of the first half year since opening that the full dividend contemplated was paid to the GW, and the following year even the ordinary shareholders received 2½%.

The railway was a success, particularly when compared with similar independent lines. Furthermore, figures maintained an upward trend, with the number of passengers (upwards of 90,000) increasing every year.

The directors were evidently a good team and justly proud of their achievements, but, sadly, in 1882 Capt. Bulkeley died. He had represented the GWR's interest, but such was his contribution that Borgnis, himself suffering from failing health, was moved to testify of his 'warm interest in their little company'. He had 'often put himself to personal inconvenience on their behalf. Although so comparatively small a child compared with the Great Western, he seemed to regard it with the same interest he did the larger company.'

Walter Robinson, another GWR representative, was appointed in Bulkeley's place. Both Batting, the secretary since Ward's death in 1872, and Wanklyn, the other GW director, had previously been replaced by Messrs. John Rawson, a local solicitor, and Richard Basset respectively. The stalwart Marlow representatives, Borgnis and Wethered, were also nearing retirement. On re-election at a meeting on March 1884, Borgnis said he had seriously thought of retiring, 'the only thing which induced him to accept the office was his desire to see some very desirable improvements at Bourne End before he finally retired from the Board.'

COLONEL WETHERED

Wethered subsequently thought it important to have more than two Marlow directors on the board:

'Borgnis and I are practically the only two local shareholders who have any knowledge of the details of the company's affairs, that the working of these details must necessarily devolve on the Marlow directors, that neither Mr. Borgnis nor I are what we were 15 years ago; and that if anything were to happen to either of us, the other would be unable to carry on the work alone; that it is consequently of the greatest importance that another Marlow shareholder should become conversant with the company's affairs, in view of such a contingency.'

The Great Western did not sympathise and said it was 'more convenient' to adhere to the existing arrangements. In 1886 Owen Wethered (promoted to Colonel that year) subsequently retired to admit A. Lawrence, a local auctioneer, to the board. He was the largest shareholder of original shares next to Wethered's. In the same year A. D. Cripps, a Marlow solicitor, also replaced Rawson on the board.

In March 1887 Borgnis, who had served as chairman since 29th September 1874, was finally forced to retire through failing health. At the same time the Great Western sanctioned the requested increase in directors and Frederick George Saunders, secretary of the GWR, was elected to the board along with another new candidate, J. H. Wright, a local paper manufacturer. Robinson was re-elected and Col. Wethered returned to take Borgnis' place. However, he only held office until 13th November 1889 when 'under medical advice' he was also forced to retire[1]. The shareholders expressed their gratitude for his service and the following July presented him with a silver salver. Both he and Borgnis were sorely missed, the shareholders, townspeople and all concerned acknowledging the undisputed success of their leadership. At the age of 78 Borgnis died within a year of retiring. He had been a great benefactor to the people of Marlow. Apart from his role in the railway company, he seems to have taken the lead in many local institutions. He was, for example, a school governor and patron of the cricket, rowing and gentlemen's clubs. He gave a magnificent cup for coxless fours at Marlow Regatta which, at the time of writing, is still rowed for.

Peter Borgnis was the great grandson of an Italian painter who settled in England about the middle of the eighteenth century when commissioned by Sir Francis Dashwood to paint murals at his home, West Wycombe Park. Dashwood wanted to make his house, inside and out, a constant reminder of the things he had seen and most admired during his tours of Italy.

The painter Borgnis undertook several other commissions including the ceiling and cove of the Ionic Temple at Duncombe Park.

Colonel Wethered was described in the *South Bucks Free Press* as 'exceedingly popular with all classes'. He was a staunch Conservative and, born in 1837, belonged to an old and highly esteemed Marlow family, was educated at

---

[1] He wintered in Teneriffe and resided there permanently before his death in 1908, only returning to Marlow for the two mid-summer months each year.

Eton and Christ Church, Oxford, before joining the family firm of Thomas Wethered & Sons, brewers.

In 1859 he had joined the Volunteer Movement inaugurated in the fear of an invasion from France. From a private he quickly passed through the ranks until in 1886 he became honorary Colonel of the First Bucks Volunteer Battalion. His other offices in Marlow, described as impossible to enumerate, included directorship of Marlow Gas Co. Ltd., he represented Marlow on the Board of Guardians and the Bucks County Council, churchwarden at the parish church, president of the Cottage Hospital, Justice of the Peace for Buckinghamshire, a governor of Sir Wm. Borlase's School, a trustee of the Marlow Parish Charities and the Almshouse Trust. He was also actively involved in various local sports.

On 23rd October 1889, when Colonel Wethered announced his intention to retire, contrary to the newspaper reports, the minute book records that he said he felt the time had come to sell out to the GWR. The

PETER BORGNIS

suggestion 'as to the advisability of the original share-holders parting with their interests in the undertaking to the Great Western Co.' was raised at another meeting the following week.

Henry Lambert, general manager of the GWR, intimated that his company would give £13 a share and also the largest portion of the reserve fund amounting to a further sum of £1 15s per share'. In being appointed the Colonel's successor, C. A. Cripps of Henley, MP and County Magistrate (not to be confused with A. D. Cripps), became responsible for guiding the company through the subsequent negotiations. However, the shareholders were not tempted with the Great Western's initial offer and, comforted by their dividends, confidently decided to remain independent.

The previous year, after much urging by the Great Western, the Marlow company had agreed to install a block telegraph system. The line had been worked on the one engine in steam principle, using a train staff, but in the summer months this severely restricted operation.

When selling the land for the railway Ellames had imposed restrictions on the erection of telegraph posts and wanted the wires buried underground. However, he subsequently withdrew his objections and the equipment was installed in time for the summer traffic. Whilst this was undoubtedly of great advantage, it cost the Marlow company £236 15s. 7d. It seems the Marlow directors were not fully aware of the Great Western's intentions, as when the telegraphic equipment had been installed, they 'found a patent locking system had been introduced. This had never been ordered from the GW and it was found to be both inconvenient and expensive'. It later transpired 'Mr. Higgins never explained to the Marlow company that the apparatus would require nearly the entire time of the porter and so materially increase the expenses at the station.'

The chairman went on to say that after a further trial, the apparatus had proved 'useless for all practical purposes' and suggested under the circumstances that the GW should remove it or 'contribute substantially towards the extra expenses necessarily incurred'.

Higgins' clerk was sent to explain its use and Saunders undertook to see Higgins and Spagnoletti, telegraph and electrical superintendent of the GWR.

In the meantime, the Marlow company approached the Board of Trade for permission to abandon the system. They consented providing they received 'a sealed undertaking by the Co. and the GWR Co. not to have more than one engine in steam on the line at the same time'. However, the Great Western's consent was not given.

In November the additional expense of 'warming the signalbox from which the electric locking apparatus was worked' also became apparent, but the following spring negotiations were still pending with the GW who finally agreed to use the apparatus only during the three busy months of the season. Whether or not this was enforced is not clear. They also agreed to accept the actual cost price of maintaining the equipment 'instead of the price based on the average cost of maintaining similar work over the whole GWR system'.

The other point of contention between the two companies was the extra payment claimed by the GWR 'for the hire of trucks beyond the number specified in the original working agreement. This was eventually settled by the annual payment of £1,090 being increased to £1,215 for the supply of any additional rolling stock that may from time to time be required'.

The original weekday service had been generous by branch line standards and consisted of ten return trains. The first departure at 8.28 a.m. made connections for Paddington, arrival being at 9.50. A through carriage for London was provided on the 10.10 a.m. departure and returned by the 5.00 p.m. Paddington. The last departure at 8.44 p.m. connected for Aylesbury whilst the final arrival, the 9.06 p.m., had connections with the 7.35 p.m. from Paddington.

At this time the Sunday service had consisted of four return trains. An early start of 7.35 a.m. enabled Paddington to be reached at 9.20, but there were apparently no trains on the branch between 10.15 a.m. and 7.35 p.m.

Details of early goods services are not clear as no full service timetables appear to have been published until the 1880s.

Whilst the frequency of the weekday service was gradually increased, there were no significant alterations to the Sunday pattern until 1882 when the 9.45 p.m. from Marlow ran through to Maidenhead.

At the same period a late return trip was provided on Saturday, leaving Marlow at 9.50 p.m. This late working became a familiar feature of the timetable during the remaining independent years.

On summer Saturdays and Sundays of 1884 the 2.20 p.m. from Paddington appears to have run through to Marlow. This was apparently only short-lived as by 1886 there was only a connectional service on the branch on Saturdays and by 1887 the Sunday working was similar.

In the same year the 6.10 p.m. from Marlow ran to Maidenhead and returned at 6.40. These appear to have been the only through weekday workings at this time but on summer Sundays there were two such trains.

By 1893 a 5.15 p.m. Paddington to Marlow ran on weekdays and there were two throughs on Sundays; one of these, the 10.00 a.m. from Paddington, in similar timings, was to become a familiar feature.

By the late 1880s the weekday service had been increased to sixteen return trains including Saturday workings, and at this period and into the 1890s increased to twenty, with some nine workings on summer Sundays.

W. C. King had died at the end of the summer of 1889 and was replaced by Lt. Col. C. E. Edgcumbe and it is hardly surprising that when F. G. Saunders was appointed Chairman of the Great Western in March 1890, he resigned from the Marlow board because of his 'increased duties'. C. T. Murdock, MP, who had been appointed a director of the GWR on 5th December 1889 in place of Sir Daniel Gooch, took his place and when Basset died the following year, he was replaced by a W. H. Wills.

The need for improvements at Bourne End had long been a talking point but when it was raised at a meeting in March 1892, the chairman stated that 'he understood the GW had in contemplation to mutually improve Bourne End Station at an early date'.

Bourne End was still only served by a single line through the station (and run round loop) with no crossing facilities; consequently trains were often delayed, particularly when a goods train occupied the section through extensive shunting operations (a frequent cause of complaint). The necessary improvements were extensive, the initial estimate of £4,151 15s. 0d. in August 1892 being superseded in December, when the 'station alterations and additions, locking and other works' were estimated at £4,743. Of this it transpired that '£315 would be spent on the property of the Marlow Railway' who agreed to pay £12 12s. 0d. p.a. as interest on the amount and thus avoid the necessity of finding further capital.

Around this time the Marlow Company incurred other additional expenditure, the engine shed needed 'rebuilding and improving', together with a new water tank. Extensive repairs were required to the bridge over a stream at Bourne End and in 1895 heavy flood damage necessitated remedial works on the line. A large amount of refencing was also undertaken for £100. The dividend of 5% and even 5½% paid on the ordinary shares dropped to 1½% for the year ending 30th June 1894 and, no doubt prompted by these circumstances, T. O. Wethered was in favour of 'coming to terms with the Great Western for the acquisition by them of the Marlow line. He felt sure it would be in the interest of their Co. and of the town to do so. If the GWR acquired the line, they would do their utmost to make Marlow an attractive place for visitors'.

The Marlow company's difficult position became only too apparent again when, in an effort to protect their funds, A. D. Cripps rejected a quantity of poor quality fence posts supplied by the Great Western and set about finding an alternative supply. For daring to question the action of the GWR the matter went straight to James Inglis, General Manager of the GWR who, in a letter to R. Nelson, solicitor of the GWR, on 7th May 1896 said:

It is evidently hopeless to satisfy Mr. Cripps in the way of maintenance. I have come to the conclusion that maintenance should be given to the Marlow Co. that they themselves maintain the line in their own way, of course this means that I should still keep an eye on the branch, and whenever I think it is not sufficiently well maintained for the stock of this Co. to run over it in safety I will advise you that such is the case so that no risks be run by the GWR.

Great Marlow station staff of 1892. *Courtesy Pendon Museum*

This photograph, an exciting chance discovery late in our researches, is thought to have been taken to show the floods of 1894. It shows the layout prior to the 1901 platform extension and associated modifications and features the original signal box. The '517' class 0—4—2T with the single carriage on the right appears to be standing on the curious short stub siding, the view confirming the absence of any buffer stops as suggested by the track plans. The engine shed is shown in its intermediate condition with the recent addition of the elevated water tank.

Courtesy Klaus Marx

Perhaps you may wonder at my decision as above but from a letter I have from Mr. Pain[1] whom the Directors of the Marlow Co. have called in to advise them with reference to maintenance of the line and also on account of the fact that Mr. Cripps is interfering with the men and lately has stopped the erection of some fencing for which the materials, posts and wire, had been delivered on the ground, and informed them that he was to purchase some different material without any communication to myself, it is clear that I cannot be responsible any longer under these conditions nor do I choose to be troubled so much with such a small matter.

Notice might be given that the GW Co. cease to maintain this branch on the 30th June next.

In the meantime Cripps wrote:

On 23rd February 1895 I gave notice to your Co. that our Co. could not agree to pay for items and materials without consent or approval.

I now find that on or about December last a lot of old timber absolutely unsuitable for post fencing was delivered and I believe charged for in your last half year's accounts against us and I am further told that your engineers dept. have instructed the gangers to use the material in fencing.

Our company really cannot consent to such waste of money. An inspection of the fencing put up during the last four or so years will surely show that the material however is quite unfit for the purpose — already much of it is decayed and therefore extravagant.

I have under the above circumstances and by direction of the chairman told the ganger to use none of the materials and I have ordered proper material to be supplied from another source for the quarter mile fencing that should now be done. The accounts for last year were settled without referring to outstanding questions and I must ask your company to take back the old material delivered as above and credit us with the value charged unless they can find any competent independent engineer to pass the timber as suitable and proper for a permanent fence.

Perhaps you will also advise your engineer that I have instructed the Ganger not to use any of the old material in question. I have not written to your engineers dept. as I am not sure with which officer I should communicate.

The termination of maintenance was referred to the Law & Parliamentary Committee of the GW whose minutes of 13th May 1896 record:

A letter from the Secretary of the Great Marlow Railway Co. was submitted complaining of the materials used in the maintenance by this Co. of the Marlow Railway, and stating that instructions had been given to the Ganger not to proceed with certain fencing on the ground that the timber was unsuitable for the purpose.

The Chief Engineer stated that the Line was maintained in the same manner as and with similar materials to those used upon the Co.'s Branch Lines, and it having been explained that the Line is provisionally maintained by this Co. merely for the convenience of the Marlow Co. and at their request, the Committee, with the concurrence of the Solicitor, agreed to recommend that notice be given to that Co. to terminate on the 30th proximo the arrangement for maintenance, and that the Marlow Co. be required after that date to maintain their own Line in accordance with the terms of the Agreement of the 26th of August 1872.

[1] Presumably Arthur Cadlick Pain, light railway engineer.

The following letter dated 20th May was sent to Cripps:

I duly received your letter of 11th instant with regard to the maintenance of the Marlow Line and have since had an opportunity of obtaining the instructions of my Board thereon.

The Directors were extremely surprised to learn that you had taken upon yourself to countermand the instructions given by the Engineer to the Company's Ganger as to the erection of the fencing to which you refer and they cannot but regard such a course of action as absolutely incompatible with the existing arrangements for the maintenance of the line.

I find on inquiry that in accordance with the usual practice old timber was used for the fencing in the line at Marlow and the Engineer advises me that it was perfectly suitable for the purpose, and such as is generally used.

You are no doubt aware that the maintenance of the line was undertaken by this Company in 1874 at the express request of our own Chairman of the Marlow Co. and to meet the account of that Company.

The line has since been dealt with on exactly the same footing as the branch lines of this Company, and while, on the one hand, no unnecessary expense has been incurred, on the other, the standard of efficiency has been duly maintained.

Having regard to the course which you have seen fit to take in the present case, and inasmuch as your Directors appear to be dissatisfied generally with the mode in which this Company has carried out the present arrangement for the maintenance of the line, my Directors think it desirable that your Company should assume their responsibility in this respect; and I am therefore instructed to give you notice that this Company will cease to maintain the Marlow Railway from the 30th June next, after which date your Company will be required to maintain it in accordance with the powers of the agreement of 26th August 1872.

I will ask you to be good enough to acknowledge the receipt of this letter.

Cripps replied:

I am indebted for your letter of yesterday which I will reply to in detail after I have received the instructions of my Directors. But in the meantime I may perhaps remind you that the original difficulty arose when it appeared to us that your Company were charging a full price for new timber where they were in the habit of supplying very indifferent material. On our protest more than a year back, you made a deduction in the last consignment of second hand material and it was then understood that no more would be supplied without the approval of our Co. But for all that, I found before I wrote my last letter to you that there was a considerable stock of most indifferent material on hand which had already been charged against us, and I think I suggested that the efficiency of the material should be left, if necessary, to the opinion of any independent gentleman you liked to name.

In the past it appears that in addition to second hand material, a considerable quantity of scotch and spruce fir has been supplied and the fact that after a few years' use such timber in the fences has given way seems the best evidence that it is perfectly unsuitable and extremely costly for the use which has been made of it.

I do not see how our line can be compared with the branch lines of your own Co. for it would be quite a different matter if the old timber belonged to us and we were using it for our own purposes rather than selling it as fine wood.

In a subsequent letter to Mills, Inglis wrote that Cripps was

> . . . not aware that the second hand timber supplied for the fence posts is yellow pine creosoted timber, which costs much more when new than the cheaper qualities of fir. Second hand timber of the above quality is more durable than larch and at the present moment we are charging the Marlow Co. for the fencing, exclusive of fixing, which is done by the men working on the Branch, at the rate of £1 6s. 0d. per chain, whereas larch fencing in the market would cost £1 10s. 0d. per chain. The cost of fixing being practically the same (i.e. about 12/- per chain) so that Mr. Cripps is complaining of the economy we are practising on behalf of this Co.
>
> Mr. Cripps also complains about Scotch Fir and Scotch Spruce having been supplied in years past, and that it only lasted a few years, that is this Co.'s experience on a much larger scale no matter what efforts were made about the best quality.
>
> I really cannot gather from Mr. Cripps' letter what he would have wanted to be done in the way of fencing, except it be that we should have considered oak posts, but even these are in many instances of doubtful life.
>
> The whole letter appears to me to clearly further show that it is impossible for me to continue the maintenance hampered as this has become.

The Marlow Company was clearly in an awkward position for in seeking value for money they had alienated the Great Western and clearly were not prepared to seek alternative arrangements for maintenance. Cripps managed to secure a meeting with J. L. Wilkinson, chairman of the GWR, and whilst the details are not recorded, Cripps managed to secure an agreement to extend the existing arrangements for another 3 months while negotiations for the Great Western purchasing the undertaking were in hand.

It is difficult to see how this unfortunate episode affected the purchase. The sale would certainly relieve both parties of the problem, but although relations between the two companies at this time were hardly ideal, the purchase was undoubtedly accelerated.

The terms appear to have been favourable to both companies, in short £12,420 or £15 for each of the 828 ordinary £10 shares. This represented an unusual arrangement as under such circumstances shares in the parent company would normally have been issued. This was accepted at an extraordinary general meeting of the Marlow Company whose minute book includes the following cutting from the *South Bucks Standard* 'in lieu of written minutes . . . It is an accurate report of the proceedings and moreover gives a correct representation of the general circumstances leading to the takeover of the local shares.'

MARLOW RAILWAY COMPANY
Transfer to the G.W.R. Company

An extraordinary general meeting of this company was held at the Crown Hotel, Great Marlow, on Saturday, the 25th July, for the purpose of considering and approving the proposal for the transfer of the undertaking of the Great Marlow Railway to the Great Western Railway Company. We commented on this proposal a week or two back, and it was apparent that the shareholders present at the meeting agreed to the view we then expressed that the proposal was much to their benefit; and from what the Chairman said we trust that the general welfare of the town will not suffer now that its interests are committed entirely to the safe keeping of the G.W.R. Company. The result of this arrangement is in short that the shareholders will receive something over £16 for each £10 ordinary share which they hold, and also their dividend up to 30th June last, as from which date the G.W.R. Company take over the business. There were present at the meeting Mr. C. A. Cripps, Q.C., M.P., chairman of the company; Lieut.-Col. the Hon. C. E. Edgcumbe and Mr. W. Robinson, who represent the G.W.R. on the directorate, and Mr. A. Lawrence and Mr. J. H. Wright, who are also directors; the Rev. M. Graves, and Messrs. T. O. Wethered, G. R. Ward, William Batting, A. Davis, J. W. Morgan, R. N. Smith, H. Collins, and Maddison, the Secretary (Mr. A. D. Cripps), &c.

The Chairman, in opening the meeting, said that it was now seven years since he had become Chairman of the Company on the retirement of Col. Wethered through ill-health. At that time negotiations had been on foot for the transfer of the Company to the G.W.R., and with Colonel Wethered he had several times met the representatives of the G.W.R. on the subject. The negotiations failed then because they thought they could not get sufficiently good terms, but ever since then his opinion had been that as soon as fair and equitable terms could be obtained the transfer should be made. The G.W.R. Company had treated them well, but he doubted whether the shareholders realised how much friction necessarily arose between a small Company like theirs and a large Company like the G.W.R., jointly managing the local line. The directors had tried to get rid of the friction and at the same time to guard the interests of their shareholders, but the difficulty increased year by year. Another difficulty which faced them was the almost immediate need of an expenditure of about £2,000, on the station. He had gone into the matter with the G.W.R. officials and they had assured him that that sum was needed to bring the station up to date. This could possibly be raised by the issue of further capital, but it would mean increasing their present capital by 25 per cent. Under those circumstances negotiations again arose, resulting in an offer which he (the Chairman) thought fair and generous. When he became Chairman the shares were selling at £8 and earning a dividend of 3 or 4 per cent, and when they learnt the proffered terms and considered that the line was now acknowledged as a 5 per cent one they would, he thought, admit that the directors had done their best for them. The terms were embodied in the minute of a meeting held between himself and Mr. Matthews, chief accountant, and Mr. Nelson, solicitor, on behalf of the G.W.R. which were as follows:—

Minutes of a meeting at Abingdon-street on Monday, 6th July, 1896. Present: Mr. Cripps, Q.C., M.P., Great Marlow Company; Messrs. Nelson and Matthews, Great Western Company.

1. It was agreed that the Great Western Company should acquire the 828 shares of £10 each held by sundry persons by a cash payment of £15 per share as soon as the necessary transfers could be completed, the present holders of such shares to be entitled to receive in addition any dividend that may be declared in respect of the period up to the 30th June last, the Great Western Company participating in respect of their preferred shares.

2. Mr. Nelson undertook with a view to prevent difficulties hereafter arising, as to the transfer of the undertaking of the Marlow Company to the G.W.R. Company to have the

conveyances to the Marlow Company examined with the land plan.

	£	s	d	£	s	d
3. In regard to the reserve fund which, on the 31st December last stood at				1,749	13	6
It was agreed to deduct therefrom the suspense account	344	18	4			
And to pay the G.W. Co. the proportion they have contributed thereto out of the dividend on their preferred shares	300	0	0	644	18	4
Leaving to be retained by the Marlow Co.				£1,104	15	2

4. The G. W. Company to adopt the debentures and preferred shares of the Marlow Company and assume the capital liabilities existing on the 30th June last.

5. Mr. Matthews undertook to render the accounts for the six months to the 30th June last as early as possible and to advise their secretary about the date they would be finished.

The general result of these terms would be that the shareholders would first of all receive £15 per £10 share on their executing transfers to the G.W.R. This money had actually been paid, and any shareholder might get his money at once on executing his transfer and handing over his share certificates. They would also receive their dividend on their shares up to the 30th June last, which would probably be the best they had ever had, perhaps 6 or 7 per cent. On the adjustment of the reserve and suspense accounts, the G.W.R. would pay them about £1,100, and with the amount paid for the stock at the station, which the G.W.R. had agreed to take over at a valuation, they would certainly receive an additional £1 5s., and possibly something between £1 5s. and £1 10s. As part of the arrangement with the G.W.R. there was a sum of £100, which might be voted to the Secretary as compensation, and to cover the additional work involved in the negotiations for and carrying out the transfer. The necessary resolution to effect this he would propose afterwards. There would also be an amount of £15 15s. to be paid to an engineer who had surveyed the line on their behalf before the present negotiations had arisen. He thought the terms should be accepted. A large amount would be paid per share, and the shareholders would have the benefit of the dividend to 30th June last; also, he considered, that benefit would accrue to the town from the

large capital expenditure that must shortly be made by the G.W.R., and which would have been impossible or very difficult for their Company. He concluded by formally moving that the minutes which had been read should be adopted by the shareholders.

Mr. T. O. Wethered, in seconding the resolution said that he must express what he thought was their unanimous approval of the minutes. He was perhaps one of the largest shareholders, and had all along, even before good dividends had been paid, been of opinion that an amalgamation was necessary in the interests of Marlow. In his view it stood to reason that if the G.W.R. obtained possession of the company they would have increased interest in the welfare of the town. It seemed to him a very fair arrangement, and felt they were all indebted to the Chairman and directors for their efforts. It gave him great pleasure to second the resolution. The proposition was then put to the meeting and carried unanimously.

The Chairman proposed that the total amount available for dividend, up to the 30th June last, should be divided among the shareholders. This was seconded by Mr. G. R. Ward and carried unanimously.

The Chairman proposed that out of the amount paid by the G.W.R. £100 should be voted to the Secretary under the circumstances he had already explained. This was seconded by Mr. J. W. Morgan, who remarked that, as one of the auditors he had always had the greatest assistance from the Secretary in the audit of the accounts, which had been presented in the most careful manner.

This was carried unanimously.

Mr. T. O. Wethered proposed that a most hearty vote of thanks be accorded to the Chairman. He had always felt his interest safe in the Chairman's hands, and he had now brought their affairs to a most successful termination.

Mr. J. W. Morgan seconded the proposition and it was carried unanimously.

When the bulk of the transfers were complete, the local directors of the Marlow Company retired and GWR directors were appointed in their place. A. D. Cripps, the local secretary, also retired and the Great Western's nominee, R. Halliday, was appointed secretary.

The Great Marlow Railway was formally amalgamated with the GWR from 1st July 1897, which was confirmed by the GWR (additional powers) Act of 6th August the same year.

Great Western Railway.

Fortnightly Season Tickets to

❧ THAMES ❧ RIVERSIDE STATIONS.

ON AND AFTER FRIDAY, MAY 1st, 1903,

SEASON TICKETS

AVAILABLE FOR

14 DAYS

WILL BE ISSUED FROM

PADDINGTON

To the following Riverside Stations.

RIVERSIDE STATIONS.	RATES.			RIVERSIDE STATIONS.	RATES.		
	First Class.	Second Class.	Third Class.		First Class.	Second Class.	Third Class.
	s. d.	s. d.	s. d.		s. d.	s. d.	s. d.
Taplow - -	38 0	28 6	22 6	Tilehurst -	64 6	48 0	26 6
Maidenhead - -	40 0	29 6	23 0	Pangbourne -	66 0	49 6	27 6
Cookham - -	43 6	32 6	24 0	Goring and Streatley	66 0	50 6	28 6
Bourne End -	44 6	32 6	26 6				
Marlow - -	49 6	36 0	26 6	Cholsey and Moulsford	66 0	51 0	29 6
Wargrave - -	50 0	37 6	26 6				
Shiplake - -	51 0	38 6	26 6	Wallingford -	78 0	53 0	30 0
Henley-on-Thames	52 6	40 0	26 6				

These Tickets will be issued on the same conditions as other Season Tickets, and may be obtained by previous application at Paddington.

PADDINGTON, *April, 1903.*   **J. L. WILKINSON**, General Manager.

WYMAN & SONS, Ltd., Printers, Fetter Lane, London, E.C., and Reading.—5841.

CHAPTER FOUR

UNDER THE GREAT WESTERN
1897—1947

WITHIN weeks of the amalgamation, at a GWR board meeting on 12th August 1897, a scheme to connect the Marlow and Henley branches was suggested. On 7th October plans were submitted for doubling the Marlow branch together with the southern part of the Wycombe line from Loudwater to Maidenhead, and extending it some 9 miles along the valley of the River Thames to connect with the recently doubled Henley branch. This would have enabled through trains to run from High Wycombe and Paddington to Henley via Marlow. The scheme was loosely estimated at £231,000 and it was resolved to give notice of the company's intention to apply for powers for construction in the ensuing session of Parliament.

One of the leading opponents to the scheme was Sir John Edwards Moss whose riverside house, Thamesfield, at Henley was threatened to become the site for a new station. The *South Bucks Free Press* claimed that in a letter to *The Field* Sir John had 'greatly over-exaggerated the facts of the case' and that to talk about spoiling the regatta course was 'rubbish pure and simple'. His letter read as follows:

I think that all amateur oarsmen should be made aware of the provisions of the Great Western Railway (New Works) Bill, 1898, Railway No. 1, and the effect which, if carried out, they will produce at Henley. The Great Western Railway proposes to make a new line from Marlow to Henley. It is to branch off from the Bourne End to Marlow line and cross the river below Marlow Lock and weir, thence pass behind Bisham and Temple, by Culham and Aston, to enter the Henley valley somewhere between Remenham Farm and Remenham Lodge (the White House). It then passes behind the latter and the cricket field, turning through the corner of the Red Lion meadow, and is to cross the Oxford-London road just where Remenham lane joins it, close to the public-house, thence through my house and grounds (Thamesfield) to Shepherd's new boathouse (where Cornell kept their boat in 1895), and so across the river, about half-way between Henley Bridge and Marsh Lock, by a two-arched bridge, the buttress being on one of the eyots, to join the existing Henley line. This bridge over the river is to be 21—21ft. 6in. above water level; that over the London-Oxford road 15ft. clear from road to bridge, 18ft. to rails. The latter bridge will, of course, have side guards, say 3—4ft. high, and as the road itself is there 7—8ft. above the level of the meadow, this structure, 6—7ft. thick, will stand, its lowest line 22ft., its highest probably over 28ft. above the level of the grounds across the road, just at the foot of the White Hill, and between it and Henley Bridge. As the rails are to be at that point 18ft. above the level of the road, and 25—26ft. above that of the meadow, it follows that upon either side of this bridge the railway must run upon a high viaduct or embankment from where it emerges from a cutting through the north end of Remenham Hill to where it crosses the river. It is understood that the present Henley Station is to be devoted solely to goods traffic, and that a new station, which, according to the plans, will be close to, if not on, the very site of this house, is to accommodate passengers. On dit that the reason for this is that the new station will be near the grand stand. Possibly the Great Western Railway directors are under the impression that at the regatta visitors throng to the stand, just as, attracted by the betting rings, they do upon racecourses. Happily, betting is a thing quite foreign to the sport of amateur oarsmanship, and the ring at Henley is conspicuous by its absence. Ninety per cent, or probably even more, of the visitors spend the day on the river in boats which they hire on the Oxfordshire shore, close to the existing station....

... The local traffic between Marlow and Henley must be practically worthless. There are neither people to travel nor goods to forward. Such are the facts. I believe that those who have rowed and won honour, if not also medals and cups at Henley have a deep affection for the scene of their labours — an affection which time does not impair — and would be seriously grieved to see its scenery marred by the hideous eyesore which the Great Western Railway are seeking Parliamentary powers to erect. I am happy to say that practically all the Landowners through whose property the line is designed to pass are unanimous in opposing it. The inhabitants of Henley and the neighbourhood are, so far as I can gather, equally antagonistic to the scheme. I cannot but think that the announcement of it will be received with horror by amateur oarsmen all over the world. And I hope that English rowing clubs may be found willing to make strong and active protest against a Bill which proposes thus to deface and desecrate a spot held by most of us oarsmen, whether of the present or the past, in no little veneration.

In response to Sir John's letter the GWR made the following statement to a press representative:

The opposition to the project is based on a somewhat hasty study of the proposed Bill. The general manager states that the proposed line from Marlow to Henley has been specially designed in order to interfere as little as possible with the river scenery. The line is to be kept well back from the stream, and at the points where it will cross the river, i.e., at Marlow and at Henley, below the Regatta course, it is proposed to construct bridges of an ornamental trellis character, so that the beauty of the river shall not be disfigured. Not in the least degree, he adds, will the railway interfere with either the racing of the competing crews or the throngs upon the water. The whole object of the scheme, indeed, it to open up the beautiful upper reaches of the Thames for boating purposes, the river having yearly grown in popularity, until in the interests of Henley itself it has become imperative that its railway facilities should be developed. One point, of which Sir J. Edwards-Moss has apparently lost sight, is the fact that if the Parliamentary powers the Company is seeking are obtained, the doubling of the present single line from Loudwater to Great Marlow, and the building of the new line from Great Marlow to Henley, will have the effect of placing the regatta town upon a main line instead of being situated at the end of a railway *cul de sac* as it is at present. The estimated cost of the construction of the line is £311,000, to which has to be added £40,000 for doubling the line from Loudwater to Great Marlow.

A letter from 'an influential resident' of Marlow, published in the *South Bucks Free Press* expressed approval of the council's course in calling a public meeting in the music room on Wednesday, 26th January 1898, to consider the proposal. It went on to say that the inhabitants 'have now an opportunity of expressing their views on this very important subject. We are told by the *Financial News* and from other sources that the scheme will be strongly opposed by the large landowners. I hope the less wealthy inhabitants, to whom the prosperity of the town is of great importance, will throw off their usual apathy and look to their own benefit. That interested landowners will have some terrible warnings to scatter broadcast as to the sad effects of the new railway I do not doubt, but I hope the intelligence of the general public will put proper value on these statements. Marlow has stood still as regards building more than any neighbouring town, and it is for Marlow people to decide whether they wish to stand still or progress.'

In his opening remarks the chairman of the Marlow meeting, Walter Lovegrove, J.P., said he thought most of those present would agree on one point, that they needed a 'better service of trains, improved accommodation for goods, and quicker service', an assumption which met with applause. He assured them that 'he had it from Mr. Wilkinson's own lips' that with the present system the GWR Company could not deal satisfactorily with either goods or passenger traffic at Marlow.

He went on to explain that the proposal entailed doubling the line from Bourne End and joining it with the 'loop line to Beaconsfield &c.' Trains would be run to Wycombe in about half-an-hour, and to Paddington in 45 minutes.* He also claimed that 'one of the causes that had influenced many people to refuse to take up residence at Marlow was the fact that they could not get to their business in London early by the present arrangement.'

Like Henley, the proposed new station at Marlow was planned on the opposite side of the river and out of the town. Whilst this was 'a matter of great regret' (it was even feared that increased traffic would soon wear out the bridge), it was resolved 'this meeting thoroughly approves of the proposed new Marlow and Henley line of the GWR company, being of the opinion that a double line giving through communication with London and considerably accelerating the train service must tend to the advantage of the town and the convenience of the residents and visitors'.

The proceedings went on at length, but in short those present were practically unanimous in their support, although a large section 'would be glad to see the station placed on the Bucks side of the river if that can be conveniently done'. To their surprise and delight Mr. Walter Wethered said that his father, Col. O. P. Wethered, was willing to give the land 'free, gratis and for nothing' to the GWR if that would keep the station on the Bucks side of the river.

Henley was not only opposed to the removal of their station to the opposite side of the river but objected to the route being so close to the regatta course. Feelings ran high, particularly from the boating fraternity. A letter from F. W. Smith of Watford which appeared in the *Daily Mail* on 31st January read as follows:

> I sincerely hope that the Great Western will not succeed in getting their Marlow and Henley Bill through the House. This feeling is shared, I am sure, by all lovers of the charming scenery of our river Thames. Stress has been laid by the advocates of this scheme on the fact that it will render portions of

the river easier of access than at present. This doubtless is true, but there is another side to this question. The railways would undoubtedly mar the beauty of one of the prettiest portions of our river, and reduce Henley to ugliness. If this disfigurement takes place, what, then, will be the advantage of enticing jaded Londoners down to contemplate the artistic effect of railway embankments and bridges. The railway accommodation, and I write from experience of many years, at all ordinary times is ample. At only one season of the year is there any extraordinary demand on the Great Western, and that is Henley Regatta. Till recent years this function was the rowing man's Mecca, and few others ever attended it. Now it is a Society affair, and the course is crowded with a fashionable host, the majority of whom do not know one end of the boat from the other, and whose interest in aquatics is nil. As an instance of this, two or three years ago my skiff was lying alongside a huge house-boat during the race that practically decided the fate of the 'Grand Challenge'. Just as the competing crews came in sight, strenuously battling with victory, the luncheon bell rang on this house-boat, and without exception down below tenants trooped, never casting a single glance at the magnificent struggle taking place before their eyes. I suppose it is for the benefit of such people as these that the railway company propose to disfigure our river, regardless of the protests of its true lovers, men who know it in all its aspects, and who have frequented it ever since they have had strength to pull an oar.

The chairman of the Marlow meeting had believed 'there was no desire on the part of the GWR Company to injure the locality. As they knew, Marlow, like every riverside place, was a good harvest for the railway company in the summer, and they had every desire to encourage visitors to come there'. However, a correspondent in the *Pall Mall Gazette* was not at all convinced of the GWR's conscience:

> I notice in your issue of 25th ult., under the heading, that Mr. Wilkinson, General Manager of the Great Western Railway, stated to your representatives that 'The Great Western Railway is as much interested as anybody in preserving the natural beauties of the district through which its system passes'. It has not done much at present to preserve the natural beauties of the Thames by building that hideous viaduct at Windsor, the most unsightly embankment running parallel with the water at Tilehurst, and the two dreadful iron bridges lately erected at Bourne End and Shiplake. If these and other eyesores put up by the Great Western Railway are Mr. Wilkinson's idea of improving the natural beauty of the Thames scenery, we shall know what to expect in the proposed ornamental bridge across the river at Henley. No wonder there is so much outcry raised by all lovers of the river scenery against future schemes proposed by the Great Western Railway.

The Leander Club, who had just spent £5,000 on building a clubhouse, a boat-house and laying out the grounds, resolved:

1. That the committee of the Leander Club most strongly deprecate the scheme of the Great Western Railway Company for bringing a new line into Henley-on-Thames by a high embankment across the meadows in front of the entrance to the Leander Club House and within 120yds. thereof, as prejudicially affecting the value and amenities of the club property, and destroying the beauty of the Henley Valley.
2. That the committee take such steps as they may be advised by petitioning Parliament or otherwise to oppose that part of the scheme.

---

*This presumably referred to a proposed loop from Loudwater to Beaconsfield shown on 1897 deposited plans for Harrow, Uxbridge & High Wycombe Railway.

Mr. W. B. Woodgate, a well-known rowing authority, was also moved to write to the *St. James's Gazette* as follows:

HENLEY REGATTA AND G.W.R. VANDALS

The rowing world, the Thames Conservancy, Henley town, and riparian owners between Henley and Marlow are jointly and severally in arms against the proposal of the Great Western Railway to construct a new line of railway to connect their Wycombe branch line with the Henley branch by means of a line diverging from the Marlow sub-branch of the Wycombe line and joining the Henley branch at Henley. The plans for the new line, as deposited at Westminster under standing orders, preliminary to the introduction of the Bill, show that the route is to cross the Thames just below Marlow lock, go behind Bisham and Temple, and enter the Henley valley somewhere about opposite to Fawley Court. It is to cross the London and Oxford road just east of Henley bridge, at an elevation of eighteen feet; and to recross the Thames at the islands below Marsh lock, on which the Immisch electric charging station now stands. A new railway station is to be built somewhere in what are at present the grounds of Sir John Edwards-Moss's residence of 'Thamesfield', opposite to the old station, which is in future to be a goods depot.

The people of Marlow approve of this scheme, and naturally so. It will give them an improved access to their neighbours, and especially to the north and west. At present they have to journey to Maidenhead, and pick up there slow trains when they want to go to Oxford or Bristol way; or they can crawl round to Oxford via Bourne End and Thame. Also the proposed line will not damage Marlow scenery. With Henley folk the case is different. They have but little to gain by increased facilities for reaching petty townships such as Marlow and High Wycombe; and much to lose if their station is to be shifted across the river and into another county. The existing rail suffices to fill the town choke-full for regatta days and weeks; and the new local line will not therein add much to their regatta emoluments; on the contrary, it may reduce them by enabling Henley-week parties to come up from Marlow, Bisham, and the like places, instead of residing in Henley hotels and lodgings. Still more, the scenery of Henley Reach will be painfully marred by the eyesore of embankment and rail traffic up Remenham Valley, and the attractions of Henley in non-regatta months will be thereby deteriorated. The landowners who are mainly affected by the scheme — e.g. Sir Gilbert Clayton East, the Hon. F. D. Smith, the trustees of the 'Noble' estate of Park Place, and Sir John Edwards-Moss (whose residence is demanded for the new station) — are unanimous in objecting to the invasion. Their grounds for resistance are not the same in all points as those of the Thames Conservancy or of the Henley Town Council; so that three different and yet allied forces may be expected to oppose the Bill in Committee. Henley oarsmen, past and present, have no exact *locus standi*, but they can hardly fail to view with dismay a project which will disfigure the Reach and tend to land an extra cheap mob in the Lion Meadows. The GWR may naturally hope to create an aquatic Sandown Park with rail depositing sightseers at the course; but competitors have all to lose and naught to gain by such a change.

Some critics suggest an alternative route for the line, keeping the Bucks shore all the way. Possibly Mr. Hudson, of Danesfield Court, and Mr. Mackenzie, of Fawley Court, and Mr. Scott-Murray, with the Hon. F. D. Smith, of Greenlands, as before, would then be in arms against the measure.

The *cui bono* of the scheme is not so apparent. The ordinary traffic between two small market towns such as Henley and Marlow would not pay the cost of such a line, even if the existing longer route between them via Maidenhead and Twyford did not exist; still less so when they already can reach each other by rail. When the GWR once taps Harrow traffic, it may be some gain to be able to run on thence to the main GWR line with an outlet at Twyford; but, unless this shall result in the present unmutilated large estates which intervene along the route being cut up for building land to produce suburban traffic, it is hard to see whence dividends are to accrue from this proposed new route.

It is well known that great railways, in apprehension of rivals hereafter crossing their path to tap their monopolies, often propose new branches of their own not so much in desire to pass them into law as to enable them to cite their rejection as reasons against subsequent concessions for similar routes to rivals. It is obvious that it would be injurious to GWR interests if the new and enterprising Metropolitan branch, which runs from St. John's Wood to Verney Junction, and which aims at reaching Birmingham in time and at uniting with the 'Great Central', were to obtain parliamentary powers to run into the Thames Valley and tap Marlow, Henley, and Reading. Hence it may pay the GWR to propound a losing Bill or their own betimes, so as to stop the Metropolitan promoters hereafter. But whether or not the GWR are thus riding for a fall, all who have at heart the beauty of the Thames Valley and the sanctity of Henley Regatta should co-operate with Conservancy, riparians, and Henley Town Council in fighting the Bill. Mr. R. C. Lehmann, the well-known aquatic coach and oarsman, offers in the *Field* to subscribe £100 to a defence fund to co-operate with riparians and it is to be hoped that the two University Boat Clubs and leading rowing clubs will follow his lead.

The Henley Royal Regatta Committee resolved:

1. That the Committee of Management of Henley Royal Regatta desire to express their strong objection to the Bill of the Great Western Railway Company in Parliament this Session for a new line into Henley-on-Thames, which line (as shown by the deposited plans) will require a high embankment up the valley, and across the corner of the Lion Meadow, and will cross the London-road by a bridge. And the Committee trust the town of Henley-on-Thames and the landowners, as well as all those interested in the preservation of Thames scenery, will use their utmost endeavours to prevent the Railway Company from carrying out a scheme so detrimental to the welfare of Henley.
2. That the Oxford University Boat Club, the Cambridge University Boat Club, and other principal boat and rowing clubs be invited to assist the Committee in their opposition to such a scheme, and, if deemed desirable, a public meeting of past and present oarsmen, as well as those interested in the preservation of the natural beauty of the Henley Valley, should be held to protest against the powers proposed by the Bill now before Parliament.

The Thames Conservancy petitioned against the scheme, claiming that the proposed works would interfere with the River Thames and the navigation thereof. They also felt the plans were ill designed and the works would involve an unnecessary interference with the property of the petitioners and others 'without any commensurate public advantage'. They also contended that there was no public necessity for the construction of the proposed railway.

Feelings continued to run high and in a letter to the *Times* another correspondent said:

If it is an object to have the Thames edged throughout by a railway, like the Rhine, the project helps to realise that ideal.

But it is impossible to find any other *raison d'etre* for it. It does not shorten the distance from London to either Marlow or Henley; it does not form a link in any conceivable new trunk line to Oxford or any other place; and it is impossible to suppose that there can be any such keen desire for intercourse between Marlow and Henley as would in itself make a direct communication between these places of any importance. So difficult is it to see an explanation for this costly little line that one is driven to the conclusion that it is suggested by some consideration of high railway policy not at present revealed to the million. Dark rumours are afloat of an incursion of the Midland into the preserves of the Great Western; an inroad of the Great Central or the Metropolitan is conceivable; and it may be that the little line in question — or, perhaps, merely the power to make it — is desired as an outwork against a possible aggressor.

At least one letter of support did, however, appear in the *Reading Mercury* on Saturday 26th February, when a Mr. P. H. Jones wrote:

I have noted many paragraphs in the 'Mercury' and letters in other Journals, which more or less decry the formation of the proposed Railway between Marlow and Henley. I have lived and pleasurably lingered on the banks of the Thames as both a rowing and angling man for now some 30 odd years, and am as ardent an admirer of the river and its beautiful surroundings as anyone breathing, but I fail to see or to be convinced by sheer sentimentality only that the making of this connecting link between two important riverside towns would be detrimental to either the scenery or the public, more particularly if the railway authorities are well advised and somewhat alter the route at present proposed. A better site for the new station at Marlow could not, I think, be devised than the one near the pretty suspension bridge on the Berks side. The line would then pass at the rear of Bisham and under the Woods to Hurley, and would not be seen from the river until approaching opposite Medmenham, and here the new departure should take place from the present proposed plan, and, instead of making a horse-shoe detour through Culham, Aston, Remenham and down the Regatta course, should pass out of sight by tunnel under Rose Hill and Remenham Hill and emerge at the base of White Hill, on the Wargrave-road, where a conveniently placed station could be located within 200 yards of Henley Bridge and the Regatta Course. The line would then pass over the river by osier islands and join the Twyford branch on the Oxon side without any sharp curves. This alteration of route would save a mile or more in distance, and should surely disarm all opposition, and save a lot of weeping and wailing about the 'desecration' of the Regatta Course and the so-called beautiful 'Henley Valley'. I should not imagine that boring a tunnel would be a difficult or insurmountable matter, as Rose, Remenham, and White Hills are composed of chalk, and the ballast abstracted should be thus valuable.

The Vicar of Hurley, in a letter to the 'Field', of February 8th, thus writes:— "As a resident of much more than fifty years standing at Hurley, through which village it is now planned that this ridiculous railway should pass, I say emphatically on behalf of my parishioners of all classes, that no such railway is needed." I should have thought, certainly — in my innocence perhaps — that the said parishioners of the humbler class would have benefited by railway facilities for cheaper marketing in Marlow or Henley — that the farmers and millers would feel the much-needed advantages in carriage and freight of their produce — that the hotel-keepers would benefit by the influx of visitors — and, again, that this all-round good to the inhabitants of this unfrequented pretty village would incidentally enhance the Church offertories!

Not a sixteenth part of the millions who toil and toil lower down the Thames know of, or ever see, the lovely bit of greenery with 'just a little sunshine and just a little shade' to be found in the upper reaches of the grand old Thames, and any obstacles, sentimental or otherwise, thrown in the way of facilities to view and enjoy such oases, can only, in my humble opinion, be characterised as both petty and pitiable.

In a determined effort to overcome the opposition from Henley, the Great Western amended their plans to include a tunnel through Remenham Hill and site the station on the Oxfordshire side of the river, the tunnel alone costing an additional £50,000. However, although winning the support of the townspeople, the Thames Conservancy and the boating interest had in the meantime raised fierce opposition and, led by Sir Frederick Dixon-Hartland, M.P., lodged a petition at the Private Bill Office at the House of Commons. Their obstructive attitude had previously been severely criticised in *Herepath's Railway Journal* of February 11th, 'All this in special pleading for those who do not want their boat houses disturbed.'

In face of the opposition the GWR wrote to the Mayor of Henley stating that it had been found impracticable to overcome the opposition and that the company were therefore compelled to defer their application to Parliament. Whether the Mayor of Marlow received a similar communication is not clear.

The *South Bucks Free Press* for 1st April carried the following letters which had previously appeared in the London Press.

Now that the Great Western Railway Company have announced the withdrawal of the Marlow and Henley Railway, will you kindly allow me to thank, through your columns, those who gave their valuable and timely assistance in opposition to the scheme?

It is gratifying to find there has been such a consensus of opinion against the proposal, and the result shows that an opposition, in defence of the beauties of Thames scenery, can be successfully offered to an unsightly railway, for which no good or sufficient reasons are given. In conclusion, permit me to thank you for your aid by kindly allowing the matter to be brought forward.

I am, sir, your obedient servant,
HERBT. THOS. STEWARD

Mr. Steward's letter of to-day forms a fitting epitaph to the defunct Great Western Marlow and Henley Railway Bill, a hastily-conceived and wholly foolish measure, the project, apparently, of a coalition of the Marlow and Henley tradespeople alone and the company. Fortunately their selfish ends are defeated.

It is difficult to imagine what benefits either party expected to gain by this new railway. We know what was promised to lovers of the scenery along its track — viz., sundry embankments and two iron railway bridges, one bridge being at Marlow Lock and 'painted red!'; but it is, I say, difficult to see the advantages from the promoters' point. Marlow tradesmen point to Maidenhead as an example of a town made prosperous by its situation on a main line of a railway; but they forget that Maidenhead Station forms a convenient centre to a large outlying district, a position that Marlow, by reason of its locality, could never attain. The projected railway would, no doubt, have given some slightly increased travelling facilities to these towns, but these can surely be obtained without constructing a new railway; and also there would probably have ensued a

An unidentified 2—2—2 entering the recently improved Bourne End station c.1898. *Collection J. E. Kite*

large increase in the number of visitors to the town — admittedly 'Trippers', the increasing influx of whom is a circumstance already heartily deplored by the principal tradesmen there. The Great Western Railway, on their part, could never have anticipated obtaining any adequate returns for their enormous outlay; one can only conclude that the project was conceived by them solely with the view of keeping rivals out of the field at all costs.

I am, sir, your obedient servant,

ARTHUR E. THOMPSON

In 1899 the Great Western dropped 'Great' from the station name* which thereafter was simply referred to as Marlow, the official name of the town since the formation of the Urban District Council. Marlow continued to gain popularity as a Thameside resort and whilst facilities were no doubt adequate for day to day traffic the GWR was hard pressed to cope with the crowds, particularly during 'Marlow Week'.

On 28th March 1901 the directors authorised alterations and improvements to the Marlow terminus amounting to £2,226. The work primarily involved extending the platform and run round loop to accommodate longer trains, the provision of a bay platform for special traffic, two new sidings, and a short extension to the station building. However, these and other changes are detailed in the stations section on pages 109-141.

While the alterations were in progress 'delightful weather' at Whitsuntide attracted many visitors to Marlow

*effective from 14th February 1899

by rail, river and road. The railway traffic was unusually heavy and on the Saturday through carriages to Marlow were run on most of the ordinary trains, and duplicate trains were run for the return traffic on Monday evening. The *South Bucks Free Press* reported: 'All the hotels in the town were full to overflowing'. Some 8,450 passengers left Paddington that weekend for Windsor and the Thames Valley and Boulter's Lock had a record 110 steam and electric launches and 1,000 boats passing through. The Whitsuntide railway traffic at Marlow was a record, the GWR bringing in 2,500 passengers over the three days.

By 14th June considerable progress had been made with the alterations, the platform extension being brought into use for the first train on Sunday, 9th June, a large gang of permanent way men having carried out track and signalling alterations over the preceding night.

A new signal box was also provided in connection with the improvements, the lock and block and ordinary train staff and ticket system regulating traffic over the line at the same time being replaced by electric train staff working introduced the same day.

The improved facilities eased the demands of the summer traffic and on the Saturday of the Marlow Regatta, 10th August, 2,300 passengers were brought in.

As part of the improvements the GWR had intended to remodel and enlarge the station buildings at Marlow, but despite having gone as far as receiving tenders, they deferred the work because of outstanding capital outlay

British Railways

Bourne End Regatta in Edwardian times.

597   MARLOW LOCK. — LL.

Marlow Lock.   *C. E. Turner Collection*

to which the company was already committed. However, according to the *South Bucks Free Press* for 4th October 1901, the directors altered their decision and accepted the tender of Mr. G. H. Tucker of Reading for enlarging the booking office, general waiting room and parcels office, providing a new waiting room for ladies together with new and larger lavatories for both sexes. The work was completed in March 1902.

Whilst not comparable with the international event at Henley, the Marlow Amateur Regatta was nevertheless well patronised and required similar, if more modest, arrangements. The 1902 event, held on Saturday, 8th August, boasted a 'Venetian Fete, Illuminations, and Grand Display of Fireworks'.

Extra staff drafted in to cope with the arrangements were as follows:

BOURNE END
A telegraph clerk from 10.00 a.m. until after departure of last train.
Policeman Cassell to assist.
1 Porter throughout the day.
2 Ticket collectors, 11.00 a.m. to 10.00 p.m.
A Waiting room attendant all day.

MARLOW
2 Porters throughout the day.
Policeman Neale to assist.
A Lampman from 4.00 p.m. until after departure of last train.
A Waiting room attendant all day.
The Gas Man stationed at Windsor to be in attendance at Marlow during the afternoon and evening.

Again in common with arrangements for Henley, goods and coal trucks were cleared out of the terminus on Friday night and taken to Maidenhead where they were held until Sunday night. The goods yard was needed to accommodate complete trains which were held at Marlow during the afternoon until required for their return journeys. According to official instructions the Marlow branch train was made up to eight vehicles, presumably using extra four-wheeled stock. Special through trains were run from Paddington and Wycombe and to assist with running round trains and any shunting requirements a pilot engine from Slough shed was stationed at Bourne End from 11.00 a.m. 'until released'.

The General Manager's report records that the arrangements 'met the requirements very well' except that it was necessary to return one of the specials to High Wycombe at 3.10 p.m. to provide another service, but otherwise no other difficulties of any kind occurred. Staff arrangements were described as 'satisfactory', new pattern blue serge uniforms, issued all over the GWR on King Edward's birthday on 30th May, undoubtedly giving the men a very smart appearance, inspectors, guards, ticket collectors, signalmen and porters being among those affected. Although some 2,300 tickets were collected on the Saturday, this was about 250 less than the previous year, apparently because of the weather.

Mention must also be made of the annual Bourne End Regatta which, held earlier on 19th July, required similar arrangements, the Marlow branch train again being

MARLOW FROM QUARRY WOODS.

C. E. Turner Collection

strengthened and running an extra late night trip. Passengers travelling from Paddington, Wycombe, Marlow, etc. totalled about 2,600.

In 1905 it was suggested that the GWR might further exploit the tourist traffic by running a service of motor buses between Henley and Marlow during the summer months. The company apparently decided to experiment by running such a service between Oxford and Henley during Henley week and it was suggested that the 'cars might continue their journey from Henley to Maidenhead, via Marlow'. It is not clear what arrangements took place that season, but the GWR certainly ran a service between Marlow and Henley during the Henley Regatta, in subsequent years, 249 passengers being carried in 1906 and 345 in 1907 for example.

Edwardian summers enjoyed by countless numbers of elegantly attired men and women flocking to the Thames were not always so idyllic. Intending tourists therefore had to take advantage of any good weather whenever they could as witnessed by the *South Bucks Free Press* on 30th June 1905:

ASCOT SUNDAY ON THE RIVER.
A BRILLIANT SCENE.

A more animated scene than that presented on Sunday by the stretch of Thames of which Boulter's Lock is the centre can scarely be imagined. The brilliant sunshine had brought everybody out, and the ladies' dresses that had glittered on the lawns at Ascot shone once more in the reflections of the silver stream on Ascot Sunday. Boats were in constant demand all day, from nine o'clock in the morning onwards; before seven in

the evening at least 1,600 craft of various sorts and sizes had been dealt with at Boulter's Lock, and one boat-letter alone had disposed of 150 small craft and 17 launches. People seemed determined to take advantage of the sudden rush of summer before the weather changed again; and it was difficult to realise, in watching the variegated crowd of happy merrymakers, that any note of discord could be possible in a scene where all seemed determined to make holiday. But some of the boats and launches held passengers who could — and did — unfold a tale of woe. Some of them had been kept waiting no less than four hours before they could get through the lock.

Among those who found the beauty of the Upper Thames so irresistible was the renowned prima donna, Madame Nellie Melba, who from at least 1899 spent several summers at Marlow. In order that she might return to Quarry Wood Cottage after a performance, she sometimes chartered a special train from Paddington to Marlow about midnight. One Saturday night in June 1899 after a performance of *Lucia de Lammermoor*, the train completed the journey in 48 minutes which included running round at Bourne End.

During what was undoubtedly the line's heyday, the idea of connecting Uxbridge and Marlow with the Wycombe line was still attractive and, even at this late stage in railway history, at a board meeting on 10th November 1904, James Inglis, the General Manager of the Great Western, 'considered it essential that powers should be sought for the construction of a new line from Uxbridge in the direction of Bourne End'. The directors accepted the suggestion and the proposal was included in the

G.W.R.

Henley Royal Regatta,

Wednesday, Thursday, Friday and Saturday,
JULY 1st, 2nd, 3rd and 4th, 1914.

ON THE ABOVE DATES A

ROAD MOTOR CAR SERVICE

WILL BE RUN BETWEEN

MARLOW & HENLEY

AS SHEWN BELOW:—

	a.m.	a.m.	p.m.	p.m.	p.m.
Marlow Station dep.	9 0	10 30	1 55	6 20	8A 0
Medmenham arr. about	9 15	10 45	2 10	6 35	8A15
Henley Station arr.	9 45	11 15	2 40	7 5	8A45

	a.m.	a.m.	p.m.	p.m.	Thursday and Friday only. p.m.	Saturday only. p.m.
Henley Station … dep.	9 45	11 15	5 30	7 10	9 0	10 30
Medmenham arr. about	10 15	11 45	6	7 40	9 30	11 0
		noon.				
Marlow Station … arr.	10 30	12 0	6 15	7 55	9 45	11 15

A Does not run on Wednesday, July 1st.

SINGLE FARES between—

			s.	d.
Marlow and Henley	…	…	**2**	**0**
Medmenham and Henley	…		**1**	**6**
Medmenham and Marlow	…		**1**	**0**

The number of seats will be limited and Passengers will only be conveyed from Medmenham on the condition that there is room in the Cars; Passengers will only be booked to Medmenham after through Passengers have taken their seats.

Seats may be retained.

Special Cars for the conveyance of private parties can be provided at reasonable charges.

For General Notices and Regulations relating to the Company's Road Motor Cars, see separate bill or announcement in Company's Time Table, or apply to Mr. C. Aldington, Paddington Station, or the Stationmaster at Henley-on-Thames, or Marlow.

PADDINGTON, June, 1914.   FRANK POTTER, General Manager.

WYMAN & SONS LTD., Printers, Fetter Lane, London, E.C., and Reading.—1947.

This picture appeared in the *GWR Magazine* in 1908 captioned 'Preparing for a long journey — swallows at Marlow' and provides a rare glimpse of the approach to Marlow station. The bracketed signal arms are of a centrally balanced type and contrast with the standard 'short' arms used on the bracket signal erected here in 1928 (see page 108).   *A. Pitman*

company's new works Bill for the next session of Parliament. However, when it was discovered that 'all the present landowners would be opponents to the Bill' it was withdrawn.

The last expenditure on the line of any size was the reconstruction of the viaduct at 28 miles 79 chains just outside Bourne End in 1913. This unavoidable expense amounted to some £3,237.

The six-week coal strike which began in March 1912 brought about a curtailment of services all over the GWR and no less than five trains from Marlow and four from London to Marlow were withdrawn, together with the midnight train on Wednesdays and Saturdays, whilst on Sundays there was no train until the evening.

The effect of the strike damaged the reputation of the GWR who were criticised in some quarters for not having a larger coal reserve or for adopting 'a false policy of economy by cutting down the train service to a minimum', Some of the company's employees were given enforced holidays whilst others were dismissed. Easter arrangements were described by the *South Bucks Free Press* as 'deplorable', some of the trains running over half an hour late and in most cases 'packed to suffocation'. The withdrawal of all weekend and excursion tickets and 'the failure to run special trains for the Football Final at Wycombe' also caused much unfavourable comment.

Even after the strike, the GW, which had suffered a large financial loss, was criticised for not displaying any undue haste in resuming the full service until the end of July. The glorious weather over the Whitsuntide ensured the returns at Marlow were 'practically the same as last year', but when fares were increased on 1st July the local press was not slow to point out that this was 'not likely to be popular'. Fares from Marlow to Paddington were increased from 3/5d and 6/9d to 3/11d and 8/- for 1st and 3rd class respectively. The reporter also pointed out that 'Marlow, one might almost say of course, has been dealt with more drastically than other stations. The first class return Marlow to Paddington is now 3d more than the combined total of Marlow-Bourne End and Bourne End-Paddington returns. In other words money can be saved by booking twice. Similar unfair treatment was meted out to Marlow when the season ticket rates were recently revised, the percentage increase being double that for the other local stations. The action taken by the Urban Council on that occasion secured more reasonable treatment.'

Another criticism of the GWR was voiced through the columns of the *Maidenhead Advertizer*:

In the company of two friends, I proceeded on Sunday afternoon last [3rd November] to Marlow railway station. The booking office window was in due course opened for the issue of tickets. I asked for 'three-thirds' for Maidenhead. 'Seven twenty-six' was the brief reply of the youthful clerk-in-charge. This meant a wait of over an hour, the train 'in' being a down train and proceeding as far as Bourne End only. 'Oh! very well,' said a companion, 'we'll take the tickets and make a call at the Railway Hotel at Bourne End and then join the train for Maidenhead.' But the clerk coolly informed us that if we took tickets for Maidenhead we should not be allowed to leave Bourne End platform!! 'Very well' was the retort, 'let us have three tickets for Bourne End, and please may we walk from Bourne End to Maidenhead?' The tickets were issued and the company's takings that day were less by three fares from Bourne End to Maidenhead than they would otherwise have been. No wonder the travelling public welcomes trams and buses when a railway company frame and insist upon the observance of such vexatious regulations.

Such complaints soon lost their importance against the course of events leading to the Great War. Locally the preliminary movement in the concentration of troops for

Marlow station c.1910.   *Lens of Sutton*

The presence of soldiers, the visiting 0–6–0 and the commodious 'Dreadnought' coach suggests this little mishap probably occurred during the Great War.

Courtesy Ronald Goodearl

Troops drilling at Marlow. June 4th. 1915.

the autumn manoeuvres took place on Saturday, 30th August 1913, when the 4th Infantry Brigade (London Foot Guards) assembled at Marlow, a camp being established on open ground between Bovingdon Green and Marlow Common where some 4,000 men were under canvas.

Special trains had arrived at Marlow station on the previous Monday with tents and stores, and another from Kensington at 10.30 on the Saturday brought in the 2nd Battalion Scots Guards, who marched through the town playing drums and bagpipes. Another train arriving from Kensington about 11.30 brought in the 1st Irish Guards,

defenders of the right. The sight we witnessed on Wednesday morning at our Railway Station, as our men left to do their part, will never be forgotten by us as townspeople, for all political differences were forgotten, and we realised that the sons of this beloved Empire, to which we are proud to belong, are going forth united to meet a common foe. Marlow and the County of Buckinghamshire (which has played a prominent part in the history of this country before) will do so again. May each one of us remember the wives and loved ones whom they have left behind in our prayers, and out of this War may come lasting peace for Europe.

By December over 400 men from Marlow were serving with the forces and nearly 10,000 employees from the

Soldiers of the 3rd Battalion Grenadier Guards at Marlow station setting out for their march to Bovingdon Green Camp shortly after arrival on 4th June 1915.
Lens of Sutton

who marched from the station to 'lively ragtime music' with the regimental dog preceding the band. The 2nd and 3rd Coldstream Guards marched from Purbright and Windsor respectively.

In a send-off reminiscent of that given in 1900 to volunteers for the South African war, following the call-up of the Army reserve, a great crowd assembled at the railway station on the morning of Wednesday, 5th August 1914, to see the local Territorials off. Before the men entrained, a Mr. Langley, on behalf of the council, made a brief speech to wish them God-speed and a safe return. There was a great cheering when the train steamed out of the station. The Bucks Yeomanry, who left for Wycombe by the 10.7 train, were also given a good send-off.

In writing to the editor of the *South Bucks Free Press*, a Mr. Harvey of Marlow wrote:

Thank God the sons of Britain have bravely responded to the call, and are marching to the conflict with a brave heart to uphold our promise, and prove to the world that we are

Great Western, over 4,000 coming from the locomotive department alone, all blissfully unaware of the huge numbers that would never return.

Train services were reduced and women were employed as booking clerks and ticket collectors to aid the depleted workforce, a Miss Buckell being appointed booking clerk at Marlow.

With the nearby camp at Bovingdon Green, the station became the scene of more military arrivals and departures, the 3rd Battalion Grenadier Guards, about 1,200 strong, arriving in two special trains from Wellington Barracks, Chelsea, and marching to the camp on 4th June 1915. The Reserve battalion also arrived on Saturday, 4th September, and an hour later at midday the company, which had been at the camp for a month, left by special train.

A draft of 70 men from the Grenadier Guards left for the front on Friday, 8th October, apparently in the highest spirits and, according to the press, 'eager to get to work

Marlow station from Dedmere Road in 1919.   *L & GRP, courtesy David & Charles*

on the Germans'. They were followed a week later by the last of the Grenadiers and the Welsh Guards. Further send-offs included drafts of the Home Counties Royal Engineers, who left for the front on 15th June and 23rd August 1916, large numbers of residents again assembling at the station and cheering their departure.

By October 1917 Marlow, in common with other towns to the west of the Metropolis, had been 'invaded' by Londoners anxious to escape the air raids. The town was packed, all the hotels and boarding houses were full, together with any rooms to let in private houses.

At a time when the service was being cut back even more, trains to and from London were packed, the number of passengers exceeding record summer seasons in pre-war days.

News of the Armistice reached Marlow at 11 a.m. on Monday, 11th November 1918, the glad tidings spreading through the town 'like wildfire'. Flags and bunting were displayed from nearly every house and the bells of the parish church were rung morning, afternoon and evening, and the hooter at Wethered's Brewery was blown until all the steam in the boilers was exhausted. The inhabitants were summoned to the market place by the town crier and after an address on behalf of the council, sung the Doxology and the National Anthem. It was indeed a

joyous and memorable occasion and a thanksgiving service was held at the parish church in the evening.

The local people had suffered the rationing of coal and other supplies and, as a precaution against possible air raids, lighting restrictions, but these were minor hardships. More than 1,000 men from Marlow braved the trenches and over 180 lost their lives.

Not even a year passed before train services were disrupted again, this time by the sudden 1919 railway strike on Friday, 26th September. The last train which ran from Marlow that day was the 10.50 p.m. which was scheduled to connect with the 10.5 p.m. from Paddington. Because of strike action the latter did not run and the Marlow train also failed to return. However, this was not due to any action on the part of the Marlow crew, but because the signalman at Bourne End had left his post. The stranded locomotive returned the following morning but the whole of the Marlow staff went on strike and the water tank was emptied to thwart any attempt at restoring a service.

A retired driver and a number of other volunteers came forward to work the line, and during what can only have been quite an adventure for those concerned, trains were run on Monday and Tuesday afternoons to bring in mail and goods from Bourne End. On the Wednesday two trips were made in the afternoon for passengers, mail and parcels, but after pickets managed to interview the driver, he retired from the position. Consequently, although a service was maintained between Maidenhead and Wycombe, there were no trains on the branch on Thursday.

A telegram of support was sent from the town to the Prime Minister and a food control committee organised rationing of food. Milk was sent to London by road and the utmost economy in fuel and light was urged by the authorities. On Friday, 3rd October, the branch was re-opened in the afternoon, a strike service of eleven trains also being run on Saturday.

The strike was settled on Sunday, 5th October, but the normal timetable was not in full operation until Tuesday. The services of those volunteers who drove the engine during the strike was recognised by a collection in the town w'.ich realized £40 8s. 6d.

Branch services were also reduced during the 1920 and 1921 coal strikes and withdrawn completely during the 1924 railway strike. In his New Year's message for 1925, Sir Felix Pole, General Manager of the GWR, appealed to the 'good sense' of the employees and stated:

> As Great Western Railway employees we have a reputation to uphold. It is no small thing to be a member of the staff of this great company. We must jealously guard the good name which

has been built up by generations of railwaymen second to none in their endeavours to respond to the demands made upon them and to serve their company loyally. The product of our efforts is Great Western Railway service, and the more efficient that service becomes the better will be our standing with the public. We must foster good will by good service, and the best advertisement of our service is a job well done. A business succeeds only as it serves.

The branch service was lost yet again during the General Strike of 1926. Not all the staff went on strike, however, for during the service, again operated by volunteers, the station master, Mr. J. Morgan, acted as signalman and Mr. H. Belcher, the only uniformed man at Marlow to remain on duty, acted as guard. The press reported 'quite a good service was maintained to connect with the trains on the Maidenhead-Wycombe line.

Branch locomotives were provided by Slough shed and changed each week for boiler wash-outs and other maintenance carried out at the parent depot. Since the turn of the century 'Metro' class 2—4—0Ts were sub-shedded at Marlow almost exclusively, the list of official allocations on page 186 giving the known exceptions. It appears that '517' class 0—4—2Ts worked the line before 1900 with only the occasional 'Metro', but records of the earlier period are scarce.

Another view of Marlow station in 1919.

L & GRP, courtesy David & Charles

'Metro' class 2—4—0T No. 1497 at Marlow with a train of four-wheeled stock, probably c.1930, shortly before the introduction of auto-trailers on the branch.
Collection P. Karau

There were normally two drivers based at Marlow and three firemen who took turns to work the night shift to clean and prepare the loco for the following day's services. After the last train, the departing crew would leave the engine over the pit outside the shed for the night man who booked on at 11.30 p.m. and began his duty by cleaning the fire.

George Parsons as a young fireman.

George Parsons, who started at Marlow as a young fireman in 1920, remembered this duty well. After cleaning the fire he would usually lift three of the firebars and drop any clinker and surplus fire through the gap into the ashpan. After he had raked the contents of the ashpan into the pit and emptied the smokebox, he would start to build the fire up again ready for pumping water. In his day, the branch locomotives were always in steam. While the fire was pulling through, he filled the bunker directly from the coal stage and after this arduous work moved the loco into the shed and stopped for 'a sit down and a smoke'.

Later the small pumping engine, which was used to fill the water tank outside the shed, was connected to the loco by means of a flexible pipe coupled in place of the brake whistle. The pump was housed in an adjacent hut whilst the water supply came from a well alongside. Once the pump was in action, George went into the shed pit and under the engine to clean the frames and motion, leaving the paintwork above the footplate until afterwards. When all was clean, he would take the opportunity of another rest until the driver arrived at about 4.50 a.m.

Sometimes, during the summer months, George took the loco outside again into the early morning sunlight and emptied the loco coal wagon alongside the coal stage. Often by the time the driver arrived he would have oiled up and even coupled onto the coaches in 'Khartoum' siding. In any event, the crew were frequently sitting in the loop with the assembled train of three bogie coaches waiting for the arrival of the signalman to let them out.

The clerk at this time was Percy Peyman, who later became station master at Paddington. He cycled in from Bourne End each morning to open the ticket office for the first train, the 5.40 a.m., which primarily conveyed workers for Jackson's Mill Board at Bourne End, usually about 20 women and 25 men.

The overnight fireman worked this first trip, which involved considerable shunting at Bourne End to collect wagons for Marlow. The mixed train (unadvertised) was assembled there in the down main platform with two of the branch coaches next to the engine, followed by various wagons and the third coach, a brake end, at the

This 1920 aerial view clearly shows the position of the station on the edge of the town.

Aerofilms

'Large Metro' 2—4—0T No. 3592 running round its train at Marlow in May 1935.
Reg Daniells

rear. George Parsons also remembered returning sometimes with all three coaches behind the wagons, presumably when there were no passengers.

The workmen's train dated from November 1917 when it replaced an early morning goods train which had run since the independent years. However, the return trip continued to bring goods into Marlow, in addition, that is, to three mixed and two other goods trains. Outwards goods in 1917 ran at 3.30 p.m. and 8.38 p.m. with one mixed train on Sundays until the Second World War. The return of the workmen's train became a mixed train from October 1940 timed to depart Bourne End at 6.35 a.m.

The working day is considered more fully in the next chapter but to conclude the overnight fireman's duty, on returning to Marlow he was relieved from the footplate by the early turn fireman, who then accompanied the driver in placing the wagons in the goods yard while the overnight man finished his duty between 7 and 8 a.m. by shovelling ashes from the pit, cleaning the shed and, if he hadn't already done so, unloading the loco coal wagon.

The 'Metro' tanks continued working the branch with hardly an exception until 1935 when, from July, the familiar push and pull trains (without a branch guard) became a regular feature and the newly introduced Collett '48XX' class 0—4—2Ts took over. According to official records, they maintained the same exclusive dominance as their predecessors, only displaced in 1947 by one of the old 'Metros', no. 3562, which returned to Marlow for a brief sojourn for the first time since the Great War.

Auto trains had appeared on the line from at least 1927 when an early morning train supplied from Reading left Bourne End at 7.05, returning to Maidenhead at 7.26. From 1930 the stock worked from Reading as the 6.25 a.m. passenger train. It appears that the service was introduced because the Marlow branch engine was otherwise

Miss E. Roberts in one of the 4-wheel branch coaches.   *Cty. Mrs. E. Genery*

engaged with the early morning goods which arrived from Bourne End immediately before the departure of the 7.26 a.m.

In addition to the early morning services, five other trains ran with auto coaches in the summer of 1930, three via Maidenhead. In 1935 some 19 return trips on the branch were covered by auto trains including the early morning Reading service which was to survive until 1940.

In the years prior to the Great War the GWR had maintained the service frequency of the 1890s and more 'through' workings were introduced particularly at summer weekends.

July 1899 saw two trains from Paddington to Marlow; the 10.25 a.m. on Sundays and the 1.00 p.m. on Saturdays. There was also a mid morning departure to Maidenhead leaving at 9.35. By the summer of 1907 seven 'through' workings existed; four to and from Paddington, two Maidenhead workings and a Sunday trip from High Wycombe at 2.50 p.m. The Maidenhead trains were the only through workings during the week.

Through carriages were still running in July 1900 when they were advertised to run on the 8.50 and 10.15 a.m. trains from Marlow, returning by the 4.00, 4.50 and 5.50 p.m. London services.

In the years immediately prior to the Great War 'through' workings became complex. In the summer of 1914, for example, ten existed including a weekday Paddington to Marlow service leaving the Metropolis at 10.00 a.m.

The mid-morning Marlow to Maidenhead service, departing at 9.45 a.m., continued during the Great War and by October 1920 had been supplemented by four others albeit mainly on Sundays. In 1918 the 10.05 p.m. Paddington ran through to Marlow.

The 1920s saw the revival of 'through' workings in some numbers, eight in 1922, nine in 1923 and thirteen by the late '20s. A regular Marlow to Paddington weekday service in the guise of the 9.18 a.m. had been introduced from the early 1920s and in 1927 was balanced by the 6.15 p.m. (6.08 p.m. the following year) from Paddington which became a well-known train. The intensive 1929 service reveals a 9.17 a.m. High Wycombe to Marlow on weekdays and a 9.53 a.m. Marlow to Slough. In this period the weekend visitor to Marlow was well catered for with six Sunday 'throughs' to Maidenhead and Slough.

Return workings on the branch had reached some 20-25 trips by the late 1920s, a frequency that was to be maintained through the war years and until nationalisation. Sunday services over the same period amounted to 11-16 returns depending on the time of year.

The early morning return goods train which ran during the independent years continued until November 1917 when the first departure from Marlow became the 5.40 passenger train. The return goods service remained, departing at 7.10 a.m.

In July 1899 as well as the early morning trains there had been a mixed and a further goods working to and from Bourne End. A Sunday goods service was also provided but this was short-lived.

In November 1917 there were two goods departures at 3.30 p.m. and 8.38 p.m. with one mixed at 6.23 p.m. There were no less than six arrivals; three mixed and

One of Collett's new 0—4—2Ts which replaced the 'Metro' class 2—4—0Ts on branch services from 1935 until dieselisation.

Courtesy Mrs. E. Hobbs

An undated photograph with only a few members of the Marlow staff identified. Second from left, behind the front row is parcel porter Len Stroud, followed by driver Henry Napper and outside foreman Walt Lester. Station master John Morgan is seated in the front row.

Cty. L. Stroud

Above left: Miss Kathleen Neighbour who also entered the company's service at the commencement of the war, relinquishing her position in 1920 to make way for an ex-soldier. 'She was much liked for her cheery manner and invariable courtesy'. *Above right:* W. J. Mealings was station master at Marlow from 1928 to 1942. The eldest of three brothers who were all station masters, he was succeeded by Freddie Funnell.

Left: Miss Buckell at Marlow in 1915. She was the first woman employed at the station. *Cty. S. Clark*

Marlow station staff in 1911. They are from left to right: *Back row* — Harry Belcher, carman; unidentified; Len Stroud, parcel porter; unidentified; A. Belcher. *Front row* — Freddie Funnell, who (shown here as a junior clerk) returned to Marlow in 1942 as station master; Ted Coventry, guard; Walt Lester, outside foreman; C. Akers; unidentified; Jimmy Norton, outside porter.
Cty. L. Stroud

Above left: Ivor Morgan senior, signalman. *Above right:* Fred Wethered, porter. *Cty. Mrs. D. Emmett*

Right: A face familiar to most older residents of Marlow, Len Stroud who worked at the station as a porter and leading parcels porter for some 40 years before retiring shortly before nationalization. He was one of the few who saw continuous service at Marlow throughout the Second World War and during the female staffing. *Cty. Mrs. D. Emmett*

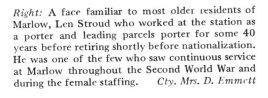

Marlow station slumbering in the midday sun c.1930.

C. L. Mowat

three goods. A Sunday mixed train also ran from Bourne End to Marlow at 9.51 a.m. This Sunday service had run when required just prior to the Great War and ran regularly during peacetime. It did not apparently run during the Second World War and was not revived afterwards.

The familiar 6.35 a.m. mixed train from Bourne End to Marlow (return of the 5.40 a.m. Marlow passenger train) commenced running in October 1940, continuing into the BR era. From March 1941 workmen's trains ran as required on Sundays, leaving Marlow at 5.40 a.m. and 9.45 p.m., returning at 6.15 a.m. and 10.10 p.m.

In 1946/47, in addition to the 6.35, there were 9.40 a.m. mixed and 3.30 p.m. goods departures. A 9.00 p.m. goods departure also ran when required. Shortly before nationalisation the 9.40 a.m. was apparently suspended.

In common with several other lines, the GWR ran late trains on Wednesday and Saturday nights, aimed mainly at cinema and theatre-goers. They first became a feature of the Marlow branch in 1902, a service leaving Marlow at 12.55 a.m. for Bourne End, returning at 1.10 a.m.

Late night services continued until the winter of 1916 and were not revived until the summer of 1920. In its revived form a train ran empty to Maidenhead, returning at 12.55 and by the late 1920s at 1.20. However, these services ended in the winter of 1939 and were not revived until BR days.

Marlow might have been far off the serious unemployment experienced in industrial centres during the 1930s, but in 1932 the 'severity of unemployment' was such that the following year a Marlow Unemployment Relief Com-

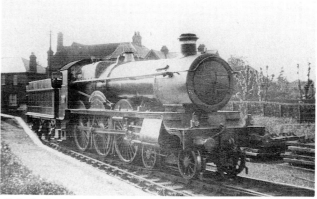

'Saint' class 4–6–0 No. 2916 *Saint Benedict* running round an excursion train at Marlow in May 1935.   *Reg Daniells*

mittee was formed to raise funds and carry out any schemes 'of a suitable public character which should provide work for the unemployed'. Among its achievements voluntary house to house canvassers generated enough money to fund the raising of Regatta Meadow by about 4 feet, the material being won by cutting back the bank on the Oxford Road side near the waterworks some seven feet over a length of 600 feet.

Yet against this background tourist traffic flourished, over 70 special trains running into Marlow during the summer of 1935, for instance, bringing excursionists from all over the country including Newcastle, Manchester, Bury, Weymouth and the West of England. These were in addition to the regular services, many of which connected with Salters steamers, the GWR continuing to advertise combined rail and river trips each summer since at least the early 1920s and at Maidenhead even in Victorian times. The lure of the river was unfailing and even during the Second World War the *Bucks Free Press* reported that holiday buses and trains were 'as crowded as ever'.

The Bank Holiday excursions of 1939 probably serve as well as any to illustrate the variety of this traffic, albeit that the threatening clouds of international conflict were looming on the horizon. On Saturday, 27th May, a special train from Derby brought a party from the Abbey Street Boys School to Bourne End, an LNER loco and three coaches, working through with a pilotman, arriving at 10.58 a.m. The coaches, which were stabled at Bourne End while the loco ran light back to High Wycombe, were later attached to the rear of the 5.45 p.m. from Paddington. At Wycombe they were picked up again by the LNER loco for the return journey to Derby.

On Whit Monday, 29th May, two specials ran from Harecastle (via Leamington) and Northampton (via Oxford) to Windsor, arriving at 12.00 a.m. and 1.37 p.m. respectively. The empty stock was worked through to Marlow where the passengers walked from the river to rejoin their trains which left at 7.09 p.m. and 9.31 p.m. respectively. On the same day a party from the *Newcastle Chronicle* travelled to Marlow via Banbury and High Wycombe, arriving at 8.56 a.m. and rejoining their train at Windsor and travelling back via Paddington, High Wycombe and Banbury. Another special that day ran

from Longton Bridge (via Leamington) to Bourne End, arriving at 12.14 p.m. and returning via Windsor etc.

On Tuesday, 30th May, a train from Colne, Lancashire, (via Leamington LMS) dropped a party from the Burnley Chamber of Trade at Bourne End and continued empty stock to Windsor. The party travelled to Windsor along the Thames, presumably in one of Salter's steamers, and returned via Paddington and Euston. The empty stock left at Paddington was later retrieved by the LMS at Kensington Addison Road. On the same day two other specials brought parties from Leicester to Windsor, returning via Marlow, and from Bradford and Huddersfield to Windsor, again returning from Marlow after a river trip.

The final such excursion that holiday was a special from Radcliffe (via Leamington) to Windsor, returning from Marlow at 7.09 p.m. This and some of the other trains included a dining car, which on such trips would be gassed and watered at either Windsor or Slough.

During the August Bank Holiday period that year specials ran on Sunday, 6th August, from Macclesfield to Windsor, returning from Marlow; Monday 7th from Manchester (LMS) to Windsor, returning via Marlow; Tuesday 8th two trains from Leicester (LMS) (via Acton) to Windsor, returning via Marlow; and Thursday 10th from Nuneaton (via Oxford) to Windsor, again returning from Marlow.

In addition to these excursions from 'foreign' companies, the Great Western also ran its own excursions to Windsor, returning from Marlow from such places as

No. 4959 *Purley Hall* pulling into Bourne End with empty stock from a rail/river excursion from the Midlands to Marlow in 1939. The train is crossing from the Marlow branch to the up line platform.

Trevor Bailey

An undated view showing the branch train strengthened with an additional trailer at the terminus, probably in the late 1930s.

Lens of Sutton

Wolverhampton and even Weston-super-Mare, a town which was more usually the recipient of excursions from all over the system.

Another means by which Thames Valley explorers could arrive at one destination and return from another was the bicycle tour ticket. This innovation dated from at least the turn of the century, a 1901 publicity leaflet listing, for example, two tours involving Marlow: one to Staines, Uxbridge or Windsor, and another to Henley, returning from Marlow or vice-versa. Fares at the time ranged from 4/6d to 10/-, depending on the class of travel.

There had been no let up in services during the 1930s. In the summer of 1935, for example, there were some thirteen through workings, and through coaches were attached to the 8.34 a.m. to Bourne End and 6.42 p.m. return. A similar pattern was maintained until 1938/39 when, apart from the familiar morning and early evening Paddington services, there were seven to and from Maidenhead, one from High Wycombe, one from Reading and one from Slough.

The war years inevitably curtailed through working. In February 1940 only four services involving Maidenhead and Reading remained, together with the morning and evening through coaches. By the following summer only the latter workings survived, and in 1942 there were no 'throughs' of any description.

With the possible exception of excursion traffic, through workings were not revived during the remaining GWR period.

Marlow became a 'reception' area under the Government's evacuation scheme, mothers and children being billeted throughout the town on the outbreak of hostilities. Whilst this initial move proved rather a false alarm, evacuees arrived again in July 1940 followed by more in March 1941. There was also a drive to persuade those who could to offer billets for 'the new and growing army of women war workers'.

While men left to join the forces women were 'vitally needed for work in war industries in the area'. Loud-speaker appeals were given and included one accompanied by a Hurricane fighter mounted on a trailer and another from a motor launch touring the Thames between Windsor and Maidenhead. Their contribution and accomplishments in many arduous occupations is generally well known, particularly at a time when women were not so 'liberated'.

Many of the jobs at the railway station were taken over by conscripted women, the first, Joan Clayton, becoming a porter. Other positions were gradually filled until by 1944 about ten were employed.

Undoubtedly the most responsible of the positions held by the women at Marlow was that of signalwoman, a demanding task which required much training and comprehension. The first was Glenys Morgan from South Wales. Glenys started about February 1944 and for six weeks was trained at the signalling school at Reading. She then worked at Marlow under Ivor Morgan, a Marlow signalman who had himself moved up from South Wales to fill what was initially a porter/signalman's vacancy (a grade below his position) during the 1930s Depression. A loss of grade was the penalty for such a move on the GWR. She also worked under Norman Mabbits, a senior relief signalman.

Soon two other girls, Judy Tyler and Evelyn Harris, were also trained and eventually the box was manned throughout the day by female staff in three shifts, 5.20 a.m. to 1.20 p.m., 1.20 p.m. to 4 p.m. and 4 p.m. to midnight. The middle duty was only part of an 8 a.m. to 4 p.m. shift, the first part of which was served as porter's duties on the platform. By mutual arrangement the women changed over at 1 p.m. on Saturdays to give each other a long weekend every third week. Previously the box was manned for a period by just two signalmen in shifts of 5.20 a.m. to 2.40, and 2.40 p.m. to the last train, hours which always involved overtime payment. The early turn signalman booked the passengers for the workmen's train with tickets, and a 'float' left by the clerk the previous day as the booking clerk did not come on duty until 7 a.m. Sometimes they also had to evict personnel attached to RAF Medmenham from the coaches beforehand. These men were often late returning to Marlow and, with no transport available to the camp, they were unofficially allowed to sleep in the stock overnight. Many of them cycled to the station, which created storage problems, and the Ministry of War Transport eventually funded a new bicycle shed in 1944 for the purpose. The sum of £44 15s 7d was also expended on the 'adaptation of General Waiting Room to provide shelter accommo-

Joan Clayton, a porter at Marlow during the war years.
Courtesy Mrs. J. Staton

dation for staff. ARP measure.' The work was completed on 18th August 1943.

Judy Tyler kept a diary for 1944 and we are fortunate in gaining an insight of her personal feelings during this period.

Wednesday, 9th February
Cold, wet. . . . . Dear old Father met me at school and took me over to Wycombe for my call-up interview. It was all rather strange and I don't think I did very well.

Thursday, 9th March
Cold, wet. I'm afraid I will always look back on this day as one of the worst and most depressing . . . . . Then I went for my interview and was told by some indifferent woman that I was to leave school and be a mobile factory worker. I completely broke down . . . . . .

Monday, 13th March
Sunny, cold. School, I can't really believe all this call-up business has happened . . . . . .

Wednesday, 15th March
Sunny, cold. . . . . . . I went to Marlow Labour Exchange which was bristling with importance, and they told me I must go where I was sent . . . . . . can think of nothing except this call-up.

Tuesday, 21st March
Wet and depressing. . . . . . . Wish they would let me know when I was to be called up or where I was going.

Tuesday, 28th March
Misty and sunny later. . , . , , , I went to the Wycombe Labour Exchange and was told that as I was mobile I couldn't take a job at a Marlow Factory . . . . . . Depressing evening picturing myself living at a hostel for factory workers . . . . . .

Tuesday, 4th April
Wet, muggy. Last day at school . . . . . .

Wednesday, 12th April
Sunny, showery. The fateful letter arrived this morning. I was expecting it so it wasn't much of a shock. I went to see Matthews at 11 with Father feeling like nothing on earth, and he told me I was to be a signal woman at Marlow Station — such a relief. Dear old Father took me round to see the Station Master who fixed everything up — lovely to have someone to look after you . . . . . .

Thursday, 13th April
Unsettled. . . . . . I had a very happy day. Wrote lots of letters and told everyone about my new job.

Monday, 24th April
Warm and cloudy. First day in my box and I quite enjoyed it — refused to let myself think of the year ahead with the holidays. Everyone was very affable but I think the work is very complicated — came home to lunch and then went back till 6. I would like to write a lot about it, but I'm so tired and anyway least said soonest mended.

Tuesday, 25th April
Sunny, windy and cold. Caught the 8.33 train for Reading. Mother packed up a lovely lunch. We had quite an interesting class in a big dusty room. Then we had lunchtime off and went to the canteen which was rather fun, but only as a short experi-

ence. The other girls are very amusing. Shopgirl, service and hairdressing. Came home at 5. Felt very cheerful and happy. Nice. Spent evening going over my notes.

Wednesday, 26th April
Sunny and warm. Met the girls at Maidenhead and had a good day at Reading. We found a park and sat on a deck chair which was nice and peaceful. Home 5.30 — tea in the garden . . . . . .

Thursday, 27th April
Very sunny and warm. Lovely morning, breakfast outside. Rather a hot day in Reading — it seemed a waste of a lovely day. Went to see Dr. Henry and he gave me a medical certificate. Lovely evening . . . . . .

Friday, 28th April
Sunny intervals. Box at 8 this morning. Dear old Father got everything ready. Uneventful morning, but a nice tea-party in the afternoon with all the gang . . . . . .

Saturday, 29th April
Cloudy, windy. Peaceful morning in the box. Helped Mr. Morgan, indeed to tidy up, and wrote a letter. Our boss said we could have the afternoon off . . . . . .

Monday, 1st May
Sunny, windy. Off to Reading with the 'girls'. 4 new ones today. Lecture was rather dry but I enjoyed the day on the whole . . . . . .

Tuesday, 2nd May
Very windy. Good day at Reading. Very amusing and fun. Came back about 6.

Wednesday, 3rd May
Fine and warm. Took sandwiches to eat with Michael in Forbury Gardens in Reading. Quite missed the canteen . . . . .

Thursday, 4th May
Cold, wet in evening. Day in box. Nice signalman on duty, quite amusing morning but I couldn't get any letters written.

Friday, 5th May
Windy, cold, sunny. Back to the box . . . . . . enjoyed the morning but the afternoon was irritating. The Inspector came and fired questions at us. Mr. Morgan was very trying. Felt depressed when I got home . . . . . .

Tuesday, 9th May
Sunny and very warm. Met Michael in the gardens after lunch at the canteen . . . . . .

Friday, 12th May
Sunny and warm. Reading again with the girls. The Inspector kept me ages asking me questions — he took till 12.30 . . . . . .

Saturday, 13th May
Warm. Rain in evening. Box as usual. It's very annoying having to break into a Saturday . . . . . .

Monday, 15th May
Cold in evening. Morning in box with Glenys — quite nice. Home to a lovely lunch with Father. Came back to the box to find the Inspector waiting to tell me I wasn't to go to Reading any more but to take late shift in the box tomorrow. Rather a blow . . . . . .

Marlow signal box.   *Courtesy S. Brooks*

Tuesday, 16th May
Wet and very cold. . . . . . . Went down to the box at 4 o'clock. Am writing this now. It is quite fun.

Wednesday, 17th May
Very cold . . . . . . rained all evening and I felt quite cosy in the signal box . . . . . .

Thursday, 18th May
Very cold . . . . . . I had to be down in the box at 4.

Saturday, 20th May
Sunny morning . . . . . . Evening in the box again till 12; felt very sleepy.

Monday, 22nd May
Cold, sunny. Enjoyed my early start — everyone very witty at the station for so early on — reminded me of the end of a dance. Morning went by very quickly . . . . . .

Wednesday, 24th May
Sunny, misty first thing. Very foggy and cold. Evelyn came for the morning. Am looking forward to being on my own. Some Inspectors came to make improvements on the box . . . . . .

Tuesday, 30th May
Hot and sunny . . . . . . Back to the box at 4 — seemed quite a tie after the holiday and the hours dragged. Lovely moonlight night.

Wednesday, 31st May
Warm, windy. Back to my box at 4. Very warm still. Quite a good evening playing cards.

Thursday, 1st June
Rain in morning. Father took me down to the box. Restless day waiting for Inspectors who didn't come.

Friday, 2nd June
Sunny, wind, cold. Went to Bourne End on the engine and the Station Master was furious, deducted an hour and sent me up the box. Most unfair. Gruelling morning with the Inspector but I got on alright.

Saturday, 3rd June
Cold. Rather bored in the box with Glenys, Evelyn and Jack. Also Cox got my goat by watching every time I went on the platform . . . . . .

Monday, 5th June
Cold, sunny. Found I was on with Jack Hammond at 6 o'clock this morning. So pleased as he is great company and very clever. Morning flashed by and I enjoyed it . . . . . .

Invasion Day. Tuesday, 6th June
Very cold. Jack told me I had to change my shift tomorrow and that another Inspector was coming down. He came and it was alright and I may go to Paddington on Saturday.

Wednesday, 7th June
Cold, but less windy. Helped on the platform at 8 this morning. Went to Bourne End with the cash and generally mooched about mopping out rooms and grumbling. Came back to the box at 1 and had amusing time being teased . . . . . .

Thursday, 8th June
Cold, showers. Rather bored on platform. Received £5 10 for wages and they had been taking off too much tax.

Friday, 9th June
Very wet. A troop train left Marlow early this morning and caused a great to-do. Lots of Inspectors and things. Quite an amusing day at station being asked questions by Jack. Bed early for the great day tomorrow.

The interior of Marlow signal box.

Cty. Monica Jones

Saturday, 10th June
Unsettled. To London on the 7.20. Doug, Jack and all others saw me off. The exam was quite fun at Paddington — very amusing . . . . . .

Monday, 12th June
Cold wind & sunny. Amusing morning. Shunter on the engine. Freddie said I was to take over tomorrow. Hope I get on alright . . . . . .

Tuesday, 13th June
Wet. Inspector Harland passed me out this morning. I took on the box all by myself — quite nerve racking! . . . . . .

Wednesday, 14th June
Windy and wet. Went to Bourne End to pass the time — quite amusing. Saw Alison and about 3 signalmen. An old lady fell down on the platform and cut herself and caused quite a commotion.

Friday, 16th June
Cold. Amusing morning in the box with two linemen who were awfully nice. Old Harland came down to throw his weight about.

Saturday, 17th June
Cold, sunny. Another day at the station — better than usual . . . . . .

Sunday, 18th June
Sunny, cold early. To the station at 5. Quite enjoyed it, as it was a new experience for me — morning passed quickly and quietly . . . . . .

Monday, 19th June
Sunny, cold. Started the trains off early again . . . . . .

Tuesday, 20th June
Cold, wind & sun. Irritating morning doing nothing on the platform. I hope this shift doesn't last long . . . . . .

Friday, 23rd June
Cold, overcast. . . . . . . Inspector Harland came down about next week's turns and was very affable . . . . . .

Saturday, 24th June
Sunny, warm, settled. Lovely warm Midsummer day, tried not to be fed up at the station all day. I'm glad I'm on early turn next week.

Thursday, 28th June
Showery. Same sort of morning as usual — they go very quickly. Father came to see me in the box for a cup of cocoa . . . . . .

Friday, 30th June
Overcast. Station full of dramas as usual. It's rather like being back at school — they are all jealous tell-tales but I suppose it adds to the spice of life . . . . . .

Saturday, 1st July
Wet, muggy. Pouring with rain and I got soaked going down. Doug lit me a fire to warm by. Very busy morning cleaning the box, and endless things to do with the engines — but it made the time pass quickly. Mr. Funnell has put me on late turn tomorrow which seems hard . . . . . .

Sunday, 2nd July
Showers. . . . . . . Mother came to the box for supper. Very wet evening. I enjoyed having her. She left at 9. I got back at 11.

Wednesday, 5th July.
Showery. . . . . . . The siren went 3 times and we actually saw a Doodlebug for the first time. Jack had supper with me in the box and brought me home at night.

Friday, 7th July
Wet. Fine later. . . . . . . caught the 10.20 to Maidenhead and there I was escorted to the signal box to see Jack who was expecting me. Spent a very amusing hour with all of them. Came back to the box at 4. Lots of alerts.

Saturday, 8th July
Sunny at times. . . . . . . Father brought my chair down for me. Quite a nice evening. Jack brought me home very late as the fireman didn't turn up.

Signalwoman Glenys Morgan on the steps of Marlow signal box.
Courtesy Mrs. G. Church

Tuesday, 11th July
Wet & cold. Rather dreary morning on the platform then to the box at 1 . . . . . .

Wednesday, 12th July
Cloudy & cold. Same sort of morning as usual. Several signalmen rang me up and it was quite amusing. Doug had an accident last night, so he couldn't come for his shift. Joined the Union today . . . . . .

Friday, 14th July
Cloudy and muggy. Spring-cleaned the platform a bit this morning, so the time passed a little more quickly. All the usual dramas occurred. Peter turned up in the box at 4 and took me home in his car . . . . . .

Saturday, 15th July
Very wet. . . . . . . some mysterious telephone call in the box at 1.30. Glenys went off to Wales . . . . . .

Sunday, 16th July
Unsettled. Early start to the box . . . . . . Quite a good morning. Dave and lots of signalmen rang up . . . . . .

Monday, 17th July
Very warm. Really warm day. Thick mist at 5 and rather 'coca'. Worked till 1.20. Quite amusing but very hot . . . . . .

Tuesday, 18th July
Warm and heavy. To the box at 10 as Ivor had to go off for a funeral or something. Day passed very quickly . . . . . .

Wednesday, 19th July
Warm. . . . . . . enjoyed the platform work.

Thursday, 20th July
Warm. . . . . . . the Inspector came to see Evelyn. He stayed for ages. He is very frightening and don't know whether Evelyn passed or not. Anyway he is coming down again next week.

Friday, 21st July
Warm. Quite fun at work today as a truck was derailed and caused quite a paraphernalia and I was able to meet a lot of new people. Wish I could travel about on the railway a bit more.

Saturday, 22nd July
Cold, wet. Doodlebug landed (and bombs?).*

Monday, 24th July
Cloudy. Rather amusing morning. Nice new fireman, and I had a long chat with Doug and lots of signalmen. Morning went very quickly . . . . . .

Tuesday, 25th July
Warm, cloudy later. Usual morning in box. I'm getting quite attached to it.

Thursday, 27th July
Cloudy. Depressing start as I left the key of my locker behind, so I had to break it open. Ben came to the box at 1 and we went and had drinks with Charlie and Doug at the Wheatsheaf.

Friday, 28th July
Overcast, muggy. Only one more early start. Went on the train to Bourne End for a trip and got the Inspector's name in my book . . . . . .

*A German V1 landed on the north side of Chalk Pit Hill. The explosion injured Jim Platt, a young lad of 10.

Saturday, 29th July
Wet. Very cross and depressed this morning because old Freddie put me on to work on Sunday . . . . . .

Monday, 31st July
Warm later. . . . . . . Quite enjoyed getting back to my box after my long holiday! Lots of my signalmen rang up which helped to pass the time away.

Wednesday, 2nd August
Warm, sunny later. . . . . . . Box pleasant and amusing. I enjoy it more and more . . . . . .

Thursday, 3rd August
Overcast, warm later. . . . . . . Evelyn passed her signal exam.

Sunday, 6th August
Sunny and very warm. . . . . had a long session in the box. Quite nice. Slough firemen and drivers helped pass the day away . . . . . .

Tuesday, 8th August
Hot, cloudy midday. Back to the station but not so bad as I thought.

Thursday, 10th August
Cloudy, muggy. . . . . . . Came to the box at 1. A P.W. Inspector came and talked to me for a long time. Home at 4 . . . . . .

Friday, 11th August
Warm. . . . . . . Mrs. Roberts came to the platform and gave me a tip. Mr. Harland came down and fixed up Evelyn next week on the porter turn, so she'll be early next week which just suits me.

Saturday, 12th August
Cloudy and warm. . . . . . . I came on to do a dreary platform shift wasting my time. Felt tired and fed up for almost the first time in the box.

Sunday, 13th August
Warm. Early start to the box. Joan came down to see me which was nice and lots of people phoned up and dropped in . . . . . .

Monday, 14th August
Fine and sunny. Lovely hot day, so glad I'm on early shift.

Thursday, 17th August
Muggy and cloudy. . . . . . . Doug (the lineman) and Bert spent the morning in the box, and it was fun and it went very quickly . . . . . .

Tuesday, 22nd August
Muggy and cloudy. . . . . . . Spent from 5 o'clock in the box and arranged to give some greengages to some obscure person on the phone.

Friday, 25th August
Muggy. . . . . . . rushed down to the box again. Joan looked in to see me, and Mother came to supper. Train was late again.

Saturday, 26th August
Hot and sunny. . . . . . . Spent most of the day sunbathing and came to the box at 4. Joan came to supper and was lovely. Glenys looked in too. Quite a good, non-boring evening.

Sunday, 3rd September
Sunny then rain. Bright moonlight to come to the box in and then a lovely sunny morning. Extraordinary to think the war

has been on for 5 years today — I remember that first Sunday so well when we all sat on the verandah and listened in . . . . . .

Tuesday, 19th September
Two men came down to do the telephone and lavatory, and my uniform arrived all in one foul swoop. Caused a great stir on the platform. Quite amusing afternoon with the two linemen in the box.

Wednesday, 20th September
Misty early. Wore my uniform — messed about all morning with two funny men who came to finish fitting up the phone. Quite funny. They fitted up a lavatory in the box afterwards.

Tuesday, 26th September.
Quite a 'do' on this morning as the engine wouldn't go and they had to send for another one from Slough. Anyway it all helped to pass the time and I rather enjoyed it . . . . . .

Thursday, 28th September.
. . . . . . £3 6d was my pay this week . . . . . .

Saturday, 30th September
Last morning of the awful early starts. Very amusing morning being told conundrums by the signalman at Bourne End South. Changed at 12 and caught the 12.20 . . . . . .

Thursday, 5th October
. . . . . . Noisy shift in the box — some bombs dropped quite close. But luckily I finished early which made up for it.

Monday, 9th October
Platform shift and it didn't go down too well. Freddie wouldn't let me go to Bourne End which was a bad start . . . . . .

Tuesday, 10th October
Sunny. Better day on the platform — I miss going to Bourne End . . . . . .

Wednesday, 11th October
Wet and cold. . . . . . . Inspector Allen came to the box today, which was a pity because I couldn't entertain him properly. Anyway I had a little chat. There are rats in the box I think . . .

Saturday, 14th October
Wet. Last day on the platform — not a very pleasant one either.

Tuesday, 31st October
Very cold. Went into the box to relieve the monotony of the platform (soul destroying) . . . . . .

Tuesday, 21st November
Lovely sunny day for a change. Quite pleasant and uneventful. I don't mind this shift nearly so much now. It goes very quickly . . . . . .

Friday, 24th November
Still damp and muggy and wet. . . . . . . Quiet platform shift with no dramas.

A selection of autographs from Judy's diary.

Sunday, 26th November
Very early start and very cold — morning went quite quickly — how thankful I shall be when this exam is over. I shan't really cheer up until it is . . . . . .

Saturday, 2nd December
Lovely sunny day . . . . . . left the box at 12.

Monday, 4th December
In the box again tonight, rather lonely without my wireless . . . . . . the 2nd exam wasn't too bad . . . . . .

Tuesday, 5th December
. . . . . . my wireless was ready tonight — and I enjoyed it in the box.

Wednesday, 6th December
. . . . . . The box was quite pleasant — I didn't leave it all evening. The train was late . . . . . .

Thursday, 7th December
Last day of the exam, thank God! . . . . . .

Wednesday, 13th December
Cold & foggy. . . . . . . to the box at One . . . . . . very foggy evening. All trains late.

Friday, 15th December
Cold & foggy. Last day on the platform — quite busy . . . . . .

Saturday, 16th December
To the box at 8 today. Glenys went on the 8.34. Rather a lazy day . . . . . . but quite fun just the same, and one or two odd things happened . . . . . .

Monday, 18th December
Early start and the fire in the box was out which was a bit of a sod . . . . . .

Tuesday, 19th December
Foggy and cold. Busy morning in box with 2 linemen and some policemen who came and asked me questions — I think there's been a burglary . . . . . .

Wednesday, 20th December
Very foggy morning, all trains hopelessly late. My phone was out of order which was a bit worrying. They mended it for me later . . . . . .

Saturday, 23rd December
Sunny and cold. Last early start. Finished at 12 . . . . . .

Monday, 25th December
. . . . . . down to the box from 2 to 10 . . . . . .

Tuesday, 26th December
Early start to the box 7 o'clock. Very very cold morning . . . . .

Wednesday, 27th December
. . . . . . came to box at 4 . . . . . .

All the staff at Marlow worked hard during these difficult times and undertook a variety of duties in addition to their normal work. Station master Funnell (who took over from Mealings in 1942) must have been proud of his team who each made a contribution to the war effort.

The travelling public were obviously appreciative of the service given, since, for example, in 1944 a Christmas tree in the booking hall became adorned with gifts for the staff who continued to run a train service throughout the holiday period.

Among firms evacuated to Marlow were Sandeman's (port) and Courtauld's. Greenwich Sawmills Ltd. also established a new depot there. Mr. Garfield Weston of the Canadian Biscuit Manufacturers lived at Whittington during the war and entertained air crews at weekends. Doreen Emmett (*née* Stroud), who worked as a clerk at Marlow station, remembers Guy Gibson of Dambusters fame standing by the fire in the booking office. Mr. Weston apparently donated the money for seven fighter planes, one for each of his children.

Wethered's old mineral water factory was used as a buffer depot for the storage of tinned milk and sugar, the Ministry of War sending supplies to places of need such as

Joan Clayton again and Florence Rimmell who carried out porters duties, usually on the same shift, seen here with Len Stroud.   *Cty. Mrs. J. Staton*

Flood water threatening the branch train near Spade Oak on 15th March 1947.   *R. Goodearl*

Plymouth which sustained heavy air raids. With supplies of food and fuel remaining in short supply in the post-war years, the notorious winter during the early months of 1947 came as a particularly harsh blow. When the snows melted the worst floods in memory occurred in the Thames Valley, isolating entire villages. The river was reported as three miles wide in some places and at Marlow passed the hitherto record levels of the 1894 disaster.

Ken Lovett, goods clerk at Marlow, remembers the river overflowing its banks and how each day as he went to work on the train he could see the water gradually spreading across the fields towards the line. Since the embankment had been raised in GMR days, the railway had managed to stay just above the winter floods, but on Saturday, 16th March, the water had reached the boundary fence just on the Bourne End side of Fieldhouse crossing, just outside Marlow. The ganger kept watch on it during the morning and by about noon it was washing the ballast at that point and an hour later it was considered unsafe to continue running the train as it was still rising.

Mr. Funnell, the station master, was apparently off that weekend and Ken was due off duty at 1.15 p.m. However, he stayed on and contacted Mr. Tame, the station master at Bourne End, about closing the line.

Arrangements were made with the Thames Valley Bus Company to provide a service between the stations at train times, or as near as possible, and Ken finally went home about 4.00 p.m. The details are not clear now, but the local newspaper reported the line closed from 6.30 p.m. that day until 6.00 a.m. on the 25th, and despite the bus service the town experienced another serious fuel shortage as railborne coal supplies were stranded. Indeed such was the damage to the line that permanent closure was rumoured, but fortunately this was not to be.

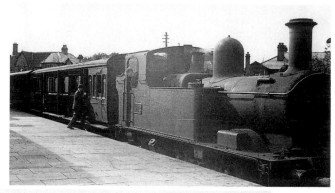

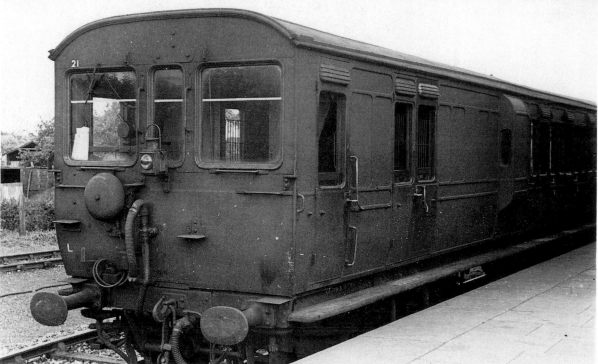

It has been difficult to establish when the Clifton Down push-pull stock was first sent to Marlow but it would appear to have been used from the late 1930s, through the war until Nationalization, and is believed to have been sent to Swindon for scrapping in 1948. In his well-known 'Railway Topics' column in *Model Railway News* for July 1947 the editor J. N. Maskelyne wrote: 'In spite of their age, the two coaches of this train are kept well groomed, and the responsibility for this is the care of an energetic lady, Miss Cicely Bateman by name, who appears to possess strong ideas on the subject of railway-carriage cleanliness! She it was who was interviewed by Roy Rich in the "In Town Tonight" broadcast . . . . . and we learned, among other things, that she goes on duty at 7 a.m., sees that the train is in proper trim for its first trip at 7.30 a.m., and then makes a number of trips on it herself, taking every opportunity to wash and dust the compartments, polish door-handles and other brasswork and keep the windows clean. The result is that a trip on the "Marlow Donkey" is a real joy for most of the passengers. Miss Bateman goes off duty at 3 p.m.; but she says she enjoys her job, which she has now held for seven years, and I must say that the spotless condition of the compartments does her credit.' These two pictures show the Clifton Down stock at Marlow in 1947.

J. H. Russell

CHAPTER FIVE

BOURNE END TO MARLOW
BOURNE END STATION

THE appearance of the station as remodelled by the Great Western makes its modest origin far from obvious. For the first years of its life Marlow Road, as it was then called, was a simple wayside station which, as described on page 15, was almost crudely modified to provide junction facilities for the Great Marlow Railway.

Up to this time it was staffed by a booking porter and three porters, two each for day and night duties. One of the porters was appointed switchman to man the new 'locking gear box' when the branch junction was installed which, according to an official report, left only one man besides the booking porter 'to do all the station work such as collecting tickets, booking parcels, attending to the trains, luggage etc. and the other various duties on the stations, and this was more than he was able to get through'. In 1874, therefore, a lad porter was also appointed.

The signal box referred to is probably the same as that featured on a plan for the installation of a run-round loop for branch trains in 1879. This shows the cabin with a 27 lever frame (12 signals, 14 points and 1 spare) situated on the fork of the junction.

The shortcomings of the modified station were becoming more obvious and bearing out the Marlow Company's directors' initial doubts. Even the officer inspecting the new run-round loop for the BOT on 28th March 1879 pointed out:

1. The platform is too short.
2. All the sidings should be controlled with safety points.
3. All facing points should be fitted with lifting bars and locking bolts.
4. Clocks should be provided in the Junction Cabin and at the station so as to be seen from the platform.

The booking office was enlarged in 1887 for £10 and the booking porters' houses, both here and at Wooburn Green, were enlarged in 1889 by S. Robertson for the sum of £370, but otherwise it was some years before any substantial improvement took place. In 1892 the Great Western evidently decided they could no longer stave off

An Edwardian scene at Bourne End level crossing.

Bourne End Residents Association Collection

BOURNE END

Taken after the installation of gas lighting in 1904, this postcard, dated July 1906, provides an excellent view of the station after the 1894 improvements and before the lengthening of the crossing loop at the Wycombe end in 1907. The down starting signal for the North signal box, with the distant signal for Cores End Crossing beneath, is visible beyond the gates. A new signal, without the distant arm, was provided, further from the station, as part of the 1907 work. Billinghurst's horse-drawn van is also featured at the end of the up platform.

Authors' Collection

the provision of at least a second platform and extensively revised the whole site in true GWR style for an estimated £4,743. The work included provision of an 'up' platform, a double junction providing direct access to the branch, extension of the branch bay by slewing the bay line to run behind the station, thus widening the platform, and a new run-round loop for branch trains. The new layout was consequently resignalled and operated from two new signal boxes, north and south, at each end of the site. William Goodchild successfully tendered for the erection of new platform coverings, waiting shed, footbridge, etc. for £1,235 10s 0d, the GWR presumably carrying out the remainder of the work.

Before the improvements were completed, a fatal accident, which occurred at Bourne End on 5th May 1894, prompted a census of traffic using the level crossing which was cited as 'much frequented'. Vehicular traffic was said to have been subjected to delays as long as 20 minutes during shunting operations which was 'most complained of'. Ironically, the accident had no real connection with this problem, the victim, under the influence of drink and having illicitly ridden in a truck of a goods train from

Marlow, walked down the platform ramp and, despite a warning from a man outside the gates, he crawled under the wheels of a goods train stopped on the crossing. Before he cleared the other side, the train moved and he lost his legs and died the following day.

However, despite the extraordinary circumstances of the incident, which appears to have been irrelevant to the general complaints, a survey was carried out from 24th to 31st July (including a weekend), revealing that during the eight day period a total of 9,692 passengers, 269 animals, and 787 vehicles were subject to 27 delays of between 3 and 6 minutes. A committee from the parish, apparently aided or led by Rev. Sladen, carried out their own survey during the Marlow Regatta week, the higher results of which the GWR did not agree with, pointing out to the Board of Trade that the period was hardly typical.

The new facilities, which included interlocking the crossing gates with the signalling, were most impressive, but on his inspection for the Board of Trade on 8th January 1895, Colonel Yorke expressed surprise and said:

'. . . . in view of the large number of pedestrians who are reported to use the public road level crossing at the north end

The Railway Hotel.

Bourne End Residents Association Collection

An undated photograph looking over the Marlow branch curve from the end of the bay platform around the turn of the century. The train is on the Bay Loop line and has just passed the Up Bay Loop line up stop signal. In the background are (from left to right) the South box Up Branch Stop signal with North box Up Branch Repeating Distant arm beneath, the Down Branch Stop and Down Bay line to Branch Stop signals (see plan on page 200).

J. E. Kite

of this station during a certain season of the year, it is unfortunate that the new footbridge was not constructed in such a position as to be available for such persons, as well as for passengers by train. To have done this would have involved some interference with the station master's house and would have increased the expenditure already incurred in making the alterations at this station. But having regard to the complaints which have been made by the local authorities on the subject of this level crossing, I feel some surprise that the company will not see their way to incur the necessary expenditure to effect this further improvement. But as it is probable that the alterations in the arrangements at the station will considerably lessen the amount of shunting over the level crossing, and as the gates are now controlled from the signal box which is close to the crossing, I am not at present prepared to recommend the Board of Trade to press upon the company the sanction of a second footbridge for the use of persons passing along the highway.'

Bourne End was certainly the subject of considerable expenditure for at the same time the old timber viaduct over the Thames, already rebuilt in 1873, was due for renewal, the estimated cost of which amounted to £9,000.

It had long been the subject of local concern, one correspondent in *The Times* as early as 1866 writing:

'Sir, — Being a constant traveller on the Great Western Railway, on their branch line from Maidenhead to High Wycombe, I desire through your columns, to inform the public who use the line of the great risk they run of being killed or seriously injured each time the train passes over the bridge at the Marlow Road station. It is notorious that this bridge has been for a long time in a very dangerous state, but no repair has been done, and it is evident that before long the bridge will give way. The river at this place is deep and wide, and should an accident occur while the train is passing over, the loss of life would be terrible. If you would make this known through your paper, the directors may see the necessity of repairing this bridge and many others that I hear are in an equally bad condition on the Great Western Railway.

I remain, sir, your obedient servant,
George Heatley

41 Seething Lane
Crutched Friars
Oct. 9th

The new structure, built by F. C. Caffins for £8,388, employed steel lattice girders on wrought iron cylinders filled with concrete. Three main spans, 85 ft 10 ins on the square, carried the line over the Thames whilst another five shorter segmental arches on the Maidenhead end and

Another undated view, this time featuring the empty Marlow branch bay photographed soon after the installation of gas lighting in 1904.
Bourne End Residents Association Collection

The newly completed viaduct carrying the Wycombe Railway over the Thames. At the far end of the viaduct is the South box Down Home signal with the North box Distant arm beneath. At this date distant signal arms were still painted red.

British Railways

two at the Wycombe end connected it with the approaches. It was constructed immediately adjacent to, and upstream of, the original which, before its removal, was suggested as a 'very convenient standing for examining the new one'. The subsequent realignment of the track required the replacement of the new facing point, giving entry to the station, and slewing the ends of the refuge sidings.

Colonel Yorke inspected what he described as 'this handsome viaduct' on 30th December 1895. He was evidently impressed and went on to say 'The work generally seems to be of a high class character'. Consideration had been given to the provision of two extra cylinders for the second line, and, although these were not built, one of the girders was 'designed with sufficient strength for a central girder, should the line be doubled at some future date'.

The station had thus reached the ultimate form in which it remained until the post Second World War decline, that is apart from the extension of the existing two 'down' or south sidings, the addition of a third,

and, it appears, an extension of the 'up' end of the crossing loop and the associated modification of the yard entry, presumably when 'additional siding accommodation' was authorised for £444 in May 1902. If this is correct, the crossing loop was further extended in 1907 for £219 and the 'up' platform extended in 1913. These and comparatively minor changes are described in the remainder of this section. The level crossings evidently continued to be of sufficient concern for plans to be prepared in 1930 for a new road bridge, approaches and attendant road alteration. Certainly it was intended to replace the Cores End crossing and presumably the main Station Road crossing. Although the plans have been examined, further details have not come to light, but it was evidently still under consideration when the new 'up' carriage siding was proposed in 1935.

By 1934 the staff comprised a station master class 2, goods clerk class 5, booking clerk class 5, general clerk, junior, station foreman class 2, parcel porter, 4 porters class 4 (including 1 junior), goods checker, goods shunter

British Railways

A local postcard view of the station and level crossing, probably taken around the time of the Great War, looking north along Station Road with the double entrance to the goods yard in the foreground and the Railway Hotel in the background. The establishment has in recent years been renamed 'The Firefly'. The doubling of the original station house is particularly apparent here, the plain brick contrasting with the flint and brick of the first.

Cty. Mrs. E. Hobbs

class 4, 3 signalmen class 4 (north box), 3 signalmen class 3 (south box) and 3 crossing keepers for Cores End crossing.

TRAFFIC

Milk
Details of milk carrying prior to the turn of the century are not clear but by 1903 empty churns were being returned to Bourne End mainly from Paddington. Churns transhipped from the Marlow branch often involved taking them over the line near the level crossing. Milk traffic appears to have reduced considerably after the Second World War and by the 1950s had virtually ceased.

Smalls & Passenger Parcels Traffic
Before the introduction of the zonal system, Webster's, the GWR's appointed agents, distributed 'smalls' which arriving in station trucks, were unloaded at the platform. This included all manner of local requirements including the proverbial kitchen sink. Predictably in such an area, traffic was mostly inward but one of the station rate books for the 1930s and '40s has survived and indicates that large quantities of watercress (mainly from Putnams, a local grower) were despatched to such places as Birmingham, Leamington, Manchester and York as well as the inner London area. Other traffic during this period included cheese to Aylesbury and plants to Bedford and Diss. Fish was received from Fraserburgh, Grimsby and Tynemouth.

In the 1950s 'Floor Treatment' of Wharf Lane sent their products by rail.

Before the introduction of the zonal scheme many 'smalls' items were received and despatched using the station truck (sometimes referred to as roadside wagon). In 1915, for example, a truck ran from Bourne End to Hockley and by 1922 one ran in the reverse direction but to Maidenhead. The trucks were loaded and unloaded *en route*, usually in station platforms as was the case at Bourne End.

No station truck working appears to have served the Marlow Branch, consignments being transhipped at Bourne End.

Delivery Arrangements
It seems that James Johnson of Chapel Street, Marlow, who in 1869 offered a carrying service to and from Marlow Road station, was superseded by John Flexman, another local man. In 1883 he was described in local directories as a general carrier and coal merchant.

By 1887 Thomas William Beach was listed as carrier and railway agent at Bourne End and between 1903 and 1911 Charles J. Billingshurst, who was also a corn merchant. A horse-drawn wagon belonging to him features in the picture on page 66, the display on his canvas tilt reading 'C. J. Billingshurst, Cartage Contractor, Agent to the GWR, Bourne End & Wooburn Green'.

It appears that the well-known firm of R. Webster and Son took over from Billingshurst about 1911 and held the agency until the advent of the zonal scheme. Both Marlow and Bourne End stations were served by the Maidenhead sub railhead, a lorry calling mid morning after its rounds to deal with local parcels traffic and returning to Maidenhead about 4 p.m.

However, railway lorries from Reading also served Bourne End direct when necessary, as with Marlow, Harry Rose calling in. Arrangements apparently varied over the years as staff remember Harry calling most days, via Henley, arriving about 2 p.m. and returning at 3 p.m., or alternatively arriving earlier at about 11 a.m. and serving the area. Before the war, heavier items were handled by Webster's but in later years Jack Goodgame used a Scammell which was shared with Marlow for these.

Wagon Load Traffic

Thomas & Green's paper mill, with its own private siding, undoubtedly brought the most goods traffic to Bourne End. Situated some distance to the north of the station, it really falls outside the intended scope of this book. However, mention must be made of the special trains, sometimes 20-25 sheeted wagons, of Esparto grass received from Brentford Docks for use in the manufacture of high quality writing paper. The company's produce was generally despatched in box vans, often destined for London and Birmingham. Regular supplies of coal for the mill are mentioned elsewhere but other supplies included the occasional tank wagon of caustic soda. Care had to be taken when moving these vehicles around when loaded to avoid any of this potent liquid spilling onto the horse provided by Websters for shunting the company's siding. Coal was dropped off at the siding by the Oxford to Taplow goods which also picked up empties, but most of the other traffic was apparently sent via the goods yard, a loco and van servicing the siding from the station. During the Second World War the siding accommodation was increased for the Ministry of Works on behalf of the Ministry of Food and the premises improved and used as a 'buffer depot', Wooburn Food Storage Depot, although in the event stores were mainly roaded.

C. J. Billingshurst's office in Station Road in 1909.
Cty. Bourne End Residents Association Collection

Local requirements were not very demanding. Seasonal farm produce, such as hay and sugar beet, were despatched but other traffic was otherwise of a special short-term nature. For example, in the late 1930s Thorn Buildings used the goods shed as a rail distribution point for their products which included garden sheds. When Jackson's Millboard extended their premises, the little used Bourne End yard crane was used to unload material which arrived by rail. During the 1950s metal radiators from Sweden arrived in ferry wagons and were unloaded in the goods shed. It appears that little, if any, container traffic was handled, but predictably boats were despatched and received from time to time.

Some full load consignments were occasionally despatched from Jackson's and paper in box vans, but generally such traffic was roaded to Reading.

Coal

John Flexman has already been mentioned as both carrier and coal merchant at Bourne End in the 1880s but by the turn of the century Joseph Child traded in coal from the station. He is said to have had three railway wagons, the livery of which is believed to have been red with black lettering. However, whilst early trade directories only acknowledge R. Webster and Son of Maidenhead as corn merchants, they undoubtedly dealt with the largest amounts of domestic coal at Bourne End and had an office opposite Bourne End station and at one time stables alongside The Railway Hotel. As already mentioned, they were also railway cartage agents and undertook various contract work in the area including the hire of horses to Thomas and Green's for shunting wagons at their sidings.

After undertaking delivery work for Webster's from around 1910 to 1927, H. Carr set up his own coal business at Flackwell Heath in 1927. Starting with a horse and cart and later using various lorries including a Ford, Bedford and Morris, he traded mainly in domestic coal and received about two or three wagon loads a week at Bourne End. He didn't own any wagons but instead hired from Galicks of High Wycombe. Shortly before the Second World War when his sons joined him, the company traded as H. Carr and Sons, H. Carr Snr retiring in the late 1950s when his sons took over the business. Supplies continued to arrive by rail until the closure of the sidings when coal was received by road direct from the collieries.

R. Toomer & Co., well known in the area, had an order office near the station for a short period in the late 1920s, but this was closed shortly after the opening of the new one at Marlow station. No coal is believed to have been received at Bourne End by rail.

Apart from coal to Thomas and Green's Paper Mill, between Bourne End and Wooburn Green, the largest consumers of coal were Jackson's Millboard Ltd. of Furlong Road. Prior to the Second World War their supplies were received at Bourne End goods yard and roaded to the factory by G. H. Baker, but later coal was received at the North Sidings and dealt with by F. G. Roberts and Son. The area between this siding and Furlong Road later became a coal storage area and in the 1960s Carr's also received supplies here.

Looking south from the crossing on 14th May 1921 with the Marlow branch train of 4-wheeled coaches in the platform. The section of up platform in the foreground was a later addition of 1913, the platform previously having ended under the footbridge. This new extension, which included alterations to the goods shed, cost £356. Whilst the up platform had been built hard up to the building, what modifications were necessary for this extension are not apparent. The enclosure beneath the left hand footbridge steps was used as a station store shed. In the left foreground, just out of the picture, was a double gateway used for loading directly on and off the agent's lorry. The station awnings seriously interfered with the sighting of the signals at the south end of the station, as this view shows, and a number of alterations were tried in the following years to overcome the problem.

L & GRP, courtesy David & Charles

The all-embracing platform canopy and covered footbridge certainly obscured the simple architecture of the old Wycombe Railway station building. Great Western standardisation managed to align even this formerly modest country station. Accommodation, which had been modified primarily during the 1894 improvements, included the rearrangement of doors and windows and a new extension, and ultimately provided a parcels office (also extended in 1901 for £30) tucked behind the stairs of the footbridge, adjoining two cycle sheds. The 1894 extension at the rear end of the main buildings housed a gentlemen's lavatory, adjoined by a ladies' waiting room and lavatory (formerly a general waiting room), booking office and waiting room (the former enlarged in 1914 for £75), connected to the clerks' offices by a ticket window, followed by the private living quarters. The weighing and chocolate machines adjacent to the footbridge steps also show in this c.1950 view, and the short up starting signal immediately below the end of the canopy. The gas lighting dated from 1904 when, following frequent complaints that 'the old oil lamps were utterly inadequate', it was installed at a cost of £198. It survived until 1969 when it was finally displaced by electric equipment.   *J. H. Russell*

The booking hall in 1958. The building featured on the opposite side of the station served as Toomer's coal office in the late 1920s. It later became a café.

British Railways

Looking north from the footbridge c.1950. The gates at Cores End crossing are visible in the distance. The up relief carriage siding (more formally called the Up Sidings North) dated from 1936 and was probably the additional siding accommodation authorised in November 1935 'for H.M. Government' although the government's need is not clear. For some years it was used for the stabling of coaches from the 10 p.m. ex-Paddington. A Slough engine was sent to collect them the following morning and, after heating them, worked a through service back to London. Jackson's siding alongside the carriage siding was added in 1943 and appears to have also been provided for the government, or 'private siding for the Ministry of Works' to be exact, for £1,215. Again the government's need is not apparent. It was used for the receipt of coal supplies for Jackson's Millboard Ltd., manufacturers of fibreboard for radio and television backs, car linings, etc. They also received coconut matting in sheeted wagons. Previously, coal supplies for Jacksons were unloaded in the goods yard and ferried to the factory by G. H. Baker of Wooburn Green, his horse and carts being driven by Sam Burton and Bill Whiteman. However, a road was laid alongside the siding and F. G. Roberts used lorries and a mechanical grab, to ferry supplies to Jacksons. Certainly in later years the road alongside became a coal storage area and in the 1960s Carrs also received supplies here. The shop on the right was the station fruiterers provided under an agreement dated 15th August 1912, and between this and the signal box was a footpath to Cores End. There was a small barber's shop adjacent to the level crossing, on the left and out of the picture, and alongside that was Webster's coal, corn and seed merchants office. Milk from up trains for Marlow was wheeled via North End Road level crossing across the forecourt and through the double gateway to the branch bay platform. This view shows the signalling which allowed trains to leave for Wycombe from the London-bound (up) platform. The higher arm on the bracket signal read to a stop signal on the up line, sandwiched between the running line and the sidings, which acted as the starting signal for down trains on the up line, and also protected Cores End crossing. Note that there is no arm on the stop signal from High Wycombe adjacent to Cores End crossing to allow a train from Wycombe to run into the down platform — that was not provided until the 1956

remodelling. Adjacent to the foot of the steps of the signal box was the horn on which the fireman could set down the token carrier when arriving from the Wycombe direction. The pick-up post was on the opposite side of the running lines (see the facing page).

J. H. Russell

Cores End crossing, at the north end of the layout at Bourne End, had signals to protect it, certainly before 1869, if not from the opening of the Wycombe Railway. By 1936 the frame in the crossing keeper's hut was of just two levers, one to lock the gates, and one to work with the interlocking lever in the North signal box. Even so, there was not much room to move round in the hut, which was only 8 ft square. The small corrugated iron shed alongside served as a lamp hut.

D. J. Hyde

A view of Bourne End North signal box after the extension to take the new frame for the 1956 remodelling. The box was originally 18 ft 6 in by 12 ft, and could not take the new 44-lever frame. The extension is evidenced by the new brickwork, the patchy roof, and the nameplate which, having been central on the original box, was now very noticeably off-centre. The small 'wicket' gates beside the main road gates permitted pedestrians to continue to cross after the gates had been closed to vehicles — the signalman locked the wicket gates when a train was closely approaching. The wicket lock levers were included in the lever frame in 1894, but after 1956 the wickets were locked by two small levers in a separate frame in the box.   *A. Hall-Patch*

The fireman of a Wycombe-bound train collecting the token for the single line section to Wooburn Green from the pick-up post just north of the crossing in the 1930s.   *British Railways*

No. 1450 alongside the down platform in 1958, a view taken from the North signal box two years after the remodelling of the track layout and the abolition of the South box. The signal in the foreground is the up main down (direction) inner home signal bracket. The higher arm (signal 9) applied to movements along the up line towards High Wycombe – the shorter arm read into the Up Sidings North.

British Railways

Looking north through the station from the main down platform in
1947. *J. H. Russell*

A closer view of the station nameboard and fire buckets illuminated
with the electric lighting installed in 1963. *A. E. Smith*

Looking south from the footbridge towards Maidenhead in the 1920s showing the small 'up' waiting room before enlargement. This was probably carried out at the beginning of 1931 following authorisation in December 1930 for improved waiting room accommodation estimated at £200. The work evidently included the provision of a ladies' lavatory and a larger canopy. The boarded crossing was diverted in 1935 to the route shown on page 82, probably at the same time that the steps were moved to the north end of the box (see below). The bay line signal has the word 'Bay' painted on the arm as well as the usual white stripe.   *L & GRP, cty. David & Charles*

Looking over the junction towards Maidenhead c.1950, by which time all the signals in view had replaced those featured above. The bracket signal on the down platform (on the right) — which allowed trains to be started in the up direction — had been changed from a right-hand to a left-hand bracket, making it a little more visible from the down platform than the one shown above. Even so, the sighting remained poor and during the 1956 remodelling the configuration of the signal was changed yet again by the fitting of centre balanced signal arms in a further attempt at improvement. The 'wrong direction' movements out of the down platform required a profusion of locking bolts, as evidenced by their covers (the small ramps over the switch blade stretcher bars).   *J. H. Russell*

Some down trains terminated at Bourne End and this mid-1950s view is thought to show one of them. If this assumption is correct, this may be the 1.02 p.m. from Maidenhead (Saturdays only) and, after arrival in the down platform, No. 6123 has already run round the train for the return working at 1.54. The '94XX' running into the up platform (with no headcode) would be the 1.25 p.m. freight (Saturdays only) from Bourne End to Taplow.

Lens of Sutton

The interior of the up waiting shelter in 1958. It doesn't take much imagination to picture the scene inside here on a winter's morning when the smell of newsprint mingled with damp clothes, wet gloves and dripping umbrellas as workers, shoppers and schoolchildren all sought the comfort offered by the coal-fired stove carefully tended by the station staff.

British Railways

82

J. H. Russell

The view from the footbridge c.1950.

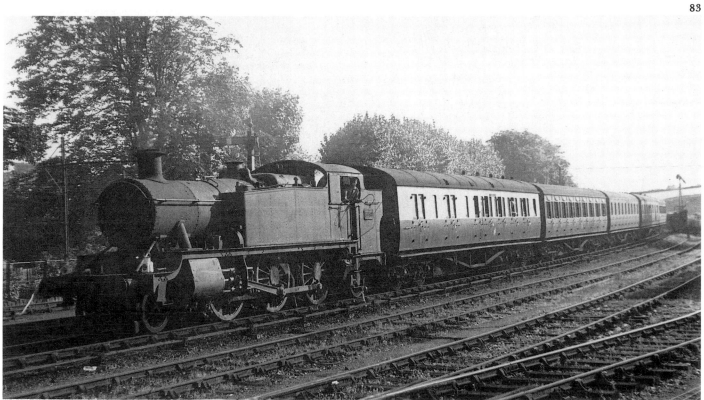

The fireman of a Wycombe-bound train with Class A headcode, about to surrender the token on approaching the station in 1947.

J. H. Russell

An official posed view of the token being set down by the South box on an earlier occasion. The 55-lever box was erected during the 1894 revisions and had internal dimensions to locking room of 38 ft 5 in x 12 ft x 9 ft high. The entrance steps and porch were moved from the opposite end of the building in the mid-1930s. The South box was closed on 28-30th January 1956.   *British Railways*

This old postcard shows the station on a fine winter's morning c.1910. *Courtesy Mrs. E. Hobbs*

Two views of Bourne End goods yard in 1927 with porter Ernie Hobbs who later became a signalman at Marlow. *Courtesy Mrs. E. Hobbs*

This snapshot of Ernie Hobbs, taken on the same occasion, provides a view of the goods office and coal store. From at least the 1930s the office was in use as a store, the paperwork being dealt with at the station. The 1 ton 10 cwt crane can just be seen inside the building.

Courtesy Mrs. E. Hobbs

The goods yard looking comparatively deserted in 1955. Unusually, according to plans, the siding serving the goods shed appears to have always terminated inside the building. The 'back siding' was used for unloading coal supplies, although there were no wharves, and the 3-ton yard crane was provided in 1929 by Messrs. Holt & Willett. There was previously only a 1 ton 10 cwt crane in the goods shed between 1877 and 1899, variously recorded as 2 ton and 1 ton 10 cwt. The Marlow bay was used for the few horses handled here and cattle pens, formerly at the end of the middle siding, were little used and removed when £2,550 10s 0d was spent on mileage accommodation. The work, ordered by the Ministry of War Transport and completed on 20th December 1943, evidently included relaying the middle siding using the concrete blocks and tiebars shown. The 12-ton weighing machine GW 273 (12 ft x 8 ft plate) and office at the end of the back siding were replaced by a 20-ton machine and new office in 1946-7. The goods shed was little used in later years other than for the storage and distribution of garden sheds etc. from Thorn Buildings just before the Second World War. However, even this traffic was brief and only lasted for a few months, the components arriving in the firm's lorries and being sent out by rail.

A. Hall-Patch

Looking south from the foot of the down platform ramp towards Maidenhead with the Thames Viaduct just discernible in the distance. The three south or 'down' sidings on the right of the running lines with capacities of 17, 14 and 14 wagons respectively, were squeezed in the confines of the junction and the river bank and used for Marlow branch traffic, general purposes and hot boxes, but particularly wagons for Marlow. The two sidings shown on 1895 plans were added to in 1902. However, despite these improvements congestion was still a problem and at times the Marlow branch was used as a refuge, to hold passing goods trains. The goods yard headshunt on the left was added in 1935 and, with a capacity of 15 wagons, made it possible to continue shunting without interfering with movements on the running line. Its instalment necessitated a new (the third) realigned yard entry crossover. During the late 1940s when the PW gang were burning stubble behind the signal box, flames spread on the paraffin-soaked ground and set fire to the lamp hut. The local volunteer fire brigade from Wooburn arrived first but with no water! They then apparently ran their hose from the goods yard over the main line. However, a second appliance came to the rescue. This was not the first time such an incident had occurred there as the first corrugated iron lamp shed had been destroyed by fire in December 1899. According to a newspaper report, water supply had been a problem on that occasion too and the South box was threatened during the two hour blaze. This picture was taken c.1950.   *J. H. Russell*

A closer view of the HQ of the Bourne End PW gang (No. 100) situated at the edge of the goods yard as seen in the previous view.
D. J. Hyde

The doubled station house is particularly evident in this 1955 forecourt view of the station. *A. Hall-Patch*

This 1960 view after the removal of the run-round loop, nevertheless shows how the 1894 extended branch bay was slewed to avoid the station and skirted the forecourt, separated by familiar iron railings. As already mentioned, the gateway at the top of the platform ramp was occasionally used for loading horses. *Lens of Sutton*

An earlier view of the bay complete with run-round loop in 1947. This loop also dated from the 1894 rebuild when it replaced another beyond the platform on the branch curve. Due to the severe curvature alongside the platform, the centre doors of the 70 ft trailers that succeeded the Clifton set were locked and passengers boarded through the driver's vestibule to avoid the dangerous gap. *J. H. Russell*

The distinctive Clifton Down push-pull fitted stock and a conventional auto-trailer on branch service in the bay in 1947.   *J. H. Russell*

A closer view of Collett 0—4—2T No. 1442 sandwiched between the branch stock.   *J. H. Russell*

The signalman's view from the South box, again in 1947. In the foreground right is the token receiving apparatus, with the horn and net on one post, and the lamp (to illuminate the horn and 10 mph speed restriction notice) on the other post. In the foreground left is the rear of the 5 mph GWR pattern internally illuminated speed restriction board, the rectangular lamp housing of which can be clearly seen. The appearance of the front of the board can be seen on page 87.

J. H. Russell

The Marlow branch train comprising Collett 0—4—2T No. 1442 and auto-trailer W201 propelling a horse-box onto a High Wycombe train at Bourne End on 30th July 1949. Comparison with the photo on page 68 shows how, in the 1930s remodelling here, the branch starting signals were moved nearer the box, and the bay loop line extended round the curve towards Marlow.   *J. H. Meredith*

No. 1448 arriving with the branch auto on 1st August 1955. By the time this photograph was taken, the token receiving apparatus had been removed — it was of no use for train staff working — and the signalman had to come over from the box to receive the staff as the train passed.   *J. N. Faulkner*

The approach to Bourne End and Brooksby crossing viewed from Marina crossing on 21st April 1956. The internally illuminated board warning of the permanent speed restriction was very much a characteristic of the GWR. The board applying to trains proceeding to Marlow was adjacent to the South signal box (for front and rear views see the preceding page). These relics of the GWR were replaced by standard BR signs on 29th March 1965. The signals in view were the Bourne End Up Branch homes — signal 5 (the higher arm) read to the main line and 21 to the bay. The signal bracket was renewed to modern standards in December 1958.

M. F. Yarwood

ALONG THE LINE

Bourne End on 7th September 1954 showing the Wycombe line crossing the Thames and the Marlow branch commencing its riverside course. *Aerofilms*

The long tortuous curve taking the branch westwards away from the Wycombe line enables the line to assume its easy level riverside course to Marlow. Even the familiar Collett tanks squealed their flanges against the check rail as they eased round this undignified exit from the station, obeying the 10 mph speed restriction. All other classes were further restricted to 5 mph. Soon, in the shade of trees screening the railway from the 'fashionable' riverside properties, the line changes direction gently, and at 0 miles 18½ chains, beyond the limit of the former run round loop and the up Marlow branch home signal, is the first of a number of minor road and footpath level crossings. Known as Brooksby (once known as Frys or Fryers) after one of the large residences, this drive is followed barely sixty yards further on at 0 miles 21¼ chains by another known as Marina. Drivers of approaching trains whistle for all crossings. This second and wider crossing, once protected by larger gates and wickets, led to Bourne End or Wooburn Wharf, more commonly named after the owners of the boatyards there. In 1880 Horshams established a boat-building business, bringing new activity to the site which had languished since the railways killed off much of the barge traffic. Several launches were built here including *Alaska*, the first steam launch used by Salters Steamers to operate a passenger service on the Thames.

The river was becoming popular at that time and the Railway Hotel, adjacent to Bourne End station, had prospered under good management. However, others saw their chance and in the late 1880s two more hotels were built in the area, the first, the Quarry Hotel, on the Berkshire bank just upstream from the Wycombe railway bridge, and the other at Spade Oak. The 3-storey Quarry Hotel, renowned for its cuisine, was served by a ferry from the wharf which, from the late 1880s, had been taken over by Shaw and Townsend, whose names have since been adopted for the yards and associated crossings. No doubt for some years after Horsham's departure, that company's name similarly lingered on.

The Quarry Hotel was destroyed by fire in 1938 and the ferry, which offered the opportunity of a leisurely stroll across Cockmarsh to Cookham, has since disappeared, but the line still slips past the corrugated iron and wooden buildings which survive to accommodate a yacht chandlers, boat builders and the Bourne End Cruiser and Yacht Club.

On the opposite side of the line from the boatyard, dense foliage secretes the shady gardens of what had been regarded as a model 'garden estate' of the late Victorian and Edwardian eras. The Abbotsbrook estate, now a conservation area, was once the scene of river fetes and regattas. In 1899, for example, a Venetian fete was held there and amongst the attractions were illuminated boats threading their way through the backwaters. In *Theirs were but human hearts*, local historian Brian Wheals records that 'gondoliers were invoked to duck as they

93

Townsend's boatyard.

Another view of the boatyard at Bourne End Wharf.

British Railways

propelled their craft beneath the low railway bridge separating the estate from the Thames!' This bridge is the substantial plate girder viaduct carrying the Marlow branch over the Abbotsbrook backwater. In order that visitors from London could stay and enjoy the spectacle, the GWR ran a special late train leaving Bourne End for Paddington at 11 p.m.

From the end of the viaduct the line plunges into another short stretch shaded by poplars and emerges at

Shaw's Crossing at 0 miles 31 chains. This provided independent access to Shaw's boatyard, separated from Townsends by the Abbotsbrook backwater, but united by a small bridge maintaining the towpath. Incidentally, Ted Shaw was a famous Marlow footballer.

Another crossing at 0 miles 37 chains serves the Thames Sailing Club grounds. Founded in 1884, this club reflects the popularity of sailing on this part of the river just above Bourne End viaduct. These premises had

No. 1448 crossing the Abbotsbrook Viaduct.

N. M. Lera

No. 1448 passing the Thames Sailing Club car park on 4th October 1959.

been served by what was little more than a footpath crossing, cars being left on the opposite side of the line. However, since the late 1960s a second wider access has been arranged.

The line continues on a gentle left-hand curve past a row of riverside bungalows established on the narrow strip of land between the railway and the river. The first of the sleeper-built PW huts now demolished was situated behind these dwellings on the right-hand side of the track, and shortly after is another crossing at 0 miles 48½ chains, taking a footpath from Cold Moorholme Lane to the river.

Looking back at this point, we can see a screen of poplars enclosing the Abbotsbrook estate, and defining the outskirts of Bourne End. As we continue towards Marlow, the straggling riverside homes peter out and the line assumes a different character, taking a more remote course on a low embankment over the flood plain, with the river and towpath in sight. On hot summer days, when the sun beats down on sleepy pastures, with cattle grazing at the water's edge, hosts of ramblers, picnicking familes and courting couples all watching the canvas sails of the many river craft, the character and atmosphere of these surroundings is one of blissful leisure. Yet in the heavy mists of winter this deserted, exposed and often muddy plain can seem lonely, a place to seek solace and put problems into perspective, alongside the ceaseless flow of the deep Thames.

The overall speed limit on the branch was 40 mph for the Collett tanks and 20 mph for other classes, but the approach to the notorious Spade Oak Crossing at 0 miles

Cold Moorholme (today spelt as one word) Lane crossing.   *Paul Karau*

Although this scene is worthy of a romantic album of the 1940s, it was in fact taken as recently as July 1970.

R. Goodearl

The approach to Spade Oak crossing.

Paul Karau

58½ chains always requires extra vigilance for this had been the site of many accidents over the years.

Before the railways penetrated the area each parish had its own wharf and Spade Oak was the landing point for Little Marlow. Coldmoorholme Lane connecting the village to the river is now simply a pleasant walk, but it had been a vital link. Today it is not so easy for us to imagine the river before the invasion of pleasure craft, when heavily laden barges, almost 130 ft long, plied up and down with their bulky loads. Although fitted with sails, they were often towed by up to sixty men, known as halers. These armies of burly, reputedly lawless, characters struggling along the muddy river banks with one of these great barges in tow could hardly have contrasted more with the Edwardian scene of later years when elegantly attired ladies with parasols were accompanied along the same riverbanks. The crews of these barges slept on board and ate their meals beneath hooped canvases.

During the 18th century horses had taken over from the halers and teams were available from Spade Oak. Again according to Brian Wheals, 'the tenant farmer of Spade Oak, a Mr. Rose, did sufficiently well out of the venture to build himself an elegant home in Well End, now known as Vineleigh House, and this still bears a wall plaque carrying his initials 'R.R. 1701'.'

So in this pre-railway age Spade Oak presented a very different scene for this was important to, if not the focal point of, Little Marlow. It may not have been over busy, for hauling these barges was a major undertaking but the odd one must have tied up alongside the slowly decaying timbers of a wharf projecting from the muddy unkempt reeds and lilies of an age before river authorities. Doubtless cattle grazed in lush meadows crowded with buttercups, while teams of horses were changed and perhaps the crews were provided with some refreshment. The wharf would surely have been soiled with bark and other debris from loads of timber, dust from any coal landed here, hay and straw, and unavoidably horse and cattle dung, all accompanied by the odour of leather harnesses and the smell of the river itself. All this is long gone and the cares of that age remote from us now.

In later years a ferry was established here and the Upper Flam on the opposite bank, a watering place for cattle on Cockmarsh, became a popular place for bathing as the wide sandy shallow here extended almost halfway across the river and bathers could wade out to its edge without going any deeper than waist height. This popular spot was served by the two ferries mentioned and around 1890 a hotel was built nearby in Coldmoorholme Lane to cater for the growing number of visitors. It was called Ye Ferry Hotel and boasted a rather grand entrance and nameboard at the landing stage, which one can only imagine was intended to suggest a gateway to some kind of paradise. If anyone actually arrived by steamer or launch, this illusion probably soon faded for the hotel was barely in sight, and certainly today the building is not really visible from the river.

Spade Oak Crossing was equipped with large gates and wickets, and at one time only tenants and owners of bungalows held keys to the padlocks and chains securing the larger gates. Anyone else wishing to use the crossing had to apply to the adjacent farmhouse to borrow the

Driven from the trailer, the branch train is seen here at Spade Oak crossing c.1960 on its way to Marlow.   *M. Esau*

keys. A notice on the gates warned that any person leaving these unfastened or unlocked would be liable to a penalty of 40 shillings. This arrangement was in force in 1914 and on 11th August that year a car became stuck on the crossing. The driver, Mrs. Devenish, was on her way from a houseboat moored nearby to Bourne End for some shopping. Whether she was busy securing one gate behind her before completing the crossing is not clear, but the car was stranded and the Marlow branch train, running bunker first from Bourne End, smashed into it. Mrs. Devenish escaped unharmed.

On another occasion, on 18th August 1922, J. White, contractor of Dean Street, Marlow, was busy with his lorries, carting ballast from Spade Oak ferry. He had stopped his lorry on the crossing while the second gate was opened, and the 11.20 a.m. from Bourne End came round the curve and smashed into it, also bringing down a telegraph pole. The driver escaped with cuts and bruises but owing to 'slight damage' the branch service was suspended until another loco came from Slough.

This crossing was also a notorious spot for suicides. Thirty-year old Rose Pesteridge put her head on the rails in front of the 6.50 a.m. goods on Wednesday, 8th May 1907, 68-year old unemployed gardener George White, who was described as being depressed, was killed here on 3rd May 1921, and 52-year old Stanley Bridger fell in front of a train about 9.00 p.m. on 27th July 1938, leaving a note apologising for the trouble caused.

A more recent tragedy took place on Sunday, 14th January 1962 when the branch train killed the driver of a Volkswagon saloon, which had apparently stopped on the crossing with a boat trailer while the two occupants, father and ten-year old son, opened the gates.

Before dismissing this morbid toll, it is as well to point out that incidents also occurred at Townsend's Crossing. These included a narrow escape for the driver of a horse-drawn vehicle belonging to grocer W. N. Ford. Again, the vehicle had been left on the crossing before the second gate was opened, but on this occasion, 25th May 1907, the driver managed to stop the train in time. However, on 3rd July 1918 32-year old Ada Maud Boddy was killed when she attempted to run across the line on the same crossing. Today 'Marina' crossing is ungated and protected only by flashing lights whilst the approaches to the galvanised tubular steel gated, remote but heavily used, Spade Oak Crossing are subject to a 10 mph restriction.

Ye Ferry Hotel, now known as Spade Oak Hotel, still stands and large car parks on the northern side of the line now cater for the steady flow of visitors to the river. The ferry here was a double one, a punt for pedestrians and a chain ferry for horses and carts, and cattle. However, today they no longer survive and visitors are no longer sculled across the water to 'Ferry House' and the nearby sandy shallow. Instead the less attractive bank at Spade Oak is used for bathing, although cattle grazing at the water's edge are still a comforting tradition.

From Spade Oak the line continues on through the site of Sandals Crossing at 0 miles 72½ chains. The name was probably a corruption of Sandhills. This crossing became redundant when the land bordering the northern

This aerial view taken on 19th June 1957 shows how the railway traverses the flood plain on its low embankment. *Aerofilms*

Vineyards Crossings.   *Paul Karau*

boundary of the railway was lost in favour of a huge artificial lake formed to repair the landscape after extensive gravel extraction. This new feature has rather changed the character of the area which might be regarded as surprising if one reflects on the fierce protection of the Thameside scenery during the proposals to link the Henley and Marlow branches. Conservationists have evidently given way to popular opinion here and the site of ancient lazy pastures are lost for ever and instead become a playground for various water sports. Perhaps it is fortunate that the course of the railway which from Spade Oak has distanced itself from the towpath, has held these lakes at bay from the Thames.

Beyond the one mile post the line veers slightly left before straightening out again to continue on its low embankment skirting the lush meadows overlooked by the wooded Winter Hill and further west the more dense Quarry Woods, entirely typical of the high ground forming such a pleasant backdrop to this stretch of the Thames. The adjacent Vineyards Crossings 1 and 2 at 1 m. 8 ch. and 1 m. 8½ ch., carry a farm crossing and footpath from Little Marlow over the line. They are named after an area reputed to have been the location of grape vines in the Middle Ages.

A high chain link fence following immediately on our right encloses Little Marlow sewage works which was built in the 1950s to serve Marlow (superseding the UDC works mentioned on page 105), Little Marlow, Bourne End and Wooburn, etc. Another sleeper-built platelayers' hut just beyond Ten Acre Crossing, at 1 mile 23¾ chains, was pulled down when a 4 ft pipe was laid from the sewage works to the river. It was apparently replaced by a 'vandal-proof' cabin which has since disappeared.

Two pictures of Calcot Lane crossing on 10th December 1951.

British Railways

A second artificial lake borders the line until Calcot Lane Crossing at 1 mile 44¾ chains, named after a one-time local farmer. The farm lane here survives, stranded between the second and third artificial lakes.

Between the 1½ and 2 mile posts another three crossings punctuate the line, all named after Ivory Field. Distinguished only by numbers, they occur at 1 mile 55¼ chains, 1 mile 75½ chains and 1 mile 76¼ chains, the second two a mere 15 yards apart. These are on a right-hand curve taking the line right away from the monotony of the flood plain, the river having by this time faded from view. Indeed, this corner marks the beginning of a shallow cutting and another distinct change in the character of the route on the approach to Marlow. The sleeper-

WINTER HILL.

This undated postcard, looking west from Winter Hill (perhaps in the 1930s?), shows the line's final approach to Marlow, past the sewage works and disappearing behind the trees screening filter beds of the 'Brewery Irrigation Meadow' which belonged to Wethereds and is now a small market garden.

Authors' Collection

No. 1421 passing over Ivory Field crossings Nos. 2 and 3 in June 1961.   *S. C. Crook*

built platelayers hut that latterly stood in the shade of trees on the outside of this bend probably replaced one recorded on an early survey of the line as being situated further round the corner at the end of the cutting on the right-hand side of the track. Marlow rugby ground, adjoining the southern boundary of the line at this point, occupies the site of Marlow racecourse, a casualty of the pre-railway age.

After this short cutting the line straightens out to run almost due west into Marlow, passing the site of an old gravel working on the right-hand boundary. As this pit is shown on the first edition Ordnance Survey Map of 1876, it is tempting to suggest that this may have been the one connected with the construction of the line and served by a siding, but this is speculation. The 1932 revision of the Ordnance Survey shows the sewage works of the Marlow Urban District Council adjacent to the site of the old pit and this area appears to have been the nucleus of Folley Brothers' activities in the 1950s.

Another farm crossing at 2 miles 15¼ chains, unnamed and no longer apparent, preceded the fixed distant for

Marlow, once supplemented by a fogman's hut. Today the outskirts of Marlow are clearly defined by the hideous concrete bridge striding over the line bearing the incongruous bypass, but in more pleasant times, before characterless industrial estates, a group of poplars and other trees secreting a sewage farm heralded a more rural approach and the last crossing of any significance at 2 miles 29½ chains, variously known after Field House Lane, Bloom Corner, Folley's (at least by the staff), and today Mill Lane.

It appears to have started life as an accommodation crossing under a conveyance dated 27th December 1870 between Eliza Atkinson and the Great Marlow Railway Co. The brick-built hip-roofed crossing keeper's lodge, featured in the picture overleaf, was provided when the line was first built: 'One crossing only will require a lodge for a keeper. This will be built of bricks and if required by the Board of Trade to be provided with signals and gates to close across the line.' Perhaps because of the quiet traffic it was later demolished. However, when Messrs. Folley Brothers Ltd. started to excavate gravel, sand and ballast from nearby land to the north of the line, the crossing took on a new importance. Folley Brothers paid to have it strengthened to stand up to the pounding of their fleet of lorries plying back and forth with their heavy loads. The frequency of their operations called for the provision of a telephone link with Marlow signal box and a hut for a gatekeeper who was stationed there for long periods. The railway carried out the necessary work at the crossing, and provided the necessary 'signalling instruments' at the hut at Folley Brothers' expense. They also charged for the wages of the member of the PW staff, usually George Chapple, who acted as gatekeeper, whilst Folley Bros. built and maintained the crossing keeper's hut, a sizeable brick structure with metal casements and a flat roof. Whenever the train left Marlow or Bourne End the Marlow signalman had to press a button which sounded a buzzer in the crossing keeper's hut but the company gave an undertaking to the railway that the crossing would not be used during periods of fog.

By 1951, whenever the crossing keeper was not on duty, the gates were locked for safety reasons, an action which met with considerable controversy. In the early part of the year there were letters to the *Bucks Free Press*, comments at meetings of the Marlow Urban District Council, and correspondence between Mr. John Haire, MP for the Wycombe division, and the Transport Com-

This official photograph, taken to show 'flange rails' at Marlow in 1906 is the only view discovered of the keeper's lodge at Field House Lane crossing.   *British Railways*

Evidence of Folley Brothers' activities c.1951.

Courtesy R. Stephenson

One of Folley Brothers' ballast lorries crossing the line in the wake of the branch train on 23rd July 1951. *Collection R. S. Carpenter*

Folley Brothers' crossing and hut in the late 1950s. The strengthening work had been completed in September 1948 for £96 19s 10d.
B. W. Leslie

mission. According to the *Bucks Free Press* for 23rd February 1951, the resulting correspondence revealed that from 1921 to 1934 users of the crossing were 'challenged' annually at Eastertime, but in 1934 Rights of Way Act notices were erected at the crossing. The following was also quoted from the British Transport Commission's letter: 'Our chief, who has fully considered the history and user of the crossing, now advises us, however, that between 1871 and 1921 the public have, at common law, acquired a right of way over the crossing for pedestrians, perambulators, and possibly bicycles.' The significance of the year 1921 is not apparent but it may provide a clue as to when the original crossing keeper's lodge was removed.

The crossing was at the centre of quite a puzzle one hot summer when neither of the signalmen, Ivor Morgan senior or junior, could get any response from the token instrument in the cooler temperatures of the early morning or late evening. Bert Nash, the linesman, was called out each time and day after day he walked the line checking the wires etc. Joe Whitelock was acting as pilotman and station master Freddie Funnell was getting more and more frustrated over the continued disruption. It eventually turned out to be a tiny break in the wire under the busy crossing. Despite the ballast lorries pounding the crossing, the heat during the day still allowed the wire to touch and the intermittent fault all the more difficult to find.

Folley Brothers continued to use the crossing until 23rd January 1954.

Standing in for the usual Collett auto-fitted tank, 0—6—0PT No. 9653 is seen here arriving at Marlow in 1951. *J. H. Venn*

MARLOW STATION

Looking east over the station from the buffer stops c.1950. Two vehicles at a time could be loaded from the cattle pens on the right of this 1947 view. The pens were also used for horses, the concrete posts and tubular rails dating from a pre-1919 rebuild. Livestock declined fairly steadily through the 1930s from 390 wagons in 1929 to just 13 in 1938. In 1957 just two were recorded.   *J. H. Russell*

The development of Marlow station has been chronicled in previous chapters and is detailed in the captions which follow. These notes concentrate on deliveries and traffic handled at the terminus.

DELIVERY ARRANGEMENTS

W. T. Porter was the appointed parcels agent from the early years of the Great Marlow Railway, and James Johnson of Chapel Street, who had been a carrier to and from Marlow Road station in 1869, was a parcels and goods agent. In February 1879 an agreement was drawn up with Abraham Cresswell of Wycombe Road, Great Marlow, who was appointed cartage agent 'to all places within a radius of one mile, and shall include the Croft and Hillside'. It appears that he succeeded Johnson but the Great Marlow Railway directors were apparently not impressed with his service since he was dismissed on 16th April 1881. It was probably at this time that W. T. Porter was awarded the agency for both parcels and goods, a similar agreement drawn up with Porter later being renewed on 24th August 1909.

In the 1920s heavy goods were being delivered by Harry Belcher who worked for Porter, but around this time 'outside porters' were also employed by the railway and, amongst other duties, they delivered items in hand trolleys pushed around the town. Hampers of travellers' samples for local shops were often delivered in this fashion, for example.

Fred Nottingham took over from Harry Belcher in July 1929 as a horse driver, and, from the late 1930s to about the time of the GWR takeover, was assisted by Tom Stiles who had formerly worked for Toomers. Fred drove his first motor lorry in 1946 about three months before the GWR took over the delivery arrangements. He was taken on by the GWR who provided a new Austin lorry GYH 48.

Whilst the GWR takeover was probably in part prompted by the introduction of the zonal scheme at Marlow in late 1946, it appears that Porter was retiring anyway and had nobody to take over his business since his only son Arthur had died during the Second World War.

The zonal scheme was planned to provide a next day delivery service for 'smalls' and miscellaneous goods. This was achieved by eliminating transhipment as traffic was concentrated at fewer loading points which made more direct wagons possible. Marlow came within the Reading zone (Area No. 15) of which Maidenhead was a sub-railhead.

The use of a lorry enabled Fred to widen his delivery area to local farms, etc., but from 1947 the outlying areas were being served from Maidenhead. From 1950 the Marlow lorry was officially kept at Maidenhead each night,

110

Station Road. Marlow.

W.H.A. 3572.

Looking north along Station Road towards the station c.1919. It was not until 1901 that it was decided to complete the Station Road paving so that at least one paved footpath was provided for the main streets of the town to the station.

Authors' collection

The station approach road was owned by the railway, who at one time roped it annually, usually on Good Fridays, to maintain the company's rights. The small café on the right, which dates from about Easter 1951, was built in 1927 as Messrs. Toomer's coal office, whilst Messrs. Porter's office, on the extreme left of the picture on page 118, is immediately behind the café in this 1950s view. Both structures still survive.
A. Attewell

A late 1950s view from the buffer stops, showing the end loading dock which saw use for horses and occasionally military vehicles. The corrugated iron lamp shed is thought to date from the 1901-2 alterations. By this time the signal box had been removed and the engine release point was worked from the west ground frame which can be seen just to the right of the 2¾ mile post, with point rodding leading off towards the trap point in the loop line.
B. W. Leslie

The forecourt elevation of the station building showing the entrance to the booking office. In later years, at times when the station was not fully staffed, these doors were locked and entry restricted to the gateway to the left of the building.

A. E. Smith

Whilst dating from the opening of the Great Marlow Railway, the distinctive station building was constructed to a Great Western design similar to those at Hungerford and Taplow. The materials specified included 'best Countess slates', bricks of the 'best kind to be procured in the neighbourhood of the railway', and joints no more than ¼" in thickness, the mortar being one part fresh burnt lime to two parts clean sharp sand. A short extension in the same style, beyond the vent pipe at the far end, was added in 1902, whilst the obvious addition in the foreground, completed in March 1947 for £131 11s 2d, was built to house the station master and thus relieve the existing accommodation. This photograph was taken on 29th July 1956. *J. J. Davis*

Fred travelling to and from Marlow by train. This enabled the lorry to be loaded ready for his arrival, but, if he was late finishing at night, he kept it at Marlow and drove it to Maidenhead the next day. The lorry was often kept at Marlow during the weekends.

During this period Jack Goodgame, who drove a 3-wheel 6-ton Scammel articulated unit and trailer, carted and delivered truck loads of goods, and during busy periods or at times of staff sickness, etc., members of the Reading relief gang gave assistance.

During the war a Reading man, Harry Rose, drove a zonal lorry between Reading and High Wycombe, calling at Marlow each way. This considerably speeded deliveries, Boots the Chemists' traffic from Nottingham, for instance, arriving at its destination the next day, together with other Midlands traffic. Harry is remembered as one of 'the old GWR staff' who was keen to get work for the company.

PASSENGER RATED TRAFFIC
Both inwards and outwards parcels traffic was generally heavy, even into the BR period, and could average about 80 per day. On occasions exceptional numbers were dispatched by local firms such as Watson Marlow Air Pumps and Chelton Electrostatic (electrostatic beads). Quite often the volume of parcels was such that they could be seen through the toplight of the parcels office!

Marlow Pigeon Club despatched racing birds to many destinations, even as far afield as France. Usually birds destined for the Continent were despatched on Wednesdays and those for the mainland on Saturday. Pigeons from other towns were also sent to Marlow where they were released on the platform. Each basket had a double label which was reversed and returned to the sender.

MILK
Before the Second World War many local farmers brought milk to the station for despatch, but sadly details have been difficult to clarify. However, during the immediate post-war period two to three dozen churns of milk were

Fred Nottingham and a colleague loading the zonal lorry outside the new station master's office in the 1950s.

Courtesy Fred Nottingham

No. 1448 alongside the platform with the 3.06 p.m. mixed train in the spring of 1951.

J. H. Venn

The main shell of the building housed a ladies' waiting room and lavatory, general waiting room and booking office, and station office, which, prior to the small 1947 extension at the far end, housed the station master. The station was gas lit from the town supply throughout its life.   *A. E. Smith*

received daily from Wootton Bassett and carried in the brake vans of passenger trains. They were loaded onto barrows and transferred to the parcels dock for collection. Later, in the 1950s some supplies, possibly samples, were received by rail for the nearby branch of the Milk Marketing Board.

LIVESTOCK

Possibly the most regular flow of livestock traffic was handled by W. Pinches of Field House Farm, who was principally a horse dealer. This equine traffic, unloaded at the cattle pens and platform, included cart horses bought at auctions. Horses were also sent out for slaughter and certainly after the Second World War they were despatched to West London markets. During the war the pens were kept particularly busy with animals arriving for the slaughter house in Spittal Street. Prior to this period sheep and cattle were driven along the public highway and regularly on market days via Glade Road. They often strayed into doorways and even occasionally into shops. Until the early 1930s the cattle market was held each Monday opposite the station, and, in the early days, behind the Crown Hotel. The bay line was unofficially used to unload sheep which were driven down the main platform with sheep-dogs in attendance. In the 1920s farmer Palmer of Well End could often be seen leading his flock from the station with sheep-dogs keeping things in order behind!

A Dr. Sheehan also used the railway regularly for the receipt of horses for Irish stud farms.

'SMALLS' TRAFFIC (under 1 ton)

Vans of 'smalls' traffic arrived with the early morning goods train and were unloaded in the goods shed. By 1946 there was usually only one van from Paddington and the occasional consignment from South Lambeth. After being

Despite the provision of a bicycle shed, the platform was still cluttered in this 1950s view.   *A. Attewell*

This charming platform scene at Marlow is a still from the film 'Four Sided Triangle'. The man with the suitcase is James Hayter.

British Film Institute, courtesy Hammer Film Productions Ltd.

A Collett 0–4–2T running round another mixed train one afternoon in the late 1950s.
Lens of Sutton

A quiet moment between trains in the spring of 1951. On this occasion the locomotive was unusually one of the large-wheeled auto-fitted pannier tanks, No. 5409.
J. H. Venn

The 'Stelcon' type cycle shed on the left, ordered by the Ministry of War Transport, was completed in December 1943 for £82 14s 6d.

M. Anderson

unloaded and checked, the various goods were sorted for delivery.

Before and after the introduction of the zonal scheme, parcels arrived at Marlow in the brake vans of passenger trains and Fred Nottingham delivered them all over the town, along with the 'smalls' items. 'To be called for' traffic was recorded on a warehouse sheet and left in the goods shed awaiting collection and a signature. During the war this included stores for HQ90 Group (Signals) at RAF Medmenham. The GWR later took over deliveries to the base with their new lorry for a small charge which was dropped everywhere when nationalised.

In the immediate post-war period most of the shops still received groceries, particularly fruit, vegetables and other general supplies, by rail, so prompt deliveries were essential to meet their needs. Meat arrived on Tuesdays in an insulated van from Smithfield, but fish came in by passenger train and included kippers from the Isle of Man.

The eastern wing, part of the original structure, provided a parcels office, cloakroom, used for cycles before the provision of the separate cycle shed, staffroom used by train crews (officially designated for porters), and in the 1902 extension at the far end a gentlemen's lavatory. The brick parapet concealed a low hipped roof, the gents being enclosed with a shallow pitched roof incorporating a skylight. Loco crews left a kettle on the iron range provided in the messroom so that it was always boiling after the round trip!

A. Hall-Patch

The siding on the right, known as 'Khartoum' by the staff, was provided as part of the 1901-2 improvements. It was used for the overnight stabling of the branch coaches, standby vehicles i.e. spare coaches, cattle wagons, horse-boxes, loco coal and ash wagons, and for many years gas tank wagons used for replenishing the gas cylinders of the branch coaches. On one occasion some coaches, said to have been fly-shunted into the siding, ran through the buffer stops in the direction of Glade Road behind.   *J. H. Russell*

A closer view of one of the platform lamps, equipped with a wartime shade. During the war some of the station building windows were surrounded by breeze block walls to prevent the escape of light, and during the same period the iron railings were painted black over several days by Italian prisoners. This study also provides a view of the back of the weighbridge office.   *A. Attewell*

The dynamos of the first electrically-lit vehicles are said to have failed to recharge their batteries on the short journey between Marlow and Bourne End. The branch coaches remained gas-lit right through to the late 1950s, their tanks being replenished every day from a gas tank wagon or 'cordon' as they were known. This was usually carried out by a carriage and wagon fitter from Slough who travelled down for the purpose and checked over the wagon in the yard during his visit. The coaches were gassed while stabled in the platform via hoses laid beneath the rails and this was usually done mid-morning while the yard was being shunted. The cordons themselves were filled at the West London Gasworks and were conveyed (twice weekly) on the rear of the 5.45 p.m. passenger train from Paddington, returning behind the 1.08 p.m. from Marlow.* There were a variety of these vehicles including the multi-cylindered version featured on page 111. No. 14, built to diagram DD5 and shown here in 1947, was regularly sent to Marlow at this time, apparently arriving around 10.00 a.m. It usually lasted just over a week and was returned at the rear of the 1.40 p.m. No. 13 of the same diagram could also be seen at Marlow. These vehicles were built around 1907 using second-hand underframes from the carriage department and being conveyed by passenger train retained vacuum brakes and screw couplings.

J. H. Russell

Timings varied over the years — those quoted are from the 1935 Working of Coaches.

Looking east towards Bourne End c.1960. Apart from the immediate surrounds of station buildings, platforms of minor stations were by no means always paved throughout, and at Marlow the platform was originally brick-faced and gravelled with 'not less than 3 inches thick of good gravel'. However, traffic evidently justified the expense for as early as 1886 further paving was carried out by the independent company. At that time the platform only extended as far as the goods shed, the 1901-2 improvements providing its final length, although understandably the final 240 ft extension remained unpaved. Total length 650 ft.   *Lens of Sutton*

To save double movement, whenever possible locos were coaled directly from loco coal wagons. This 1950s shed scene shows the fireman of No. 1443 at the end of this arduous task.
                                                                    A. Attewell

'In 1914 the water tank at Marlow, erected on top and forming part of the roof of the engine shed, was in a very bad state. This tank had already been troublesome through leakage, due to the iron plates being quickly eaten away by the sulphur fumes from the engines coming into direct contact with them. The question of repairs was fully considered, but as it is found impossible to do anything of a lasting nature, a 2,000 gallon round tank was temporarily erected on sleepers in March 1915, at a site clear of the shed, and the old tank removed, it having been decided to allow the question of the provision of a new tank to remain in abeyance until after the war. Owing to the increase in traffic the capacity of the small temporary tank is now inadequate, resulting in inconvenience to the Traffic Dept., and it is, therefore, proposed to install a tank (second hand) of 11,000 gallon capacity at the site shown on Drawing 57904, at £660.' So states the Locomotive and Stores Committee minutes of 31st October 1919. The full capacity of the replacement tank, measuring 20 ft x 12 ft x 8 ft deep, was 13,000 gallons, the discrepancy presumably being explained by the drawing which shows 'capacity at 7' 6" deep = 11250 gall.'

The indicator board on the right-hand column was part of the grandly titled 'water treatment plant' of 1938. The Swindon drawings reveal a surprisingly simple arrangement which basically comprised a hand pump secured to the back of the same column feeding the main tank from a 'standard 3 gallon steel bucket' via a single pipe. 'Instructions for working plant' read as follows: 'Before pumping water, put into the 3 gall. bucket an amount of M.18 disincrustant liquid corresponding to the reading of the indicator. Fill the bucket with water and mix well. Start up the steam pump and continue pumping until the tank is FULL. Pump the M.18 solution into the tank by means of the hand pump (this MUST be done while the steam pump is working.) When the bucket is empty refill with water and pump again to flush the pipes.' The indicator board was graduated to indicate the proportion of M18 liquid required per 1000 gallons, and a supply drum was supported on timber mounts adjacent to the pump. How long this treatment was used has not been established but later, during the Second World War, driver Lewington kept a pike in the water tank!

J. H. Russell

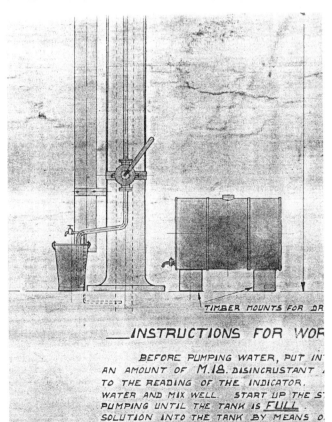

TIMBER MOUNTS FOR DR

INSTRUCTIONS FOR WOR

BEFORE PUMPING WATER, PUT IN
AN AMOUNT OF M.18. DISINCRUSTANT
TO THE READING OF THE INDICATOR.
WATER AND MIX WELL. START UP THE S
PUMPING UNTIL THE TANK IS FULL.
SOLUTION INTO THE TANK BY MEANS O
MUST BE DONE WHILE THE STEAM PUM
THE BUCKET IS EMPTY REFILL WITH
TO FLUSH THE PIPES.

The points for the shed were sprung in favour of the runround loop so it was necessary to hold them over when going on shed. On one occasion just after the war when a fireman was moving the loco and trailer onto the siding, for some inexplicable reason the driver relaxed his grip and the engine and coach took different routes. When questioned later about the incident, which occurred during the summer months, the driver claimed that while he was holding the lever a wasp had stung him on the neck and the pain had made him let go! No discipline was taken against him. This was not the only such derailment.

R. C. Riley

The timber-built coal stage is recorded as being 24 ft long, 11 ft 9 ins wide, 5 ft high to the stage floor and 9 ft 6 ins high to the top of the sides. Whether this was the original wooden 'coke platform' is not clear. Official records state that baskets were being used for coaling in 1901.

A. Attewell

The disposal pit in front of the coal stage was 34 ft 6 ins long. When it was cleared each morning the ashes were piled alongside and left until they accumulated enough to justify a wagon which was filled by a man from Slough shed. The small brick building in the background was the replacement pump house. The original timber-built structure pre-1901 had a gable roof and inside dimensions of 7 ft long, 6 ft wide and 6 ft and 8 ft 6 ins high to the top of the wall plate and ridge respectively. *A. Attewell*

It is hardly surprising that the varied and numerous small water pumps tucked away in anonymous murky sheds and wells all over the system were rarely photographed. They are consequently somewhat elusive and often referred to rather vaguely by the crews who used them — after all it was just another chore. In this instance we are privileged to see an example of a vertical engine inside the pump house at Marlow. The supply came from a well situated between the coal stage and pump house and was raised by either of two steam-driven pumps connected to the branch loco by means of a flexible pipe coupled in place of one of the whistles. One of the pumps was apparently more efficient than the other, but it seems that the tank was often only filled to about 5,000 gallons each night. When dismantled the pumps were said to have been amongst the oldest on the Western Region. For many years one of the firemen, George Harding, kept a pike that he caught in the well. He fed it on dead frogs, bread and scraps. *D. R. Smith*

The engine shed appears to have been a unique structure peculiar to the GMR. It was constructed of red brick with a slate roof and inside dimensions of 51 ft 6 ins long, 17 ft 6 ins wide and heights to the top of the wall plate and ridge of 16 ft 6 ins and 23 ft respectively. So far nothing has been discovered of its original appearance, but in September 1892 it was reported that 'some considerable expense will shortly be incurred in the rebuilding and improving the engine shed and water tank'. (The shed had already been half re-slated as steam had rotted the slate nails after only six years service.) The work concerned was completed the following spring and included the replacement of the original wooden water tank by one 'of much greater capacity'. The location of the original tank is not recorded, but certainly the replacement, later described as temporary, was incorporated in the roof over the shed entrance as seen on page 26. It is even just possible that the building may have been extended to the length quoted at the same time. The line inside was 49 ft 6 ins long incorporating a 30 ft pit and terminating with small iron wheel scotches. It was also provided with a smoke trough which between the wars was apparently a favourite haunt of some 20 or so sparrows who sheltered there for warmth. They were often to be seen on the platform during the day and were quite recognisable by their black plumage! More unusually for a small shed, the building was gas-lit from 1877.   *J. J. Davis and A. Attewell*

The shed was long enough to accommodate the branch loco and one of the coal or ash wagons which were often moved inside. However, one day about 1928-9 when a wagon had to be propelled along the loop, the points had mistakenly been left switched for the shed. The driver realized too late and the brakes locked the wheels while the loco and wagon continued straight through the building, out through the end wall and into the allotment garden situated there at the time. The tenant, one of the staff, applied for compensation for the loss of his parsnips!   *J. H. Russell*

A tranquil scene looking towards Bourne End on 30th May 1953. The bay platform on the right was served by a goods line and signalled as such. However, in the summer months, with extra excursion traffic, it was utilised for passenger trains, and the points were clipped and padlocked. The spiked track of 1902 survived until about 1949. The connection for Greenwich Sawmills' private sidings can be seen disappearing towards their premises, behind the engine shed. This is described separately on page 163.   *R. F. Roberts*

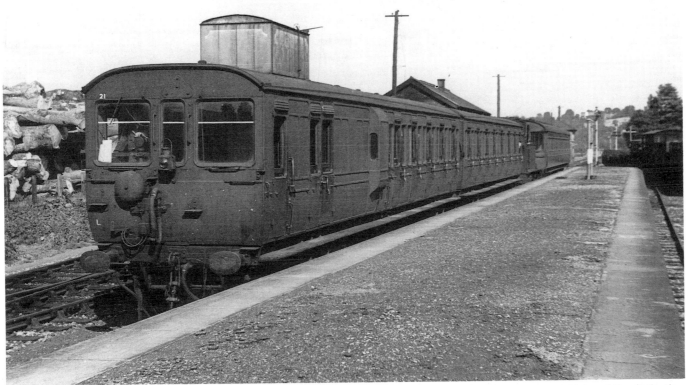

A branch train arriving at Marlow in 1947. Here the customary Collett 0–4–2T is sandwiched between two vehicles of the distinctive Clifton Down conversions and a conventional auto trailer. The stock of the neighbouring sawmill is particularly evident here.   *J. H. Russell*

126

Another view of the forecourt elevation of the station building as viewed from the goods yard c.1950. The younger brickwork of the 1902 extension shows to advantage here.

J. H. Russell

WAGON LOAD TRAFFIC

Coal was undoubtedly the main inwards wagon load traffic handled at Marlow, the companies involved being detailed on page 131.

Other inwards traffic included malt and occasionally salt for T. Wethered and Sons Brewery. New beer bottles also arrived from the Pilkington Glass Works, St. Helens, packed loose in straw in sheeted open wagons. They were unloaded directly into crates brought to the goods yard from the brewery for the purpose. Guinness was received in barrels as well as hogsheads of beer, butts and pipes of sherry and consignments of wines and spirits. Wine arrived in padlocked vans from London. For many years Wethered's drays collected items from the station, but, after the Second World War, Porters, and then the GWR, delivered using motor lorries.

Marlow Paper Mills were in operation until the war. They sent toilet rolls etc. to Glasgow by goods train for delivery the following day. After closure the mill was taken over by Lyons for storage, most of the goods arriving by rail. The 'Gables' house at the entrance to the mill was taken over by the Army who would only allow entry with a pass. Fred Nottingham would sometimes forget to carry his and had to leave his horse and load outside while he returned to the station to get it.

Seasonal agricultural supplies included fertilisers and nitro-chalk from G. Hadfield, Fisons and ICI, seed potatoes from Scotland, also dried sugar beet pulp from the British Sugar Corporation for animal foodstuffs, usually supplied to farmers who were themselves growers of sugar for the corporation. Farm machinery and baling wire for R. Batting & Son were also received along with elevators, rakes, harrows, etc.

Messrs. Y. J. Lovell, builders, established at Marlow during the late 19th century, had premises in the High Street and a yard and sawmill at Dedmere Road alongside the station. By the early 1920s they received building supplies and large quantities of timber by rail to the extent that in 1924 consideration was given for a private siding into their yard. However, this never progressed and supplies were ferried round from the goods yard by road.

Consignments of timber were also brought in when the Greenwich Sawmills set up their business at Marlow in 1941. They did arrange for a private siding and this is detailed on pages 163-177.

Pipes for the gas and water companies also arrived by rail, particularly in connection with roadworks and housing development in the area, and now and then china clay and pulp for Temple Mills paper works. Occasionally wagons arrived for Temple Mills, East London, and had to be re-directed. On one Sunday evening the penultimate arrival at Marlow conveyed 10 cattle wagons containing horses and labelled for Temple Mills. Fred Nottingham had to take them to Pinches to be fed and watered before being redirected to East London the next day.

Marlow, being a residential rather than an industrial area, generated little outwards traffic. What little there was included sugar beet to the British Sugar Corporation, the occasional load of barley for malting and fertilizer remaining from a composite load shared, for example, between a Marlow consignee and others from Loudwater and Windsor, an arrangement which gave the advantage of an exceptional carriage rate.

Bottle washing machines from Messrs. Arnold of Marlow Bottom, who assembled them on behalf of British Miller Hydro Corporation of Slough, were occasionally despatched, as were concrete greenhouses from Concrete Greenhouses Ltd. of Frieth Road.

Scrap iron and steel loaded out by J. A. Gibbons of Newtown Road went to various merchants such as Cox

The small loading platform used for the transfer of milk, mail and 'smalls' traffic between road and rail. *A. Attewell*

The 2-ton Austin lorry provided by the GWR in 1946. Believed to have been purchased from Vincents of Reading, it is seen here in BR crimson and cream livery being located for its daily round in the 1950s. Servicing was carried out by the Road Motor Engineers (RME) outstation at High Wycombe. Officially these lorries were 30 mph vehicles but apparently 'they would do 55 to 60 mph when they were nicely run in'. *Courtesy Fred Nottingham*

The entrance to the goods yard, in the late 1950s, separated from the forecourt by wooden palings.

A. Attewell

The 20-ton weighbridge and office were provided in 1928-9 to replace the 5-ton cart machine supplied by Messrs. H. Pooley early in 1875 for £96. Curiously, the original specification had stipulated a 20-ton machine. The measuring apparatus for this small machine, situated adjacent to the goods shed, was housed in what appears to have been a lean-to alongside the goods office, but unfortunately no photographs of this have yet come to light. The 5-ton machine described as obsolete and condemned was replaced by one of two redundant cart weighbridges from South Lambeth where they were no longer adequate for long road vehicles. No. 4181, measuring 16 ft x 8 ft, was sent to Marlow whilst the other one went to Chinnor. The plate shown here is the larger 20 ft x 8 ft 1953 replacement No. 10360 of the same tonnage costing £897 9s 5d. The weighbridge was also used by the public, including coal merchants, farmers, scrap merchants, even the occasional horse, or Bucks County Council checking the tare of vehicles for licensing purposes. This picture was taken in the mid-1950s.

A. Attewell

The goods shed, apparently originally equipped with a 2-ton crane, again followed GWR design and was similar to the one at West Ealing. The two loading bays were enclosed with sliding doors but the rail entrances were open, valuable goods being placed in a 'lock up' inside. The original portion of the goods office is thought to have been built at the same time as the main shell, but the obvious extension was added in 1943, at a cost of £185, to provide much needed extra accommodation. In common with Wallingford, a saloon coach for this purpose was stabled at Marlow during the war until the office was built. Following the war, the office saw little use for its intended purpose and it became a store, goods accountancy etc. being undertaken in the booking office.   *A. Attewell*

The eastern end of the building in 1965. Station coal was kept in the adjacent sleeper-built pen, 10 tons usually being received each year and unloaded by the station staff.
                                                                                                    A. E. Smith

Another view of the western end of the goods shed in the 1950s showing the porch of the 1943 extension to advantage. *A. Attewell*

A glimpse of the goods shed interior. For many years it was the home of a large white barn owl which could often be seen around the station, sitting on the boundary fence surveying the fields for prey.

A. Attewell

J. H. Venn

and Danks, George Cohen, and T. W. Ward, who in turn would send it to various steelworks. Pritchard, another scrap merchant who operated from alongside the goods yard, sent wagon loads to South Wales. Road vehicles for disposal or transfer were also occasionally sent out from RAF Medmenham.

Mr. Price sent out evergreen holly, moss, etc. to Covent Garden through an agent, George Munro. A van load was usually despatched twice a week and during the Second World War attached to the 4.20 p.m. passenger train.

Less regularly empty electric cable drums were returned to the suppliers by the Southern Electricity Board.

COAL TRAFFIC

Although Walter Porter, the owner or tenant of the Railway Hotel* was not initially successful in securing the GWR parcels agency, it did eventually pass to the family as detailed elsewhere. William Thomas Porter, Marlow's first station master and presumably son or brother of Walter (?), also ran a coal business from the hotel and by 1890 was trading as W. T. Porter and Son. Local trade directories list a High Street office in 1903 and, according to advertisements, from at least 1902 until 1909 the business was run by Charles Henry Porter, again from the

---

* His wife, Sarah Ann Porter, was apparently running the hotel by 1883.

Railway Hotel, yet by 1912 it seems to have passed to a William Thomas again. Porters rented wharfage in the yard, and from some time around 1911 transferred their headquarters from the hotel to an office in the station approach. They also had a handsome brick-built stables, which apparently held 12 horses and was situated alongside the boundary of the station goods yard. It is not clear when this was first established here but it was not until April 1903 that they arranged for the GWR to provide a gateway opposite the goods shed to allow direct access from the yard into their premises. Fred Nottingham started as one of their employees in 1929, his father, a stud groom, living in a flat above the stables. As already mentioned, Fred drove a horse-drawn parcels van, collecting and delivering around the town while another driver, Tom Stiles, dealt with larger goods with a heavy dray. William Porter, living at 'Wood Lea', Station Road, also owned a farm at Bisham. Porters also ran a Braugham from the station forecourt, a coal and general haulage business, and a small dairy, a herd of cows being kept in a long corrugated iron shed near the stables and grazed in a nearby meadow. The milk was delivered using a small trap.

Porters also ran nine 8 or 10 ton wagons lettered 'PORTER & SON' numbered 50, 60, 90, 100, 110, 120, 160, 180 and 190. No. 100 (built by S. J. Clay of Nuneaton) and Nos. 50 and 60 were painted red with

Fred Nottingham in the early years of his employment with Porters. The horse was called 'Kit'.   *Cty. Fred Nottingham*

W. T. PORTER & SON,

THE OLD-ESTABLISHED MARLOW COAL AND COKE BUSINESS.

Best Classes, House, Anthracite, Steam, Ovoids and Coke Supplied at Favourable Prices.

G.W.R. Delivery and Collection Agents.

STATION APPROACH, MARLOW.

'Phone: Marlow 51.

Bucks Free Press advert 1928

white lettering shaded black but the others were all grey with white lettering shaded black. Nos. 60, 80 and 190 were 7-plank vehicles and the remainder 5 planks. No. 160 was repainted and relettered 'W. T. PORTER & SON'. With supplies largely from the Midlands, the company survived until about 1946 when they sold out to Deans.

George Hector Dean of 21 Little Marlow Road, started in the coal and coke trade in November 1925. His father William, who was at one time a farmer, had from the late 1890s undertaken cartage work from premises in Spittal Street and on his death in May 1925 the business passed to his son. George had one 10-ton 7-plank wagon painted black with white lettering 'G. H. DEAN'.

Whilst neither George nor William appear to have been officially appointed agents for the GWR, they certainly undertook cartage work for them and possibly assisted W. T. Porter and Son.

When George died in June 1931 the business passed to his wife Edith. From around 1937 she was assisted by her son Dennis and later his brother George joined them in 1945.

Deans ran their business from Little Marlow Road until W. T. Porter and Son sold out to them in 1946 when they took over the coal office and wharves at the station. The name W. T. Porter and Son was retained until 1970 when the Reading firm of Talbot and Dunlop took over.

From the 1950s, Deans also acted as agents for the receipt of coal on behalf of Bennetts of Holyport who delivered to RAF Medmenham about once a fortnight during the winter.

Whilst the names of Porter and Toomer have for long been associated with the district, several other merchants used the railway over the years.

In 1873 the Ruabon and North Wales Colliery Company Ltd. (apparently with offices at Slough) rented a wharf which was maintained during the line's independent years. John Rutty of Marlow Fields rented a wharf from 1873 to 1882 and in 1880 had been joined by Henry Ralph Hewett, the latter acting as an agent for Toomer R. and Company, the well-known Reading fuel suppliers. From the end of 1887 Thomas Bilston Butler took over the agency following Hewett's death. Local directories indicate that Toomer occupied premises in Marlow High Street during 1893 and the agency arrangement with Butler probably ended about this time.

Toomers vacated their office at 36 High Street in favour of a new one opened at the station approach in 1927 where they traded until about 1950. They leased a wharf in the goods yard and kept stables opposite the station although latterly deliveries were made using a 3 ton Bedford lorry. Much of their supplies came from Silkstone Colliery, Derbyshire, under brand names such as 'Florence Spires' and 'Derby Bright'.

It is not known for certain how long the Ruabon Company survived at Marlow but local directories do not acknowledge their existence beyond about 1880 although they rented a wharf until at least 1896.

Other dealers and merchants in the late 19th century included Mark Wells of West Street, who retired in 1880, John Adams of High Street, James Brown of Chapel Street, George Cresswell of St. Peter's Street, Herridge and North of Chapel Street, W. J. Lovegrove of Wycombe Road, J. Smith of Little Marlow, W. V. Baines & Son and

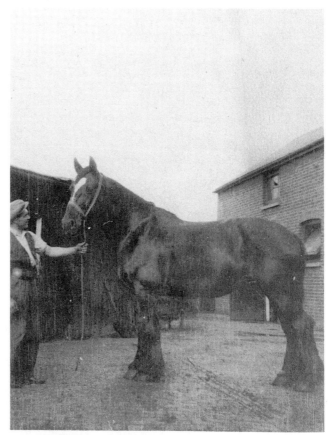

Fred Nottingham with 'Bruce'.   *Cty. Fred Nottingham*

Toomers' manager outside the Marlow office.

Albert Thomas Yates who either shared or superseded each other at 24 High Street, and John Baldwin of Station Road, who survived until about 1910. Whilst there is no record of any of these traders renting wharves, they all probably collected supplies from the railway.

Possibly one of the oldest coal businesses to subsequently use the railway was run by William Wigginton, a brewer and general dealer at Spittal Street in the 1830s. Wigginton had become a coal merchant by 1844 with a business in Dean Street, and by 1847 also at Bourne End. Robert and Thomas Wigginton, apparently the next generation of the family, were involved with the business from about 1850 and in 1854 they and William were not only traders at Marlow but coal merchants and timber dealers at Wooburn Wharf, Bourne End. During the 1880s the Spittal Street concern was being run by Mrs. Ruth Wigginton. By 1864 Robert had a coal business at 'Springs', Little Marlow, and Thomas was also a bargemaster with a wharf on the Buckinghamshire side of Marlow Bridge, where large quantities of coal were received. It is not known when the Wiggintons started to use the railway, but their Wooburn wharf was still in existence in 1881. The wharf at Marlow had been built over by 1915. Robert Wigginton, born in 1857, the eldest twin son of Thomas, died suddenly when on his rounds at the top of Seymour Court Hill in 1915 while delivering coal from the station. The *South Bucks Free Press* in Robert's obituary said that the family 'had the distinction of being the only tradesmen in Marlow to hold the Royal warrant. They have supplied wood for the royal palaces during the reigns of Queen Victoria, King Edward, and King George.'

Alfred Lee's coal business was founded c. 1907 and it passed to his sons, Walter and Alfred, in 1923. They rented

Tom Stiles' horse, 'Duke', at Quarrydale Drive, Marlow c.1930.
Cty. Mrs. D. Davis

C. Lee, G. Stiles and T. Stiles in Marlow goods yard in May 1930.

Tom Stiles' lorry in May 1930.

Another Toomers' lorry in the station approach.

Tom Stiles with his lorry c.1930.

Left: Tom Stiles outside his home in Newtown Road before Toomers used lorries.

Cty. Mrs. E. Genery & Mrs. Davis

a wharf at the station but were based at their family grocer's shop at 9 Dean Street, formerly 'The Traveller's Friend' Public House. As a youngster Walter had collected coal from the station for his mother using a pony and van. It was weighed at the shop using scoop scales, much of it being sold on Saturdays by the ¼ cwt for 4d to the poor for cooking purposes. The Lee brothers expanded the business and larger quantities of coal were received

established in 1890, was wound up by the end of the Second World War. Other merchants included Hester, Aughton, Stevens, White, Reeves and North. James North is said to have had one wagon painted grey with white letters shaded black. It was repainted when Stevens bought the firm. George Edwin Stevens of 22 Church Street, High Wycombe, was principally a corn merchant from the early 1920s. He occupied premises at 32 and 34

The coal wharves viewed from the signal box in the early 1950s.

Mrs. M. Jones

through C. & G. Ayres of Reading, mainly 'Walsall Wood' and 'London Bright', and arrived in that company's wagons. In the 1930s their horse and cart was replaced by a lorry and during the Second World War they took over from Porters the supply of coal to Wethered's Brewery, which amounted to some 10 tons per day. The brothers were nicknamed the 'midnight coalmen' since whenever possible they dealt with orders the same day, deliveries consequently overrunning into the evenings. They also ran a grocery and milk round, at one time keeping 50 pedigree cattle in fields along the Oxford Road, and even delivered wood.

Another Dean Street merchant, Alfred John Moore, was trading by the early 1920s. He had one 8-ton 5-plank wagon (believed to have been numbered 10) painted red with white lettering shaded black. He rented wharfage at the station and initially used a horse and cart for delivery of coal and timber logs. By the early 1930s, when he was using motor lorries, he was assisted by his sons George and Harold who took over and partnered the business from 1946 to 1955. George then continued to receive coal at Marlow goods yard and, at the time of writing, the family run their business from the remains of the yard alongside the present station.

Moores received their coal principally from Baddesley and Birch Coppice in the Midlands, the latter being best quality anthracite which was very popular.

John White, who had wharfage at the station, was also a cartage contractor at 74 Dean Street and his business,

Oxford Road and absorbed Reeves' business during the 1930s. Stevens apparently had 2 or 3 wagons which came to Marlow, these were painted green with white lettering shaded red.

Stevens were amongst the last merchants to receive coal by rail at Marlow in the 1960s.

Other private owner wagons frequently seen at Marlow before the war included C & G Ayres of Reading, Gas Light & Coke Co., Burr & Gibbons (Southall), Stevco (Oxford), Amalgamated Anthracite Co., and occasionally Binley (Nottingham).

Brothers George and Tom Stiles in Marlow goods yard c.1930.
Cty. Mrs. E. Genery

A not untypically busy yard in the 1950s. The rearmost of the two 'back sidings' was provided in the 1901-2 improvements and used mainly for coal traffic, an assortment of wharves and coal pens being situated along the boundary fence alongside. The siding was also used at one time for stabling the three coaches from the 6.08 p.m. from Paddington which returned again as the 9.18 a.m. through train the following morning. The siding serving the goods shed was known as the 'front road' or 'shed road' and used for forming up the goods whilst the other, alongside the platform, was the bay. The salt wagon contained bagged supplies for Wethered's brewery. In earlier years salt for domestic purposes was received in bars for sale in local shops.
A. Hall-Patch

A container being unloaded in the spring of 1951.
J. H. Venn

The 3-ton yard crane was installed about 1939, perhaps to coincide with the arrival of Greenwich Sawmills. From its appearance it was probably supplied by Messrs. Holt & Willetts. Prior to this there had only been the 2-ton fixed hand crane in the goods shed, and heavier loads including containers were unloaded by a large rail-mounted steam crane requisitioned from Reading when necessary. The old crane was removed in September 1939.

A. Hall-Patch

J. H. Venn

Shunting the yard in 1950.

The branch train passing the starting signal in the spring of 1951. The balance weight lever on the signal post has been painted white to reduce the risk of injury to the men who might stumble into it in poor light.
J. H. Venn

This permanent way hut, provided some time between 1910 and 1920, replaced its presumably timber-built predecessor shown on early plans in the yard opposite. The branch gang was based at Marlow, the men signing on at this hut each day at 7.15 a.m. There are believed to have been five members at one time, but after the Second World War there was just a ganger, Fred Burnard, a sub-ganger Walt Jolley, and two lengthmen. They were responsible for all of the branch length No. 103. After delegating work from his inspection the previous day, the ganger walked the length from Marlow examining the track, fences, lineside foliage etc. This usually took some 2½ hours, after which he was back with his men. On Sundays the whole team often combined with the Maidenhead gang for relaying work. The plate-layers were also responsible for fogmen's duties when necessary.
R. Miles

Looking towards Bourne End from the end of the platform in 1938.

Courtesy Mrs. Hobbs

The land on the edge of the yard, opposite the signal box, was partly used for garden allotments leased by the staff, including the station master. One of the firemen, George Parsons, bought a grounded horse-box body about 1924 and kept it alongside the back siding in use as a pig-sty. It may even still have remained there in 1942 when he transferred away. The yard gas lamp was apparently hardly used.

Courtesy Mrs. E. Hobbs

Between the wars Marlow signal box was manned in two shifts and reputed to have been one of the most remunerative signalmen's duties on the GWR because of the overtime involved. The box was painted in the GWR colour scheme of light and dark stone with white window frames. It closed on 26th September 1954 when the signalling was removed and the line reverted to 'one engine in steam' operation. These three photographs were all taken by Ernie Hobbs, one of the signalmen, in 1938.

Courtesy Mrs. E. Hobbs

J. H. Venn

Driver Vic Hoare enjoying a friendly exchange with passengers after arrival at Marlow in 1951.

CHAPTER SIX

A HARD PRUNING

The branch train strengthened with the spare trailer one summer Saturday in 1950. *J. H. Venn*

THE Nationalisation of the railways had little immediate effect and few could have expected the changes that followed. In that austere time, with rationing still in force, the private car was very much a luxury seldom considered by the masses to whom railway and bus services were still the accepted means of travel. Heavy goods were still carried by rail along with the majority of general supplies and foodstuffs, and the railways carried on their daily routine with a comforting regularity. Indeed, despite the various improvements and relatively minor changes over the years, the Marlow branch had continued to serve the post-war community in much the same way as it had its Victorian forefathers. It had become an accepted part of life, an institution, and as successive generations of staff fulfilled the roles of their predecessors, the permanence of the whole establishment offered unparalleled reassurance that unaccustomed generations will probably find difficult to appreciate.

Transport lecturer, James Venn, BSc Econ., spent a year employed as a clerk at Marlow station during 1950-51. He applied for the position after seeing an advert in the local paper and used the time to study the railway first-hand, his great interest also providing us with a valuable insight to his experiences there. He was interviewed by the station master, Freddie Funnell, who was about 64 year of age at the time and devoted to the railway. Mr. Funnell started his career about 1908 at Faringdon and,

after working his way up through the ranks, moved from Henley-on-Thames, where he was chief clerk, to take the station master's position at Marlow.

The station master was on call 24 hours a day, 7 days a week, and covered booking and clerical duties in addition to his own whenever required. Among other local activities, he was a member of the Chamber of Commerce, and, always keen to serve the community, he gave strict instructions to his staff not to allow a train to depart without first checking outside the station in case anyone was running to catch it. He had been staunchly dedicated to the Great Western Railway and refused to wear a British Railways badge, instead proudly retaining his regulation GWR pill-box hat as a defiant gesture of loyalty to the old company. Such devotion was more the norm than otherwise and only served to strengthen the stability of the daily routine which continued largely unchanged for so many years.

The day began with the arrival of the early turn signal-man who, as with the 1920s, usually found the locomotive already standing on the loop waiting. The auto trailer in use at this time was officially supposed to be left over-night in the platform, but for much of the 1950s it was taken on shed with the loco and even used for the over-night fireman to rest in! On opening the box at 5.20 a.m., the signalman set the road to enable the crew to move the engine on to the running line and back onto the trailer

In keeping with the spirit of wartime comradeship, the British Railways staff maintained a happy atmosphere at Marlow. Some, like the Morgans, made it a family affair. Not only were Ivan Morgan and his son signalmen but from about 1942 his daughter Ethel was a clerk. On the occasion of her marriage on 23rd April 1949, her father, in collaboration with station master Funnell and other staff, sprang a surprise. The newly-wed Maslins had intended to travel by road to Maidenhead station to commence their honeymoon journey but Ivor persuaded them to travel from Marlow where the branch train was specially decorated for the occasion. The coach was adorned with streamers and old shoes and the locomotive bore a headboard — 'Honeymoon Express'.

Cty. Mr. & Mrs. K. J. Maslin

No. 1437 leaving Marlow on 1st October 1950.

J. F. Russell Smith

ready for the first departure. Once this was done, he sent the bell code to Bourne End to open the box officially and gain release of the single line token; then, after pulling off the starting and advanced starting signals, he put the token into the carrier and took it over to the crew on his way to open the booking office. At this hour the signalman was usually the only member of the station staff on duty so he was issued with the keys to the office and left a small amount of petty cash to enable him to issue tickets for the 5.40 a.m. train which mainly catered for some 20-30 workers on their way to Jackson's Mill at Bourne End. Billy Billingham, the carriage cleaner, also travelled on the train to clean the stock of the 7.30 a.m. Bourne End to Paddington.

When he was satisfied that everyone had arrived, the signalman gave the driver the 'right away' and telephoned his colleague at Bourne End to let him know the train was in section. After locking the station again, he returned to the box, restored the signals to danger and lit the stove ready to cook his breakfast. This duty was, of course, not so agreeable during the dark mornings of a harsh winter,

when the signalbox and the station were cold and unwelcoming and remained so for some considerable time until the stove and fires respectively could take the chill out of the buildings. Steam heating the auto trailer could also take time before offering any comfort to passengers.

The train returned with the branch goods, the engine leading bunker first with the trailer and wagons in tow. Wagons for Marlow were normally assembled at Taplow and, besides the usual vans from Paddington, generally included four or five wagons from Brentford Docks for Greenwich Saw Mills. These were left for collection in the south sidings at Bourne End whilst coal wagons for Marlow, arriving with the Hinksey to Acton goods the previous afternoon, had sometimes been left in Jackson's siding.

Although unadvertised, this train also conveyed workers from the night shift at Jacksons's who, on arrival at Marlow, were met by the early turn porter who had come on duty by this time to collect the tickets. The locomotive ran onto the other end of the train to detach the wagons which were simply placed in a convenient siding in the

BOURNE END and MARLOW.

SINGLE LINE. Worked by Electric Train Token. "Red" Group Engines must not exceed 20 m.p.h. at any point on Branch

Week Days.

Dis-tances.	STATIONS.		Ruling Gra-dient 1 in	Time Allowances for H, J & K Head Code Freight Trains. (See page 346.)			G Engine ex Slough MO	B Auto Mixed. N	B Auto.	B Auto.	B Auto.	B Auto.	B Auto. K	B Auto.	B Auto. SO	B Auto.	B Auto.	B Auto.	B Auto.	G Engine. RR	B Auto.	B Auto.	B Auto.
				Point to point times. Mins.	Allow for Stop. Mins.	Allow for Start. Mins.																	
M. C. — — 2 61	Bourne End dep. Marlow .. arr.		— 132 R	— 8	— 1	1 —	a.m. 5/10 5/16	a.m. 6 35 6 43	a.m. 7 34 7 40	a.m. 8 10 8 16	a.m. 8 43 8 49	a.m. 9 6 9 9	a.m. 9 30 9 36	a.m. 9 56 10 2	a.m. 10 34 10 46	p.m. 12 34 12 15	p.m. 12 40	p.m. 1 20 1 26	p.m. 2 8 2 14	p.m. 2 34 2 40	p.m. 3 20 3 26	p.m. 3/55 4/1 1	p.m. 4 35 4 41	p.m. 5 14 5 20	p.m. 5 52 5 58

Week Days—continued. | Sundays.

STATIONS.	B Auto.	B Auto.	B Auto.	B Auto.	B Auto.	B Auto.	B Auto. SX	B Auto.	B Auto.	1152 pm M'head Auto. WSO night	B Auto.	B Auto.	B Auto.	B Auto.	B Auto.	B Auto.	B Auto.	B Auto.	B Auto.	B Auto.	B Auto.	B Auto.	B Auto.
Bourne End.. dep.	p.m. 8 42	p.m. 7 10	p.m. 7 40	p.m. 8 12	p.m. 8 53	p.m. 9 42	p.m. 10 15	p.m. 10 48	p.m. 11 17	night 12 7	a.m. 9 5	a.m. 9 42	a.m. 10 41	a.m. 11 2	a.m. 11 44	p.m. 1 6	p.m. 2 18	p.m. 2 45	p.m. 3 54	p.m. 5 6	p.m. 5 55	p.m. 7 22	p.m. 8 53	p.m. 9 50	p.m. 10 32
Marlow .. arr.	6 48	7 16	7 46	8 18	8 59	9 48	10 21	10 54	11 23	12 13	9 11	9 48	10 47	11 8	11 50	1 12	2 24	2 51	4 0	5 12	6 1	7 28	8 59	9 56	10 38

K—Suspended.   N—Not advertised.

Week Days.

STATIONS.		Ruling Gradient 1 in	Time Allowance for H, J & K Head Code Freight Trains. (See page 346.)			B Auto.	B Auto.	B Auto.	B Auto.	B Auto.	B Auto.	B Auto Mixed. K	B Auto.	B Auto. SO	B Auto.	B Auto.	B Auto.	B Auto.	K Freight RR	B Auto.	B Auto.	B Auto.
			Point to point times. Mins.	Allow for Stop. Mins.	Allow for Start. Mins.																	
Marlow .. dep.		—	—	—	—	a.m. 5 40	a.m. 7 18	a.m. 7 55	a.m. 8 52	a.m. 8 52	a.m. 9 12	a.m. 9 40	a.m. 10 16	a.m. 11 40	p.m. 12 18	p.m. 1 6	p.m. 2 22	p.m. 3 6	p.m. 3 35	p.m. 4 20	p.m. 4 50	p.m. 5 40	p.m. 6 32
Bourne End.. arr.			132 F.	8	1	1	5 46	7 24	8 1	8 38	8 58	9 18	9 48	10 22	11 46	12 24	1 12	1 48	2 28	3 12	3 45	4 26	4 56	5 46	6 28

Week Days—continued. | Sundays.

STATIONS.	B Auto.	B Auto.	B Auto.	B Auto.	B Auto.	B Auto. SX	B Auto.	B Auto.	Auto to Maiden-head WSO	B Auto.	B Auto.	B Auto.	B Auto.	B Auto.	B Auto.	B Auto.	B Auto.	B Auto.	B Auto.	B Auto.	B Auto.	G Engine to Slough
Marlow .... dep.	p.m. 6 52	p.m. 7 30	p.m. 7 50	p.m. 8 40	p.m. 9 28	p.m. 10 4	p.m. 10 30	p.m. 11 28	p.m. 11 28	a.m. 8 52	a.m. 9 30	a.m. 10 50	a.m. 11 28	p.m. 12 55	p.m. 1 55	p.m. 2 30	p.m. 3 20	p.m. 4 52	p.m. 5 44	p.m. 7 8	p.m. 8 40	p.m. 9 35	p.m. 10 15
Bourne End arr.	6 58	7 36	7 56	8 46	9 34	10 10	10 36	11 6	11 34	8 58	9 36	10 32	11 34	1 1	2 1	2 36	3 26	4 58	5 50	7 14	8 46	9 41	10 21 10/56

K—Suspended.

No. 1

307

Taken from service timetable effective 25th September 1950.

yard and sorted later, although if a good many of them were for Greenwich Sawmills and time permitted, they were shunted into their private siding by prior arrangement.

Before the war, the wagons were always placed when they arrived, particularly the box vans of general supplies and groceries. These were pushed right through the goods shed and moved back through the building using a pinch bar when each one had been emptied. The town largely depended on the railway at that time and prompt deliveries were essential, so when the mixed train arrived late one morning, it was greeted by impatient traders. On the occasion concerned there were no passengers so the crew had taken advantage of the situation and, fuelling widespread legend, had actually stopped the train in the fields and picked mushrooms.

To return to the 1950s, after disposing of the wagons, the loco was re-coupled to the trailer and the auto gear connected for the first time to work the 7.18, 7.55 and 8.32 a.m. shuttle services, the first of which connected with the 7.30 a.m. Bourne End to Paddington previously referred to. The 8.32 gave the fastest overall time to Paddington as the connecting train at Bourne End ran fast from Maidenhead to Paddington.

The timing of this train was critical as the crossing movement over the relief and onto the main at Maidenhead could cause havoc to the main line services. Paddington therefore issued instructions that the 8.32 a.m. must leave Marlow promptly.

The passengers were advised about this one evening, but the following morning one man, who had a reputation for arriving at the last minute, still only reached the station as the train was passing the signal box. Despite the instruction, when the driver Vic Hoare saw the passenger running down the platform he reversed into the station to collect him! Mr. Funnell later had a few words with the driver about the matter.

In the 1930s the 8.34 a.m. included through coaches for London. These were kept overnight in the back siding in the yard and attached to the rear of the branch set. The six-coach train ran into the 'down' platform at Bourne End where the engine from the Paddington train, having left its stock in the 'up' platform, backed onto the Marlow train, collected the through vehicles, put them on the front of its train and left for London at 8.44 a.m. The through coaches returned to Marlow with the 6.42 p.m. from Bourne End.

At one time there had also been a through train to Maidenhead at 10.15 a.m. often worked by 'County' tanks and later '61XX' class 2—6—2Ts from Slough. The stock was worked in from High Wycombe while the branch train waited in the bay.

Returning to the 1950s, a break in proceedings at about 10.40 a.m. allowed the sorting of the yard which could take anything from 15 to 60 minutes depending on the amount of traffic. The net result was the placing of all the arrivals in their respective positions and the formation of a train of outgoing empty and loaded wagons in the bay or goods shed road. The loaded vehicles were few in number and the empties mainly coal and timber wagons. Afterwards the engine spent some time at the shed taking water and coal.

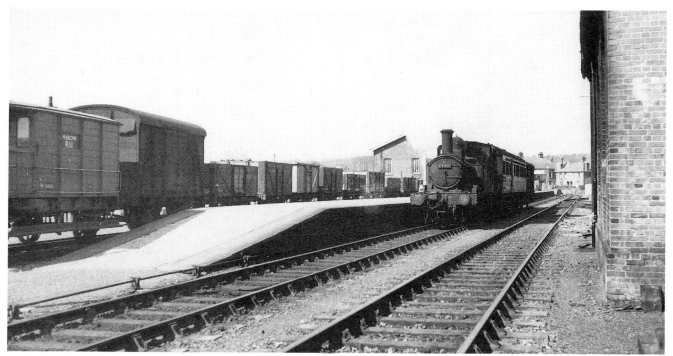

The outgoing vehicles, largely emptics, assembled in the bay for a later departure. Taken in the spring of 1951, this view shows a tail load at the rear of the departing train.

J. H. Venn

20-ton brake van or Toad No. 114760, built in September 1935 to diagram AA20 as part of Lot 1171 (24 ft long, 16 ft wheelbase), may have been sent to Watlington originally as the name began to show through during its time at Marlow. It stayed at Marlow until about 1942 when it was transferred to the Southern, being seen at Dover in 1943 and Petersfield (on Portsmouth to London goods) still branded 'Marlow'. Toad No. 17746, shown here at Marlow c.1957, was evidently a later successor. Built in December 1907 to Diagram AA2 as part of Lot 549, this 25-ton vehicle was 20 ft long with a 13 ft wheelbase.

Collection M. Anderson

No. 1411 with an afternoon mixed train near Spade Oak Crossing on 24th May 1954.
Norman Aston-Smith

In the meantime the trailer, which had been left in the platform, was being cleaned out by Billy Billingham who had returned with it from Bourne End. Billy, an old shed labourer from Slough, replaced Cicely Bateman, a wartime carriage cleaner. Ron Britten, a carriage and wagon examiner from Slough, also travelled down with it when necessary (usually every other day) to recharge the gas cylinders for the coach lighting from the 'Cordon' or gas tank wagon kept in 'Khartoum' siding. He returned on the next train when the service resumed at 12.15 p.m.

On Saturdays it was more convenient to take the goods out with this train but from Monday to Friday the 3.06 p.m. ran mixed. A separate goods train was allowed for in the working timetable at 3.35 p.m. but is not remembered ever running as such. The trailer remained attached to the engine while the wagons and goods brake van were collected from the yard, the assembled train then being backed into the main platform. There could be up to 20 or 25 wagons which meant the auto trailer was a considerable distance up the platform, perhaps opposite the engine shed. On one occasion three or four ladies, having bought tickets, asked Mr. Venn which was the train. 'At the platform', he replied, forgetting to tell them the auto coach was at the opposite end. They were probably not the first to think they were being asked to climb into the empty coal wagons!

At Bourne End the mixed train ran into the main 'down' platform where the wagons were detached by the station pilot, an engine which had worked down from Taplow and shunted Thomas and Green's siding, just north of Bourne End, then Loudwater before running on to High Wycombe where a fresh engine was provided to work a pick-up goods up the branch to Taplow. The 'pilot' returned light engine all the way from Wycombe to Slough shed. The parcels porter, Alf Taylor, worked as guard on this train, the goods brake or 'toad' being left in the south sidings for the following morning.

The rest of the day's service simply consisted of a shuttle service to and from Bourne End, but the loco going on shed for coal and water at about 5-6 p.m. made a tight schedule between the services concerned. The trailer coach remaining coupled to the engine was also taken on shed and, quite unofficially, passengers were escorted over the track to board the coach alongside the water tower! Mr. Venn remembers helping people up the boarding steps so the train could start away from the run-round loop in order that the London connection could be made at Bourne End.

Horse-boxes for Messrs. Pinches were another regular feature. They were detached from Wycombe line trains at Bourne End, picked up by the branch train, and worked to Marlow behind the engine, which was sandwiched between the trailer and tail load. Vehicles from Marlow were put into the north or south sidings for 'up' and 'down' trains respectively. On arrival at Marlow, tail vehicles were left in the platform while the loco and trailer were released onto the run-round loop. The vehicle(s) would then be pushed alongside the cattle pens by hand. Alternatively, such vehicles were propelled back up the platform clear of the loop entry points, uncoupled and moved back into the platform with a pinch bar after the loco and trailer had run onto the loop. Tail loads of fitted vehicles, such as siphons with parcels, for instance, (or horse-boxes) were a regular feature, particularly on the last service into Marlow before the late morning break in the service. A parcels vehicle remaining in the dock would often return to Paddington on the 4.50 p.m. loaded with Mr. Price's evergreens and/or parcels if required.

On Wednesdays and Saturdays for many years an extra late night service was run, the branch train working through to Maidenhead and back to connect with London services. In 1955 the branch train worked through to Maidenhead and back with the 10.05 a.m. from Marlow and that winter the 10.21 p.m. and 11.12 p.m. trains were also extended to Maidenhead on weekdays. During the last days of steam the branch train made four return trips through to Maidenhead and three to High Wycombe.

There were numerous other changes to the timetable over the years and the 1950s were certainly no exception. The summer of 1952 saw the introduction of the 12.08 p.m. Marlow-Bourne End mixed train (Sats. excepted) later retimed to 1.00 p.m. in September 1956. In 1957 a correspondent in *The Railway Observer* noted that the train

A cordon and paco (horse-box) alongside the cattle pen in the 1950s. *A. Attewell*

Another view of 0–6–0PT No. 9653 standing in for the usual Collett tank in the spring of 1951. Without auto-gear this substitution meant more work for the crew as it was necessary to run round at each end of the journey. In this scene the locomotive is just about to be uncoupled and, after running round, the horse-box would be propelled alongside the cattle pens. *J. H. Venn*

The branch train ran through to Maidenhead on certain turns and this view shows it alongside Platform 5 under the train shed on 28th February 1960.

R. Denison

Another view of No. 1447 at Maidenhead on the same occasion.   *R. Denison*

usually conveyed twelve or so wagons. The 1.00 p.m. lasted until September 1962 when mixed workings finished with the end of steam-hauled passenger services. Goods traffic was subsequently catered for by the 12.44 p.m. from Thomas and Green's siding to Bourne End being retimed and extended to Marlow, returning from Marlow to Taplow at 2.00 p.m. In 1954 the 6.35 a.m. mixed train from Bourne End to Marlow became an unadvertised passenger train retimed to leave at 6.15 p.m. to bring back overnight workers from Jackson's Mill. The 9.38 a.m. from Bourne End ran mixed instead.

Sunday services also underwent several alterations following nationalization. There had been twelve return trips including the unadvertised 9.45 p.m. ex-Marlow, but from the summer of 1949 the service was increased to 14 and even to 15 the following year, although the extra return trip was not repeated in 1951. The 1955 summer timetable made even more generous provision with eighteen return services, seven of which even worked through to Maidenhead. Of the thirteen return trips of 1955 winter Sundays, only one was confined to the branch, the others running to Maidenhead, High Wycombe, and one trip, the 6.56 p.m. ex Marlow, even to Aylesbury. A similar pattern was maintained the following summer but the Aylesbury run was dropped from the 1957 summer timetable and the High Wycombe run was taken off the following year. Thus from the 1958 summer timetable the branch train ran through to Maidenhead only, on almost half of the eleven winter and eighteen summer departures.

Again, as with the 1920s, there were two drivers working shifts of 5 a.m. to 3 p.m. and 3 p.m. to 11 p.m. and three firemen working 7 a.m. to 3 p.m., 3 p.m. to 11 p.m. and 11 p.m. to 7 a.m., the overnight fireman working the first trip each morning and the Wednesday and Saturday late services when necessary. For many years a Slough crew worked the afternoon shift on Sundays which enabled Marlow drivers to have alternate Sundays off, although the fireman effectively had only one in three as, in addition to the early turn, one of them had to report for the night duty at 11 p.m. on Sunday evening. The Slough men arrived each Sunday afternoon with a fresh engine and the stock for the 7.30 a.m. Bourne End to Paddington which was worked from Slough as a passenger service. On arrival at Bourne End, the engine ran round the train and left the stock in the north sidings, then ran light to Marlow, where it was put straight on shed. The Slough men worked the rest of the day's services with the old engine, which, after the last return trip, worked back to Slough light engine.

From the summer of 1948 the timetable shows the branch engine returning to Slough after the last arrival at Marlow. The details of these arrangements evidently varied as the fresh engine did not always arrive on Sunday afternoon. From 10th September 1951 the Marlow crew on Sunday turn No. 2 booked on at 7.50 a.m. (driver) and 8.30 a.m. (fireman) in time to work the 8.40 a.m. to Bourne End. They continued to work the remainder of the day's services until relieved by Slough men at 4.00 p.m. One can only assume that the Slough crew travelled

One of the first rail/river excursions of the 1951 season.   *J. H. Venn*

in on the cushions and took the engine back to Slough shed at the end of the day's timetable as turn No. 45 (Mondays only) of the Slough crew roster, again commencing 10th September 1951, involved booking on duty at 3.45 a.m. and working a replacement light engine from Slough at 4.30 a.m., arriving at Marlow at 5.15 a.m. to work the 5.40 a.m. return trip (known as Jackson's train). Marlow men took over for the second trip leaving the Slough crew to travel on the cushions to High Wycombe where they relieved the crew of the 8.22 a.m. Oxford to work the 10.08 from Wycombe to Maidenhead, finally returning to Slough with the light engine from Oxford.

Collett 0—4—2T Nos. 1426, 1442 and 1450 were the three regular Marlow branch engines during the early 1950s and, whilst they usually ran chimney first to Bourne End, they were sometimes turned at Slough to help even the flange wear incurred on the sharp curves leaving Bourne End.

The '48XX' class 0—4—2Ts worked the line until the withdrawal of steam, but '54XX' pannier tanks or '61XX' large prairie classes did work the line on the odd occasion.

In addition to the regular timetable, special charter trains were run to and from Marlow during the summer months, usually in connection with river trips. Such excursions came from as far afield as Devon or Lancashire and arrived in the charge of large and sometimes 'foreign' tender engines. For a time during the early 1930s there is believed to have been a regular weekly excursion from Durham. It was not uncommon to see 'Saints' and 'Halls'

working to Marlow on these 'specials' before the Second World War and later 'Castles'. The locos usually ran light engine to Slough for turning, watering, etc. but one 'Castle' took water at Marlow, emptying the tank in the process!

In the mid-1950s an LNER 'Football' class 4—6—0 arrived at Marlow crewed by local Western Region men who had taken over from the Eastern Region crew at High Wycombe. The passengers travelled on the Thames to Windsor while the empty stock was worked there to meet them and afterwards the LNER engine returned light engine to Slough for turning. Such duties with other companies' engines were quite a novelty for the crews who tended to regard unfamiliar machines with deep suspicion. Some LNER and LMS engines were fitted with rocking grates, a refinement denied to Western men, and at Slough, in cleaning the fire, the shedman succeeded in getting this particular grate stuck in the open position. Rather than tamper with such technology, a fitter was sent for from Neasden. He arrived about 4 p.m. but after managing the repairs in a very hot firebox, the crew did not have much time left to re-light the fire and build it up again for a 6.30 p.m. departure from Windsor. They only just made it!

These excursions varied, some continued from Windsor to Paddington and included a night out at a London theatre, whilst others simply took passengers to Marlow and waited while they went to, say, Henley and back on the river. Tuck-boxes issued on some trains are well remembered by the Marlow staff who shared the contents of any found surplus to requirements. Often such trains ran to Windsor first, then empty stock to Marlow to await the arrival of the trippers from their aquatic tour. One such train remembered by former staff was a 'special' chartered by Reckitt & Colman of Hull, manufacturers of 'Brasso', 'Robin' starch, etc. Having deposited the employees and

catered for simply by strengthening the branch train with a spare auto coach, the loco being sandwiched between the two vehicles and often running extra trips. The additional accommodation was also provided on the preceding Thursday and Friday evenings for the preliminary events. A second spare trailer was also sometimes held at Bourne End in case a three-coach train was necessary.

The Church and Bridge, Marlow

their families at Windsor, the LNER engine, a Thompson 'B1' class 4—6—0, worked the empty stock into Marlow to pick them up again. This was indeed an unfamiliar sight in Marlow station, with a train of six Gresley saloons and two restaurant cars all in varnished teak.

Combined rail and river tickets in co-operation with the famous Salter's Steamers had enabled passengers using the regular train service to enjoy the Thames for many years and were always popular, but excursions from outside the area were particularly well patronized. Even in the early 1950s there were occasions when as many as three chartered trains were waiting at Marlow on a summer's evening, one in the main platform and two in the goods yard. However, even when there was only one in the station, the branch train was relegated to the unsignalled bay line designated 'for special traffic', the unlocked yard points being clipped and padlocked by the signalman. Blackboard notices and careful watching over the passengers was essential on such occasions otherwise someone going to Paddington might find themselves in Birmingham, Leicester or Nottingham! Departure times could also be delayed on hot sunny days when the number or boats queuing at the locks could easily delay the steamers. Many trains had to be completely re-timed.

Other 'specials' included at one time chartered trains for Wethered's Brewery staff outings, and when Marlow football club was playing at home a 'special' was often arranged on a Saturday afternoon to bring about 500 supporters from High Wycombe. Marlow Regatta day also provided quite a boost to the takings and the booking office was kept open until midnight. Requirements were

Mr. Venn's time in the booking office was not without its amusing moments. Shortly after the departure of one train, a woman appeared at the booking office window in a very distressed state. Her husband had left her and she wanted Mr. Venn to arrange for an engine or another train to pursue him! After explaining the impracticalities of the situation she was advised to seek other means of reaching Cookham where she might intercept the connecting train.

Mr. Venn also recalls the day when a Hammer Film company official simply walked up to the booking office window to ask if it was possible to shoot a sequence at the station. This is believed to have been for 'The Four-sided Triangle' with Barbara Payton, Stephen Murray, John Van Eyssen, James Hayter, Percy Marment, Jennifer Dearman, Sean Barrett, Glyn Dearman, Kynaston Reeves, John Stuart and Edith Saville. The film was an early Hammer excursion into horror, involving the creation of a machine that would reproduce objects (and people) exactly!

Not surprisingly, the Marlow branch only played a very minor part in the film and, in the event, the passenger service was suspended for just half a day and a replacement bus service laid on. In a sequence where the heroine was being seen off by her lover, Vic Hoare had to drive the branch train in and out of the station several times before the director was satisfied and Vic received £10 for his co-operation.

Other films with sequences at Marlow station included 'Meet the Duke', described as a 'ham-fisted comedy thriller' of 1948, and 'The Miniver Story' in 1950, for which the brake compartment of the auto-trailer was commandeered to enable backscenes to be shot along the branch. This apparently caused some inconvenience to passengers with prams and bicycles. Around 1960 'Nearly a nasty accident' with Jimmy Edwards and Kenneth Connor, apparently involved the branch, and in the early 1950s a washing powder advertisement was made at Marlow station. This involved washing strung up outside the signal box while the train passed by emitting plenty of smoke! Ivor Morgan, who was on duty in the box at the time, had to duck out of sight every time the train passed, while an actor shouted to his wife to watch out for the smoke on the washing. Sadly, Ivor can't recall the name of the soap powder.

The staff on duty on Saturday mornings had to be particularly vigilant when what seemed to be something approaching 200 children from the Bourne End area arrived for the children's films at the cinema. On their return they tended to swarm all over the platform, goods yard and anywhere else they could get, often causing some consternation by sitting with their legs dangling over the edge of the platform! On quite a different occasion, some Borlase schoolboys got into the guard's compartment between Marlow and Bourne End and screwed on the handbrake. That particular auto-trailer ran with flats on the wheels for some time afterwards.

However, it was not only children who could be a hazard to safety. One young woman who had missed the train at Bourne End decided to walk to Marlow. Mr. Venn was busy in the yard labelling wagons for the 3.06 p.m. mixed train, when she appeared carrying her shoes and walking bare-footed along the sleepers. It turned out that she was the fireman's girlfriend — 'It's alright', she said, 'I've got a ticket!'

A pig which arrived for RAF Medmenham officers' club, caused chaos one day. The animal arrived in a horse-box which was left alongside the cattle dock, but without reference to the railway staff, the RAF personnel who had been advised of the arrival, set about unloading it. The pig was reluctant to move, but when it was finally

Another scene from 'Four Sided Triangle' with station master Freddie Funnell looking on.

British Film Institute, courtesy Hammer Film Productions Ltd.

extracted it went straight down onto the trackbed between the box and the dock wall and set off down the line with the RAF men in hot pursuit!

On another occasion a wagon containing casks of beer from Burton had arrived in the goods yard. It was a very hot day and, owing to a mishap in transit, one of the casks was leaking out of the wagon. On noticing this, the coalmen and other opportunists in the yard started to come forth with their mugs. However, on this occasion they were out of luck as the wagon was marked as previously carrying lime!

Mr. O. G. Trill, who also transferred from Henley-on-Thames, took over as station master when Mr. Funnell retired in 1953. However, because of staff shortages, he covered both Marlow and Bourne End for his first two years in office there. He saw the first real economy measure when Marlow signal box was closed and the signalling removed on 26th September 1954, the line reverting to the 'one engine in steam' operation used at the outset. This brought about the first reduction in staff. He was also in charge of the line during the railway strike in June 1955 when no trains were run over the branch for several days. The *Bucks Free Press* of 3rd June reported that people in the area were accepting the restrictions so far imposed 'uncomplainingly and with stoic good humour', a railway official also commenting 'Generally, people seem to be taking the restrictions wonderfully well. Everyone is co-operating without complaint.'

The branch was also in the Sunday papers that year when the 6.04 train from Marlow to Maidenhead did not run on Sunday, 9th October. The animated redress by the *Maidenhead Advertiser* which followed the distorted national press coverage read as follows:

CHUCKLES ON THE WYCOMBE BRANCH
'The driver doesn't smoke a pipe'

There were some broad grins in Marlow and Bourne End Railway Stations this week. Porters, clerks and loco. men chuckled over the picturesque reports which appeared in the Sunday papers about the 6.4 train (the 'Marlow Donkey') which did not run from Marlow to Maidenhead on Sunday, October 9, because the train had no fireman.

"Listen to this! (said one railwayman reading from a newspaper), 'He was just in time to see the driver get down from the cab, light his pipe and walk off into the night'. Funny thing. He doesn't smoke a pipe. And as for walking off into the night — he's got to get down from the cab to go to the other end of the train!"

" 'Some of the passengers walked a mile to catch a bus to their destination!' How far would you say it was to the bus-stop from Marlow Station? Half a mile?"

" 'Others waited until British Railways laid on a special bus'. Well, now, wasn't that nice! First we knew about it . . .'"

But there were indignant comments as well.

"No action is being taken against the railway fireman who went home because he was exhausted by working overtime!" read out Mr. R. House, clerk at Bourne End station.

"I should jolly well think not! He does a good turn and that's what happens. Reading these reports, you'd think he was a dreadful character".

The national press reported that 23-year-old fireman Arthur Brown, who lives at Marlow Bottom, suddenly decided to go home because he was exhausted by working three hours overtime.

The first evidence of 'rationalisation' — the removal of the signals and signal box on 26th September 1954.   *R. Course*

What in fact happened, as reported in last week's *Advertiser*, was that a fireman at Slough failed to report for duty.

Mr. Brown had been on duty since 8.30 a.m. and was due to knock off at 5 p.m. But when the position was explained to him he agreed to do an extra trip to High Wycombe and back to Marlow, thus giving them an hour in which to find a fireman to relieve him.

Slough found a substitute fireman but he missed his connection from Maidenhead and consequently, there was no one to relieve Mr. Brown when he returned to Marlow.

What did Arthur Brown think about the matter?

"Had a good laugh over it", he told an *Advertiser* reporter.

So did Mr. Oliver Trill, stationmaster for Bourne End and Marlow. "These reports are more amusing than annoying", he said.

But he was angered by the fact that they showed Mr. Brown in such a bad light.

A British Railways spokesman at Paddington told the *Advertiser* this week that a thorough investigation had been made and they were satisfied that there was no need to take any action.

No formal statement about the matter was to be issued. He was amused by a Sunday paper's report that 'claims and protests by outraged passengers' were now being considered by British Railways. So far, he said, he knew of only one claim — for 2s. 5d.

There are many stories of branch line antics, many improving as the years go by. Newspapers seek out eccentricity, seizing any quaint tales and there is often at least an element of ridicule in press coverage of railway matters.

Few visiting Bourne End during the final years of steam, as shown in this romantic portrait, could have realised that the GWR canopy, familiar all over the system, rested upon the framework of the old train shed that had sheltered Great Marlow Railway trains since the early years of the branch. Showing clearly are the centre-balanced signal arms fitted to signals 38 (the higher arm, reading to Maidenhead) and 36 (down platform to Marlow) in January 1956. The disc signal between them read to the down sidings. The down home signal (almost obscured behind the signal at the end of the up platform) is now in the form of a bracket, with an arm allowing movements from the Maidenhead direction into the up platform. The rather tortuous nature of the single line to loop facing points laid in during the 1956 remodelling is evident.

A. C. Harold

No. 1450 in the bay at Bourne End after the removal of the run-round loop in 1955. The bicycle shed, ordered by the Ministry of Works Transport and estimated at £20, was completed on 7th June 1945.   *Lens of Sutton*

Much has been made of looking out for regulars absent from the morning train, often to the extent that anyone not intending to travel the following day would feel obliged to mention it. Some would telephone and, according to one newspaper, a call from the station master's office for anyone missed 'would soon establish whether the passenger was not well — or had just overslept.' Of course, such stories became exaggerated — and in any case not many could afford a telephone in those days. The same newspaper also reported 'occasionally cyclists would arrive in the morning with a puncture — when they returned in the evening their bikes would be mended and ready waiting for them.' How many people were quite that lucky is open to question, but these stories do serve to illustrate the spirit of the whole concern.

The branch was again in the public eye when Wethered's refurbishment of the Railway Hotel, which was re-named 'The Marlow Donkey' on 29th September 1961, achieved national press coverage. According to the brewery manager, the hotel was re-named 'to stimulate local interest and to strengthen the affection which the people of Marlow have for their railway'. The same night, after a 'certain amount of jollification', three men who admitted 'having had a certain amount of drink', walked half a mile along the line and held up the train by placing cartridges on the rails which acted as detonators. When the train stopped, driver Tom Burton was confronted by three men, two of them masked and dressed in cowboy suits. They boarded the train with toy 'six shooters' and told him it was a 'stick-up'. The driver, who was alarmed at first, did

not appreciate the joke, neither did the British Transport Commission who fined them each 30 shillings for entering a carriage 'otherwise than on the side of a platform' contrary to railway by-laws; unlawfully and wilfully stopping 'a vehicle on the railway'; and wilfully obstructing the driver in the execution of his duty. According to the *Railway Magazine* after being fined, the three local men, a 40 year old electrician, a 40 year old company director and a 38 year old car salesman, went to The Marlow Donkey for a celebration drink. One who was celebrating his 39th birthday, said as they toasted the local railway: 'We have made friends again with the engine driver'.

The Marlow branch never seems to have suffered any real threat from competing bus services. In the 1920s the Chiltern Bus Company ran a service from its base in Lane End to Bourne End via Marlow and later, in the 1930s, the Wycombe and District Omnibus Company ran from Wycombe to Marlow via Bourne End, but both services were short-lived. In the late 1940s, and early 1950s the Thames Valley Traction Company's No. 18 and 19 services (with various suffixes) also ran from Bourne End to Marlow, offering a feeder service of sorts for Maidenhead. This was not an attractive arrangement as the weight restriction over Marlow's suspension bridge meant that passengers had to walk over the bridge to change buses. Consequently, the railway kept the commuter traffic, and in the circumstances it is hardly surprising that the bus service was primarily used for local journeys and fell early victim of the private car. The bus fare in 1951 from Marlow to Bourne End was 7d single and 1/- return, and

The branch train on one of its frequent journeys to Bourne End c.1960.   *M. Esau*

the railway 6d single and 8d return. From Marlow to Maidenhead (via Pinkneys Green) was 10d single as opposed to the railway's 1/2d.

Reference to the statistics on page 178 will reveal the variations in traffic, one of the most interesting periods being the spectacular peak during the Second World War when three times as many tickets were issued. Of course, much of this can be attributed to military personnel but the even more dramatic rise in season tickets from 1,214 in 1938 to 4,166 in 1944 presumably, at least partly, reflects Marlow's role in the evacuation of London. However, despite the national trends of increasing car ownership and the general growth of road haulage, the Marlow branch appears to have retained a surprisingly healthy traffic. The number of tickets issued actually *rose* from an impressive 44,730 in 1953 to 50,463 in 1957. Parcels remained at a fairly steady 20,000 per annum and even the total goods tonnage for 1957 held at 15,254 which, if not wonderful, at least compared with the immediate pre- and post-war figures. Passenger tickets fell to 37,918 in 1962, still comparing favourably with pre-war figures, but we have not come across the figures for goods traffic that year.

Sadly, changes under the name of progress have unavoidable consequences and inevitably the Marlow branch could not escape from the harsh reality that nationally more and more traffic was being lost to the roads. This is not the place to examine Beeching's policy, but the needs of local communities took a back seat in the desire to 'streamline' the handling of freight in the quest for greater national efficiency. It was thus clear that it was only a matter of time before things would have to change.

The dieselisation of the railways was also taking place and the loss of the familiar 'little steam train' from the branch in 1962 yet again attracted attention from the press and public. There was talk of a 'Donkey Preservation Society' aimed at retaining the service for sentiment or preserving the coach as a museum piece. Another group wanted to purchase 'the old Marlow Donkey steam train'

so that it could be put into a children's playground. However, what everyone seemed to overlook was that it was not just the passing of a steam locomotive that was to be mourned, but soon the very existence of the station and its dwindling complement of staff. Consequently much more was at stake. If it was simply the substitution of diesels at the head of each train, then the institution would still exist under yet another Freddie Funnel, but the changing role of the railway was irreversible and road haulage the victor.

The last day of steam-hauled services on Sunday, 7th July, attracted a number of railway enthusiasts and local people and according to the local press 'there were cheers all the way along the riverside route.' The local constabulary and railway police were there to check any exuberance but there was no trouble, only the customary detonators placed on the line, and on the Monday morning the new diesel railcar took over.

One of the booking clerks at Marlow in 1951 maintained that diesel railcars could not work the branch as efficiently as steam locos as their acceleration was too slow. This remark was undoubtedly prompted by Vic Hoare's driving technique. He would open the regulator 'pretty wide' soon after starting so that the train was travelling at about 25 mph by the time it reached the end of the platform! The speed on the run averaged about 30 miles per hour which was maintained until about Spade Oak crossing when steam was shut off.

Whether or not there was any perceptible difference to the passengers, the new railcars continue to perform well enough but the familiar sound of the sharp exhaust rapidly resounding away from the station, leaving only the lingering scent of warm oil, steam and coal, or the muffled gasp of the engine as it gently screeched its way round the shady curve on the riverbank, whistling its approach to Bourne End, are now but fading memories.

The story which follows is one of the usual 'rationalisation' or pruning. During the last two years of the old

A wet day c.1960.

M. Esau

Marlow station in 1965.

A. E. Smith

station there were just two members of staff, Reg House in the booking office and Ted Garrett on the platform. To those who knew it before, the station must have seemed like a cemetery. Freight services were withdrawn on 18th July 1966 and the old station was pulled down in favour of industrial development. A new passenger platform was erected in the goods yard and opened on 10th July 1967, proving adequate for the branch railcar to draw alongside to collect its payload.

For a while the trackwork of the old station was retained to serve the timber company which took over the site, but even this arrangement became surplus to requirements and was taken out of use on 26th July 1970 and subsequently removed. A frail office and waiting room was initially provided on the new passenger platform and opened each morning for the convenience of commuters from approximately 6.30 to 10.30 a.m., but with no staff the structure suffered from vandalism and even this short-lived accommodation was removed, although another rude shelter has since been provided.

If the Marlow Donkey was so named after the trains of pack horses, mules and donkeys carrying goods to the riverside, then in the shape of the diesel railcars which still ply back and forth across the riverside meadows, it lives on, albeit that on arrival at Marlow such 'donkeys' retrace the path of a siding into the goods yard and halt alongside a simple unadorned platform screened from new development occupying the old station site by a row of rapid growth conifers, not without resemblance to a continental scene. The old station, pride of Wethered, Borgnis and the other Great Marlow Railway directors, the long sun-soaked platform which bore volunteers for the South African War, the Great War and many servicemen from the Second World War, the fire in the booking office which once comforted Guy Gibson, the goods shed through which the town's groceries were unloaded each morning, the engine shed which sheltered the sooty sparrows, the well in which George Harding's pike was kept, and the humble iron range in the crew's mess room where the kettle perpetually boiled over a low flame, are now only memories.

The offices of the station building were inadequate enough to require extension as recently as 1947, but when the accommodation became surplus to requirements in the 1967 re-ordering, the painstaking subject of Victorian craftsmen was mercilessly torn down.

Malcolm McIntyre Ure

Servicing Greenwich Sawmills' private siding in the spring of 1951.

J. H. Venn

APPENDICES

Appendix 1 — GREENWICH SAWMILLS

The photos in this section are courtesy R. Stephenson unless otherwise stated.

In 1941 when Greenwich Sawmills secured a contract to run a dispersal site for the Ministry of Supply, handling imported Canadian softwoods and another for the import of large African hardwood logs, they needed to expand their facilities. By this time, the company, established in 1930 by Ronald Gale, who had other business interests in South East London, was jointly owned and run by his two sons and the Stephenson brothers, Leslie and Reginald. Their father had owned a sawmill at Peckham, South East London at the time of the Great War. The mill had dealt mainly with imported softwood unloaded on the Thames at Imperial Wharf, Greenwich, but it is hardly surprising that as a consequence of the war they looked away from London and established another mill alongside the railway at Marlow.

The new site occupied five acres of a large plot bought from builders Y. J. Lovell, who had already established a sawmill nearby. When Greenwich Sawmills first took over the plot, they built a transformer house adjoining a fitters shop inherited from Lovells. Constructed of brick, it had a flat concrete roof and was erected to house a transformer and associated fittings provided by Wessex Electricity Co. Initially the company acquired a horizontal band mill by Haigh-Grouven of Oldham and in 1942 the wooden building in which it was housed was extended by one bay to accommodate a band resaw. In 1945 it was extended again to house a French Guilliet AQV 44 inch vertical band mill brought down from Greenwich.

Initially supplies were landed at the GWR docks at Brentford, forwarded by rail to Marlow station and roaded the short distance around the corner into the mill. However, it was not long before the company had its own private siding, which was not only convenient but must have greatly relieved congestion in the goods yard.

The entrance to the private siding.   *Cty. Monica Jones*

163

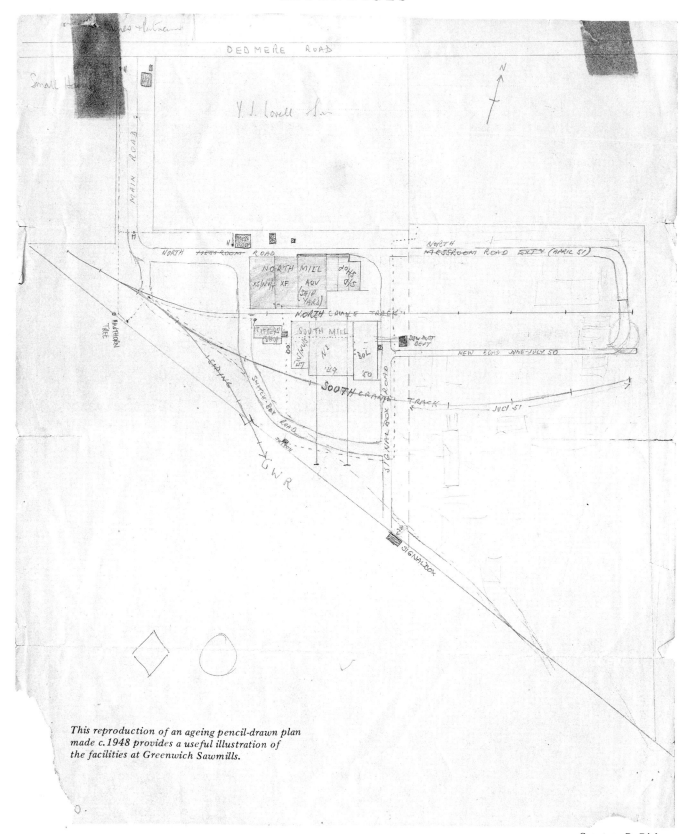

This reproduction of an ageing pencil-drawn plan made c.1948 provides a useful illustration of the facilities at Greenwich Sawmills.

Courtesy R. Rigby

Smith crane No. 10935 at work on 'No. 1 track' about 1947-8.

GWR records show the siding was first ordered on 14th May 1946 at an estimated cost of £1,120, chargeable to Greenwich Sawmills, and on 13th December that year the 'provision of additional connection to serve existing crane track, and engine stop board for the Greenwich Sawmills Ltd.' was approved, estimated at £131 11s 2d. Although the official 'into use date' was 29th January 1947, the siding agreement was not signed until 7th March. On 5th June the following year 'additional siding accommodation for Greenwich Sawmills Ltd' at £363 4s 9d was noted as completed that day.

A standard gauge railway track (the crane track referred to) had been laid in the sawmill prior to the siding connection. It was used by the mill's own rail-mounted cranes to move timber around the yard and was slewed to connect with the GWR's connection. Richard Rigby, formerly manager of Greenwich Sawmills, remembers 'many truck loads of foundry slag being brought to the site and offloaded by GWR gang by shovel. This made a beautiful top ballast.' He managed to find some correspondence that confirms the installation of the siding connection took place soon after 11th December 1946 — 'the whole of the new siding was ballasted from gate to stopblocks (GWR standard, made from bullhead rails). There was a left-hand turnout facing east about halfway along it to connect to our No. 1 track (end-on junction) and a similar turnout nearer to the gate to which we connected our No. 2 track'. He thinks the turnout for

Robinson vertical band mill XJ/NV/S inside the original wooden structure of the 'new mill'. Delivered new from the Rochdale factory, the machine was installed and operating by 21st June 1947, shortly before this picture was taken.

the No. 2 track was probably that approved on 13th December 1946. The additional siding accommodation approved in June 1948 appears to have been the extension of the siding (now effectively a headshunt) onto a newly acquired triangular plot of land to the west. All the sidings were laid with the mill's own labour, using second-hand rails and sleepers purchased either from the GWR or William Jones Ltd. of Charlton, SE7.

In 1947 another mill was erected opposite the first to house a Robinson 54 inch vertical band mill XJ/NV/S which arrived that May, and, with increasing machinery, the brick-built workshops became a sawdoctor's shop, situated alongside the old mill, expanded to three bays by 1949 when a new brick-built office/mess block was erected in the entrance off Dedmere Road. The work was executed by Lovells. In the reordering the foreman was provided with an office erected on the flat roof of the transformer house.

In February 1949 the new mill was extended to accommodate a Robinson horizontal band mill type N2/T with a 40 ft log carriage and the following year a third bay was added to house a Swedish saw frame. The new mill

An Avon electric saw mounted on a lorry, and being used to centre cut a huge oak butt in the early 1960s. It was too large a diameter to cut on the band mill which had a maximum cut of 65 inches. This type of saw, with its 8 ft long blade, had been in use since 1941, the one depicted being purchased new in about 1950. All oversize logs were handled by the Avon, and a chain saw was used for smaller logs.

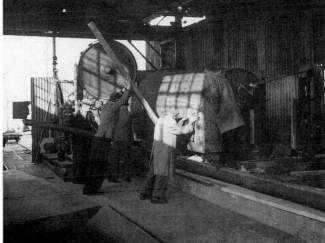

Three more views of the Robinson mill on the same site but now sheltered by the replacement steel-framed corrugated iron building of 1950. The first picture was taken looking south whilst the others are looking north. Although this was a multi-purpose machine, it usually dealt with larger logs. The pictures show slabbing in progress whereby the log is reduced to manageable proportions for handling by the horizontal machine.

Foundations being prepared for the installation of the Robinson 72 inch horizontal band mill which would be sheltered by the second bay of the new mill structure. Marlow signal box can be seen in the background.

structures employed steel framing with corrugated iron or brick walls and a corrugated asbestos roof. The 'temporary buildings' of the old mill were retained and from about 1950 became a workshop for the production of wooden pallets and packing cases.

The most obvious expansion took place in 1953 when a large plot of land adjoining the eastern boundary was purchased from Folley Brothers. Nos. 1 and 2 sidings were extended onto it and totalled 493 ft and 356 ft respectively. At the same time two more sidings, known as numbers 3 and 4 tracks, were laid onto the new land to serve storage areas, new drying kilns and associated boiler house, and new storage sheds. A new retail outlet alongside the offices at the entrance brought the site to more or less its full development, at least as far as Greenwich Sawmills is concerned.

The very nature of such an industry brought about continued changes within the site, consequent upon machine life, updating facilities, demand, etc. Even as early as 1944 the Haigh-Grouven horizontal band mill in

the first shed was replaced by a Robinson 54 inch vertical band mill XJ/NV/T with a 20 ft log carriage, and this in turn was later replaced by a 5 cutter planing machine. The Guilliet 44 inch band mill was sold to a Leicester company and in 1954 the Swedish frame saw was moved out of the third bay of the new mill into a new wooden shed alongside to make way for a new band mill. The reason for the move is not apparent, but there were doubtless other changes before Greenwich sold out.

Timber supplies were brought in with regular goods traffic and up to six wagons at a time were shunted into the mill siding and left for one of the steam cranes to collect. Empties were collected whenever it was convenient. Four-wheeled wagons were generally adequate for the purpose but bogie bolsters were used from time to time. An exceptional load remembered in the mid-1960s was a huge log from West Africa. Measuring 8 ft 6 ins across the butt and weighing some 26 tons, it had to be cut into three 12-14 ft sections for handling by the mill's cranes. Finished timber was generally distributed or collected by

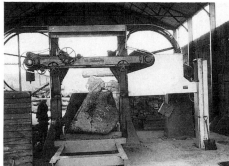

The Robinson band mill shortly after installation in February 1949. The centre left view is taken looking south and the others looking north. The narrow gauge tracks serving the band mills were laid using second-hand materials and old bogies made by Hudsons of Morley, Leeds, were used to move timber around.

Looking west towards the station about 1950 with one of the Smith 5-ton cranes at work on No. 1 track. All six mill bays are visible here, the new on the left and the old on the right, whilst the smaller brick buildings on the right were occupied by the 'saw doctor'.

The new mill c.1950. The wood in the foreground had almost certainly been received by road and was awaiting preparation and distribution.

Mahogany being stacked to air dry alongside North Road.

Looking east along the original siding (now a headshunt) with No. 1 track diverging to the left. The hawthorn tree on the extreme right was a remnant of a row of trees which formed the western boundary of GSM's site prior to the first expansion. The cranes are the Smith 5-tonners, Nos. 11698 and 10935.

A large log straddling No. 1 track being handled by the 5-ton Stothert & Pitt shunting crane. This picture provides a reasonable view of the brick-built 'saw doctor's shop'.

Top left: Greenwich Sawmills had no lorries themselves, but instead hired as required. This one, owned by Gordon Lee of Amersham, is pictured leaving the main entrance with a load of sawn timber. *Left:* Not all supplies arrived by rail, as witnessed by the load on this 4-wheel trailer. *Above:* The retail premises just inside the main entrance off Dedmere road in the mid-1950s. *Below:* Occasionally mobile cranes were hired to move timber inaccessible to railborne cranes. This picture shows a Coles crane on an AEC Matador chassis (ex RAF).

The Swedish vertical frame saw (sometimes known as a 'gang saw') newly installed in its second siting alongside the 'new mill' c.1954. An export model, callibrated in Imperial measurement, this machine could cope with logs up to 100 ft in length and 33 ins diameter. The three 'cyclones' in the background collected sawdust from the extractors serving various machines. From here the sawdust could be bagged for removal.

An earlier view of the same machine in its original position in the third (eastern) bay of the 'new mill' c.1950.

Nos. 2, 3 and 4 tracks and the entrance to the private siding in the mid-1950s. The corrugated iron building on the left is the western end of the 'new mill' whilst the buildings in the background were storage houses for timber from the kilns situated behind the large stacks. Air drying was a lengthy business, particularly when, for example, fresh sawn oak can have a moisture content of approximately 80 per cent which has to be reduced to at least 15 or 16 per cent before it is suitable for joinery and/or the furniture industry. Doubtless it was a great relief to the Greenwich company when the general licensing of new building was relaxed c.1952 sufficiently to allow the erection of the kiln in 1953 and associated drying sheds, the latter predictably Nissen huts. With coal burning, at first the boiler house was served by No. 4 track but it eventually proved more practicable to burn scrap wood from the site. Wagons were exchanged between BR and the sawmill just inside the gate, like the wagons illustrated which have been left for collection by one of the shunting cranes. In order to leave the siding free to accept deliveries, empty wagons were generally assembled on Nos. 3 and 4 tracks and only placed on the siding when required for collection by BR.

The delivery of the Stothert & Pitt 20-ton shunting crane in 1962 prompted a rare view of the engine shed and pump house.

Smith 5-ton crane No. 10935.

Stothert & Pitt 5-ton shunting crane.

road, one of the more obvious markets being the local chair industry at High Wycombe.

From 1st February 1965 the mill was sold to Y. J. Lovell (Holdings) Ltd., of which James Davies Ltd., a Swindon timber merchant, was a subsidiary. Operating as Marlow Timber Industries Ltd., the new owners only kept the business until May 1970, when Y. J. Lovell developed the site into the present day industrial estate.

CRANES

At first a pair of Smiths of Rodley contractors steam cranes of 2½ and 3 ton capacities were sent from Greenwich but neither was large enough for the work that developed at Marlow and both were returned by 1946. They were replaced by two second-hand 5-ton contractors cranes, again by Smiths, and in 1947 a 5-ton shunting crane by Stothert & Pitt. The Smiths cranes (weighing some 22-24 tons) were purchased from the London branch of Sheffield-based Thomas Ward Ltd. and the Sonning gravel pit of Messrs. Folley Brothers. The latter, in poor condition after many years' hard work, was dismantled at Sonning and rebuilt at Marlow with a 40 ft lattice jib and new boiler. The shunting crane was a particularly useful acquisition, at last providing an official means of moving the numerous railway wagons around the yard. Built in 1917 and purchased second- or even third-hand, from Stafford Timber Company in 'deplorable condition', it was rebuilt with a new standard 5-ton Smiths boiler and proved 'first class' in service, apparently handling 7-8 ton lifts! It weighed about 38 tons in working order.

In 1958 another second-hand 5-ton shunting crane, built by Smiths of Rodley, was purchased from Cox & Danks Ltd. Built about 1942 for the Admiralty, this crane had not been used much and only needed new piston rods due to bad rust pitting in storage.

Handling increasingly large timber supplies eventually brought about the purchase of a 20-ton railway breakdown crane in 1962. Built by Stothert & Pitt of Bath in

The Stothert & Pitt 5-ton crane about to perform a lift.

The Stothert & Pitt 20-ton shunting crane working alongside the 'new mill'.

A late 1950s view of the timber yard as seen from the end of the station platform. *A. Attewell*

1913, it was purchased from the Dover Harbour Board who acquired it from the War Office after the Second World War, and replaced the original 30 ft jib with a 45 ft version with a swan neck. As delivered, it exhausted its cylinders straight into the atmosphere through a vertical pipe alongside the boiler rather than through the chimney. With this unfortunate arrangement there was no draw on the fire and it was quickly winded — the pressure falling rapidly from 100 p.s.i. to 20 with one lift! Conversion to the normal blast pipe arrangements overcame the problem.

A transhipment of fresh European timber, probably from King's Lynn or Poplar Docks, being unloaded using a steel wire sling. This early 1960s picture shows the end of No. 2 track after extension onto the former Folley Bros.' land.

Appendix 2 — TRAFFIC DEALT WITH

GREAT WESTERN RAILWAY.

STATEMENT OF TRAFFIC DEALT WITH AT STATIONS (481)

STATION (Halt or Platform) **BOURNE END**

Joint with: _____ Railway

Names of other Stations, etc., Traffic and Receipts from which are included below

or Names of Stations, Halts, Platforms, supervised

DIVISION _____

SUPERVISED BY _____

	1935		1936		1937		1938		1939		1940	
YEAR	TO BE FILLED IN BY D.S.O.		TO BE FILLED IN BY D.S.O.		TO BE FILLED IN BY D.S.O.		TO BE FILLED IN BY D.S.O.		TO BE FILLED IN BY D.S.O.		TO BE FILLED IN BY D.S.O.	
NUMBER OF AUTHORISED STAFF — Clerical and Supervisory	4		4		4		4		4		4	
Wages	17		17		17		17		17		17	
Total Traffic Paybill Expenses £	3546		3597		3565		3447		232		252	
COACHING TRAFFIC.	NUMBER	RECEIPTS £	NUMBER	RECEIPTS £	NUMBER	RECEIPTS £	NUMBER	RECEIPTS £	NUMBER	RECEIPTS £	NUMBER	RECEIPTS £
Passengers Booked by Rail, including Excess Fares Collected	47328	3542	46454	3563	49456	3385	49231	3354	49495	3673	55999	4583
Season Tickets	1585	2254	1669	2360	1749	2656	1527	2399	1670	2350	2352	3234
Platform Tickets												
Seat Registration		12		12		12		14		6		5
Cab Rents and Car Parking		6		14		13		14		16		18
Lavatories		3		21		7		11		6		10
Other Receipts												
Total Passenger and Various Receipts £		587		6970		6273		5790		6061		4830
Parcels Forwarded	5257	493	5884	577	5200	463	5697	553	5494	569	4669	445
Parcels Received	10006	1	10307	2	10244		9621	2	9736		8212	
Miscellaneous Forwarded	1472	137	2113	216	2094	197	2113	180	1878	172	1989	188
Miscellaneous Received	336	48	325	50	1005	62	680	54	384	50	1427	124
Total Parcels and Misc. Traffic and Receipts £	17152	679	18629	843	18543	422	18111	789	17402	791	16292	757
TOTAL COACHING RECEIPTS £		6496		6813		6995		6579		6892		8607
GOODS TRAFFIC	FORWARDED TONS	RECEIVED TONS	FORWARDED TONS	RECEIVED TONS	FORWARDED TONS	RECEIVED TONS	FORWARDED TONS	RECEIVED TONS	FORWARDED TONS	RECEIVED TONS	FORWARDED TONS	RECEIVED TONS
Coal and Coke, Not Charged		31906		31994		36648		32536		36623		35917
Coal and Coke, Charged	8	805		1109		844	29	929	122	941		1528
Other Minerals	59	3459	93	3552	51	4018	63	3223	53	2573	205	2425
General Merchandise, Carted	3685	5477	4085	6136	4708	9755	4025	6815	4674	9376	5652	12260
General Merchandise, Agreed Charges Traffic	1831	15	1718	29	1779	2296	1453	1971	1531	1865		
General Merchandise, Not Carted	5585	4960	5896	46361	6538	53561	5570	45473	6400	50378	5857	52130
Total Tonnage Wagons	4 6328	9425	2 6650	9354	7166	10940	6377	9228	7444	9699		
Total Receipts £												
Total Goods Tonnage and Goods and Live Stock Receipts Forwarded and Received — TONNAGE	52490	15579	52267	16012	60099	18108	51043	15605	56778	17143		
RECEIPTS £												
TOTAL RECEIPTS (i.e., Coaching, Goods and £)	22275		22825		25103		22184		23995			
Other Coaching Traffic (Items not shown above)	NUMBER		NUMBER		NUMBER		NUMBER		NUMBER		NUMBER	
Forwarded Milk — Gallons / Cans / Tanks / No.												
Non-Railborne												
Permitted Tonnage	TONS		TONS		TONS		TONS		TONS		TONS	
Other Goods Traffic (Items not shown above) — Loco.	F.H. 641		F.H. 1056		F.H. 114		F.H. 239		F.H. 180		F.H. 79	
Loco, Coal and Free Hauled (Totals) £	124		146		173		171		207			
Total Other Tonnages and Receipts £					3							
Non-Railborne — FORWARDED / RECEIVED												
Permitted Tonnage												
Total Number of Invoices	9256		9202		8185		14040		15073		10765	913
Total Number of Invoice Entries	13117		13170		13591		18289		14570		13444	12951

* Also includes Receipts from Outboundary and other Cartage (excluding Non-Railborne), Weighbridge Receipts, Warehouse Rent, Siding Rent, Shunting Charges, Demurrage, and other Miscellaneous Items.

24 Bks., 2025 bks. in all.—Est. 405—4-34 (24)

GREAT WESTERN RAILWAY.

STATEMENT OF TRAFFIC DEALT WITH AT STATIONS

(481 A)

DIVISION _____

STATION (Halt or Platform) __BOURNE END__

Joint with _____

Names of other Stations, etc., Traffic and Receipts from which are included below

or Names of Stations, Halts, Platforms, supervised

_____ Railway

	1944		1942		1943		1944		1945		1946	
YEAR	TO BE FILLED	IN BY D.S.O.	TO BE FILLED	IN BY D.S.O.	TO BE FILLED	IN BY D.S.O.	TO BE FILLED	IN BY D.S.O.	TO BE FILLED	IN BY D.S.O.	TO BE FILLED	IN BY D.S.O.
SUPERVISED BY												
NUMBER OF AUTHORISED STAFF — Clerical and Supervisory	4	17	4	17	4	19	4	28	4	20	4	6
Wages												19
Total Traffic Paybill Expenses	£ 2286	5225	£ 2292	5240	£ 2362	6027	£ 2357	6020	£ 2382	6175	£ 2363	£ 7068

COACHING TRAFFIC.

	NUMBER	RECEIPTS	NUMBER	RECEIPTS	NUMBER	RECEIPTS	NUMBER	RECEIPTS	NUMBER	RECEIPTS	NUMBER	RECEIPTS
Passengers Booked by Rail, including Excess Fares Collected	64613	£ 6593	81113	£ 7246	93981	£ 8818	89912	£ 8316	84971	£ 8756	69900	£ 8508
Season Tickets	3407	£ 4714	2475	£ 3418	2259	£ 3491	3683	£ 4530	2764	£ 3413	2529	£ 4491
Platform Tickets		£		£		£		£		£		£ 16
Seat Registration		£		£		£		£		£		£
Cab Rents and Car Parking		£ 9		£ 15		£ 8		£ 2		£ 3		£ 12
Lavatories		£ 24		£ 30		£ 34		£ 32		£ 25		£ 56
Other Receipts		£ 6		£		£		£		£		£ 21
Total Passenger and Various Receipts	£	11346	£	10616	£	12351	£	12940	£	12672	£	98221
Parcels Forwarded		£ 661		£ 712		£ 1474		£ 8551		£ 8951		£ 528
Parcels Received		£ 3		£ 9		£ 5		£ 2		£ 3		£ 3
Miscellaneous Forwarded		£ 123		£		£		£		£		£ 5168
Miscellaneous Received		£ 30		£		£		£		£		£ 3
Total Parcels and Misc. Traffic and Receipts	£	817	£	921	£	1479	£	1600	£	1601	£	525
TOTAL COACHING RECEIPTS	£	12163	£	11737	£	13830	£	14540	£	14278	£	13111

GOODS TRAFFIC.

	FORWARDED TONS.	RECEIVED TONS.	FORWARDED TONS.	RECEIVED TONS.	FORWARDED TONS.	RECEIVED TONS.	FORWARDED TONS.	RECEIVED TONS.	FORWARDED TONS.	RECEIVED TONS.	FORWARDED TONS.	RECEIVED TONS.
Coal and Coke, Not Charged (on "Weight" Invoices — Charges raised by Audit Office)		36027		35828		37453		36649		30706		29457
Coal and Coke, Charged (including "Weight" Invoice traffic charges raised by Stations)	283	3439	45	2757		674	14	177	5	32	6	231
Other Minerals (Classes 1 to 6)	15	1470	55	1964	117	1710		2257	89	2322	82	505
General Merchandise (Classes 7 to 21)	5400	12374	5755	10676	6435	11972	8384	14968	7083	11092	6325	6245
Total Tonnage	5698	53310	5850	51020	6552	51809	8398	54051	7144	50194	6416	38930
Total Goods Tonnage Forwarded and Received		TONNAGE 59008		TONNAGE 56870		TONNAGE 58361		TONNAGE 62449		TONNAGE 57335		TONNAGE 45344

Live Stock Forwarded and Received

	Wagons	NUMBER	Wagons	NUMBER	Wagons	NUMBER	Wagons	NUMBER	Wagons	NUMBER	Wagons	NUMBER

Other Coaching Traffic (Items not shown above)

	Gallons	NUMBER	Gallons	NUMBER	Gallons	NUMBER	Gallons	NUMBER	Gallons	NUMBER	Gallons	NUMBER
Forwarded Milk (Included in Miscellaneous Forwarded above)	Cans	Cases	Cans	Cases	Cans	Cases	Cans	Cases	Cans	Cases	Cans	Cases
Non-Railborne	Tanks	£	Tanks	£	Tanks	£	Tanks	£	Tanks	£	Tanks	£
	No.	£	No.	£	No.	£	No.	£	No.	£	No.	£

Other Goods Traffic (Items not shown above)

	TONS.	RECEIVED.	TONS.	RECEIVED.	TONS.	RECEIVED.	TONS.	RECEIVED.	TONS.	RECEIVED.	TONS.	RECEIVED.
Loco, Coal and Free Hauled (Totals)	Loco. F.H. 20		Loco. F.H. 82		Loco. F.H. 1738		Loco. F.H. 24		Loco. F.H. 35		Loco. 42 F.H. 740	
Total Other Tonnages (i.e., Domestic, Point to Point & Tolls)											Loco. 87	
Non-Railborne												
Permitted Tonnage	FORWARDED.	RECEIVED.	FORWARDED.	RECEIVED.	FORWARDED.	RECEIVED.	FORWARDED.	RECEIVED.	FORWARDED.	RECEIVED.	FORWARDED.	RECEIVED.
Total Number of Invoices	10735	9909	10105	9300	10250	9423	10120	8575	12064	8244	13355	5009
Total Number of Invoice Entries	12839	11824	12931	11996	12742	11931	12549	10370	14226	10272	16599	5500

335

179

GREAT WESTERN RAILWAY.

STATEMENT OF TRAFFIC DEALT WITH AT STATIONS

(481 A)

_____ Railway

STATION (Halt or Platform) BOURNE END

Joint with _____

Names of other Stations, etc., Traffic and Receipts from which are included below
or Names of Stations, Halts, Platforms, supervised

DIVISION _____

SUPERVISED BY _____

		1947			1948			1949			1950			1951			1952		
NUMBER OF AUTHORISED STAFF.			TO BE FILLED IN BY D.S.O.			TO BE FILLED IN BY D.S.O.			TO BE FILLED IN BY D.S.O.			TO BE FILLED IN BY D.S.O.			TO BE FILLED IN BY D.S.O.			TO BE FILLED IN BY D.S.O.	
	Clerical and Supervisory	4			5			4									3		
	Wages	9			8			9									7		
Total Traffic Paybill Expenses		£430	£7500		£422	£9839		£447	£8861		£	£		£	£		£934	£977	
COACHING TRAFFIC.		NUMBER.	RECEIPTS.		NUMBER.	RECEIPTS.		NUMBER.	RECEIPTS.		NUMBER.	RECEIPTS.		NUMBER.	RECEIPTS.		NUMBER.	RECEIPTS.	
Passengers Booked by Rail, including Excess Fares Collected		55318	£6474		56029	£7480		47199	£6076		40136	£6349		40220	6063		37122	£406	
Season Tickets		1908	4072		1832	4294		1617	5722		1429	3808		1405	3919		1309	4105	
Platform Tickets			£			£			£			£			£			£	
Seat Registration			£			£			£			£			£			£	
Cab Rents and Car Parking			12			11			12			11			45			44	
Lavatories			20			12			16			20			15			44	
Other Receipts			£			£			£			4			16			24	
Total Passenger and Various Receipts		£	10598		£	9811		£	9616		£	9703		£	9058		£	9900	
Parcels Forwarded		7343	662			744		7444	£603		7520	£1145		7772	£1142		8225	902	
Parcels Received		8815			8808	8746		8376			7776			7471			680		
Miscellaneous Forwarded			£			£			£			£			£			£	
Miscellaneous Received			£			£			£			£			£			£	
Total Parcels and Misc. Traffic and Receipts		16158	662		17550	472		15720	£603		£	1145		15243	1142		14890	962	
TOTAL COACHING RECEIPTS		£	11260		£	12555		£	10419		£	10348		£	10200		£	9962	
GOODS TRAFFIC.		FORWARDED TONS.	RECEIVED TONS.		FORWARDED TONS.	RECEIVED TONS.		FORWARDED TONS.	RECEIVED TONS.		FORWARDED TONS.	RECEIVED TONS.		FORWARDED TONS.	RECEIVED TONS.		FORWARDED TONS.	RECEIVED TONS.	
Coal and Coke, Not Charged			31476			34537			38447			42847			44693			34070	
Coal and Coke, Charged			27			33			99			43			44			28	
Other Minerals (Classes 1 to 6)		149	219		63	1912		17	843		21	2103		10	2009		1041	
General Merchandise (Classes 7 to 21)		4116	10603		3561	12945		3724	11023		3741	8717		2805	11869		3086	0139	
Total Tonnage		4265	44347		3624	49424		3770	8738			3189	83812		2805	58435		3086	45884	
Total Goods Tonnage Forwarded and Received			48684			53066			55152			57071			61250			48970	
Live Stock Traffic Forwarded and Received		Wagons	TONNAGE.		Wagons	TONNAGE.		Wagons	TONNAGE.		Wagons	TONNAGE.		Wagons	TONNAGE.		Wagons	TONNAGE.	
Other Coaching Traffic (Items not shown above)		NUMBER.			NUMBER.			NUMBER.			NUMBER.			NUMBER.			NUMBER.		
		Gallons			Gallons			Gallons			Gallons			Gallons			Gallons		
Forwarded Milk (Included in Miscellaneous Forwarded above)		Cans	£		Cans	£		Cans	£		Cans	£		Cans	£		Cans	£	
		Tanks	£		Tanks	£		Tanks	£		Tanks	£		Tanks	£		Tanks	£	
Non-Railborne		No.			No.			No.			No.			No.			No.		
Other Goods Traffic (Items not shown above)		TONS.	TONS.		TONS.	TONS.		TONS.	TONS.		TONS.	TONS.		TONS.	TONS.		TONS.	TONS.	
Loco. Coal and Free Hauled (Totals)		Loco.	F.H. 514		Loco.	F.H. 347		Loco.	F.H. 331		Loco.	F.H. 98		Loco.	F.H. 140		Loco.	F.H. 263	
Total Other Tonnages (i.e. Domestic, Point to Point & Tolls)		1	£ 1034			£1311			£F35		7	£1673			£1443			1239	
Non-Railborne																				
Permitted Tonnage		FORWARDED.	RECEIVED.		FORWARDED.	RECEIVED.		FORWARDED.	RECEIVED.		FORWARDED.	RECEIVED.		FORWARDED.	RECEIVED.		FORWARDED.	RECEIVED.	
Total Number of Invoices		14328	1726		15738	5931		12231	1644		12877	966		10811	1302		3252	1622	
Total Number of Invoice Entries		7994	1885		891	5511		14936	1868		14941	10053		8491	1327		11382	1351	

24 bks. in £ 3,210 and 48 index leaves. B.M. 30.—1941. (28).

181 lvs. in all—Est. 405—4-34 (29)

GREAT WESTERN RAILWAY.

STATEMENT OF TRAFFIC DEALT WITH AT STATIONS (481)

DIVISION _____

SUPERVISED BY _____

STATION (Halt or Platform) __MARKOW__

Joint with _____ Railway

Names of other Stations, etc., Traffic and Receipts from which are included below
or Names of Stations, Halts, Platforms, supervised

YEAR	1935		1936		1937		1938		1939		1940	
NUMBER OF AUTHORISED STAFF	TO BE FILLED IN BY D.S.O.											
Clerical and Supervisory	4		4		4		4		4		4	
Wages	9		9		9		9		9		9	
Total Traffic Paybill Expenses	£2093		£2767/1919		£20?/1946		£206		£2103		£2505	

COACHING TRAFFIC.

	NUMBER	RECEIPTS	NUMBER	RECEIPTS	NUMBER	RECEIPTS	NUMBER	RECEIPTS	NUMBER	RECEIPTS	NUMBER	RECEIPTS
Passengers Booked by Rail, including Excess Fares Collected	36968	£3787	34389	£3865	36769	£3854	35282	£3663	34334	£3735	48162	£6096
Season Tickets	1294	1685	1266	1780	1276	1908	1214	1785	1527	1856	5530	2911
Platform Tickets		£		£		£		£		£		£
Seat Registration		£ —		£		£		£		£		£
Cab Rents and Car Parking		£15		£13		£14		£18		£15		£513
Lavatories		£9		£13		£14		£10		£9		£2
Other Receipts		£		£1		£		£		£		£3
Total Passenger and Various Receipts		£5474		£5672		£5790		£5476		£5615		£9034
Parcels Forwarded	4852	£454	5485	£511	5566	£503	4402	£383	3983	£341	5117	£479
Parcels Received	21726	£30	23799	£16	23808	£5	23389	£1	22234	£—	21969	£2
Miscellaneous Forwarded	961	£103	803	£83	816	£93	1064	£103	871	£76	810	£105
Miscellaneous Received	2260	£120	951	£111	893	£46	547	£43	617	£57	4298	£29
Total Parcels and Misc. Traffic and Receipts	29799	£707	31018	£720	20369	£647	29352	£530	27405	£474	32192	£615
TOTAL COACHING RECEIPTS		£6201		£6592		£6437		£6006		£6089		£9649

GOODS TRAFFIC.

	FORWARDED TONS	RECEIVED TONS	FORWARDED TONS	RECEIVED TONS	FORWARDED TONS	RECEIVED TONS	FORWARDED TONS	RECEIVED TONS	FORWARDED TONS	RECEIVED TONS	FORWARDED TONS	RECEIVED TONS
Coal and Coke, Not Charged (on "Weight" Invoice—Charges dealt with by Audit Office)		10154		11658		10405		10962		11392		14413
Coal and Coke, Charged (Including "Weight" Invoice traffic charges raised by Stations)		1617		1771		2400		1329		1681		1538
Other Minerals	114	3862	244	3981	406	2640	154	855	106	919	176	1035
General Merchandise, Carted (Collected, Delivered and)	565	1563	389	1523	375	1542	322	1793	345	2225	114	2845
General Merchandise, Agreed Charges Traffic					53	223	41	435	75	543	871	
General Merchandise, Not Carted	85	665	742	600	855	392	517					
Total Tonnage	568	17721	742	19169	855	17502	517	15375	520	16760	1161	20231
Total Receipts	£752	£5694	£866	£5856	£894	£5585	£692	£4644	£676	£5200	£	£
Live Stock Forwarded and Received	Wagons 123		Wagons 46	153	Wagons 27	87	Wagons 15	42	Wagons 32	42	Wagons 46	420
Total Goods Tonnage and Goods and Live Stock Receipts Forwarded and Received	TONNAGE 18289	RECEIPTS £6785	20509	£6815	18357	£6576	15892	£5278	17280	£6296	21392	£
TOTAL RECEIPTS (i.e., Coaching, Goods and Live Stock)		£12986		£13267		£12973		£11284		£12385		£

Other Coaching Traffic (Items not shown above)

	NUMBER		NUMBER		NUMBER		NUMBER		NUMBER		NUMBER	
Forwarded Milk (Included in Miscellaneous Forwarded above) Gallons	8220		9479		11104		11832		6867		1058	
Cans	780	Cases	724	Cases	731	Cases	897	Cases	771	Cases 126		Cases
Tanks				48		53		60				
No.	41									36		
Non-Railborne	£		£		£		£		£		£	

Other Goods Traffic (Items not shown above)

	TONS	F.H.	TONS	F.H.	TONS	F.H.	TONS	F.H.	TONS	F.H.	TONS	F.H.
Loco, Coal and Free Hauled (Totals) Loco.		149		522		178		261		243		118
Non-Railborne (i.e., Domestic, Point to Point & Tolls)	£165		£246		£405		£291		£261		£	
Permitted Tonnage												
Total Number of Invoices	3461	12703	3572	12912	3490	12875	3562	11468	3548	12044	3241	12719
Total Number of Invoice Entries	4642	19742	4701	19576	4316	19342	4242	19236	4326	19763	4560	19328

* Also includes Receipts from Outboundary and other Cartage (excluding Non-Railborne), Weighbridge Receipts, Warehouse Rent, Siding Rent, Shunting Charges, Demurrage, and other Miscellaneous Items.

GREAT WESTERN RAILWAY.

STATEMENT OF TRAFFIC DEALT WITH AT STATIONS

(481 A)

STATION (Halt or Platform) **MARLOW**

Joint with _____

Names of other Stations, etc., Traffic and Receipts from which are included below
or Names of Stations, Halts, Platforms, supervised

_____ Railway

DIVISION _____

SUPERVISED BY _____

YEAR	1941		1942		1943		1944		1945		1946	
	NUMBER.	TO BE FILLED IN BY D.S.O.	NUMBER.	TO BE FILLED IN BY D.S.O.	NUMBER.	TO BE FILLED IN BY D.S.O.	NUMBER.	TO BE FILLED IN BY D.S.O.	NUMBER.	TO BE FILLED IN BY D.S.O.	NUMBER.	TO BE FILLED IN BY D.S.O.
NUMBER OF AUTHORISED STAFF — Clerical and Supervisory	5		5		5		5		4		4	
Wages	9		7		11		11		11		7	
Total Traffic Paybill Expenses	£ 2935	2935	£ 3293	3293	£ 3668	3668	£ 3894	3894	£ 4041	4041	£ 4136	4136

COACHING TRAFFIC.

	NUMBER.	RECEIPTS.	NUMBER.	RECEIPTS.	NUMBER.	RECEIPTS.	NUMBER.	RECEIPTS.	NUMBER.	RECEIPTS.	NUMBER.	RECEIPTS.
Passengers Booked by Rail, including Excess Fares Collected	65905	£ 7930	87901	£ 9816	102798	£ 12563	91802	£ 12371	92698	£ 13467	66689	£ 10862
Season Tickets	3490	4512	2623	2954	2119	2894	4166	4045	3404	3437	3153	3654
Platform Tickets												
Seat Registration												
Cab Rents and Car Parking		£ 17		£ 19		£ 20		£ 19		£ 20		£ 24
Lavatories		£ 12		£ 16		£ 16		£ 17		£ 13		£ 12
Other Receipts						£ 6		£ 6		£ 7		£ 12
Total Passenger and Various Receipts	£	12471	£	12865	£	15499	£	16463	£	16939	£	14564
Parcels Forwarded	£		£		£		£		£		£	
Parcels Received	£		£		£		£		£		£	2148
Miscellaneous Forwarded	£		£		£		£		£		£	
Miscellaneous Received	£		£		£		£		£		£	
Total Parcels and Misc. Traffic and Receipts	£	708	£	921	£	1549	£	1903	£	2600	£	2148
TOTAL COACHING RECEIPTS	£	13179	£	13786	£	17048	£	18366	£	19539	£	16712

GOODS TRAFFIC.

	FORWARDED TONS.	RECEIVED TONS.	FORWARDED TONS.	RECEIVED TONS.	FORWARDED TONS.	RECEIVED TONS.	FORWARDED TONS.	RECEIVED TONS.	FORWARDED TONS.	RECEIVED TONS.	FORWARDED TONS.	RECEIVED TONS.
Coal and Coke, Not Charged (on "Weight" Invoice—Charges dealt with by Audit Office)		14479		13193		14483		15067		15583		13799
Coal and Coke, Charged (including "Weight" Invoice traffic charges raised by Stations)		3122		1985		915		378		16		25
Other Minerals (Classes 1 to 6)	69	964	82	562	11	314	126	416	123	843	282	587
General Merchandise (Classes 7 to 21)	1667	3305	1359	7134	206	11629	4051	4147	1070	7666	825	3767
Total Tonnage	1878	24870	1630	23494	2164	21912	1603	20008	1193	24108	1107	24198
Total Goods Tonnage Forwarded and Received	TONNAGE 25748		TONNAGE 25124		TONNAGE 24016		TONNAGE 21638		TONNAGE 25301		TONNAGE 19285	
Live Stock Forwarded and Received	Wagons 32		Wagons 31		Wagons		Wagons 9		Wagons 54		Wagons 43	

Other Coaching Traffic (Items not shown above)

	NUMBER.		NUMBER.		NUMBER.		NUMBER.		NUMBER.		NUMBER.	
Forwarded Milk (Included in Miscellaneous Forwarded above) — Gallons												
Cans	£		£		£		£		£		£	
Tanks	£		£		£		£		£		£	
Non-Railborne — No.	£		£		£		£		£		£	

Other Goods Traffic (Items not shown above)

	TONS.		TONS.		TONS.		TONS.		TONS.		TONS.	
Loco. Coal and Free Hauled (Totals) — Loco.	F.H.		F.H.		F.H.		F.H.		F.H. 21		F.H.	
Total Other Tonnages (i.e., Domestic, Point to Point & Totals)												
Non-Railborne												

Permitted Tonnage

	FORWARDED.	RECEIVED.	FORWARDED.	RECEIVED.	FORWARDED.	RECEIVED.	FORWARDED.	RECEIVED.	FORWARDED.	RECEIVED.	FORWARDED.	RECEIVED.
Total Number of Invoices	2389	13940	1954	12700	3016	10303	3094	30707	1733	10056	1249	8903
Total Number of Invoice Entries	3858	19177	1477	16449	3762	12366	3181	14043	3218	14440	2621	13475

GREAT WESTERN RAILWAY.

STATEMENT OF TRAFFIC DEALT WITH AT STATIONS (481 A)

15○

STATION (Halt or Platform) MARLOW

Joint with _____ Railway

Names of other Stations, etc., Traffic and Receipts from which are included below
or Names of Sections, Halts, Platforms, supervised

VISION _____ REVISED BY _____

	1947		1948		1949		1950		1951		1952	
YEAR	TO BE FILLED IN BY D.S.O.		TO BE FILLED IN BY D.S.O.		TO BE FILLED IN BY D.S.O.		TO BE FILLED IN BY D.S.O.		TO BE FILLED IN BY D.S.O.		TO BE FILLED IN BY D.S.O.	
NUMBER OF STAFF EMPLOYED — Clerical and Supervisory	46		4/6		3/6				2/9		2/9	
Wages												
Total Traffic Paybill Expenses	£	3714	£	4210	£	3988	£		£		£	
COACHING TRAFFIC	NUMBER	RECEIPTS	NUMBER	RECEIPTS	NUMBER	RECEIPTS	NUMBER	RECEIPTS	NUMBER	RECEIPTS	NUMBER	RECEIPTS
Passengers Booked by Rail, including Excess Fares Collected	52375	£8218	50070	£8946	46909	£6837	44516	£5669	46591	£5290	43758	£5300
Season Tickets	2000	£3062	1504	£2967	1246	£2705	1963	£2705	885	£2376	99	£3012
Platform Tickets												
... Registration												
... Rents and Car Parking		£38		£36		£10		£18				£12
Lavatories		£12				£13		£14		£12		£13
Other Receipts		£12		£11		£12		£6		£1		£11
Total Passenger and Various Receipts	£	11342	£	11710	£	9577	£	8641	£	7891	£	8348
Parcels Forwarded	15952	£1297	17856	£1515	7965		7157		8839	£1370	7973	£1184
Parcels Received	21546	£2	24917	£1497	25849		21930		21390	£44	20110	£93
Miscellaneous Forwarded												
Miscellaneous Received												
Total Parcels and Misc. Traffic and Receipts	36998	£1627	31953	£1565	30494	£1408	29190	£1240	30230	£1414	28082	£1277
TOTAL COACHING RECEIPTS	£	12969	£	13341	£	10985	£	9851	£	9305	£	

GOODS TRAFFIC

	1947 FORWARDED TONS	RECEIVED TONS	1948 FORWARDED TONS	RECEIVED TONS	1949 FORWARDED TONS	RECEIVED TONS	1950 FORWARDED TONS	RECEIVED TONS	1951 FORWARDED TONS	RECEIVED TONS	1952 FORWARDED TONS	RECEIVED TONS
Coal and Coke, Not Charged (on "Weight" Invoices—Charges dealt with by Audit Office)		12946		12264		10741						
Coal and Coke, Charged (including "Weight" Invoice charges raised by Stations)	302	18	73	18	73	124						
Other Minerals (Classes 1 to 6)	248	383	506	506	519	175						
General Merchandise (Classes 7 to 21)	577	953	858	3732	419	3561						
Total Tonnage	825	1353			1010	14041						
Total Goods Tonnage Forwarded and Received		18312		17954		15051						
Live Stock Forwarded and Received	Wagons 12		Wagons 43		Wagons 55		Wagons		Wagons		Wagons	

Other Coaching Traffic (Items not shown above)

	NUMBER	Cases	NUMBER	Cases	NUMBER	Cases	NUMBER	Cases	NUMBER	Cases	NUMBER	Cases
Forwarded Milk (Included in Miscellaneous Forwarded above) — Gallons / Cans / Tanks / No.												
Non-Railborne												

Other Goods Traffic (Items not shown above)

	TONS	F.H.	TONS	F.H.	TONS	F.H.	TONS	F.H.	TONS	F.H.	TONS	F.H.
Loco, Coal and Free Hauled (Totals)		175		40		76						
Total Other Tonnages (i.e., Domestic, Point to Point & Totals)	FORWARDED	RECEIVED	FORWARDED	RECEIVED	FORWARDED	RECEIVED	FORWARDED	RECEIVED	FORWARDED	RECEIVED	FORWARDED	RECEIVED
Non-Railborne												
Permitted Tonnage												
Total Number of Invoices	219	4612	292	1935	265	1449						
Total Number of Invoice Entries	234	4313	298	2055	265	1975						

805

BRITISH RAILWAYS
WESTERN REGION

STATEMENT OF TRAFFIC DEALT WITH AT STATIONS

481A

DISTRICT _London_   STATION (Halt or Platform) _Marlow_   Region _____

Joint with _____

SUPERVISED BY STATION MASTER AT _____

Names of other Stations, etc., Traffic and Receipts from which are included below
or Names of Stations, Halts, Platforms, supervised

YEAR	1953 NUMBER	1953 RECEIPTS	1954 NUMBER	1954 RECEIPTS	1955 NUMBER	1955 RECEIPTS	1956 NUMBER	1956 RECEIPTS	1957 NUMBER	1957 RECEIPTS	1958 NUMBER	1958 RECEIPTS
Number of Staff Regularly Employed :—												
Clerical and Supervisory	3		3		3		3		3		3	
Wages	6		6		3		3		3		3	
TOTAL	9		9		6		6		6		6	
COACHING TRAFFIC												
Passengers Booked by Rail, including Excess Fares Collected	44730	£5377	44812	£5485	40943	£5385	41260	£5856	50463	7863	51788	£7,217
Season Tickets	1014	£3413	1013	£3314	757	3057	769	£3270	963	3983	696	£4,661
Platform Tickets												
Seat Registration												
Cab Rents												
Car Parking		£15		£14		£19		£28		31		£41
Lavatories		£13		£13		£11		£15		15		£13
Other Receipts		£12						£6		6		£19
Total Passenger and Various Receipts		£8840		£8826		£8472		£9169		11898		£11,641
Parcels & Misc. Forwarded	8030	£1336	8272	£1543	9113	£1997		£1969	7485	1729	8715	1,799
Parcels & Misc. Received	19747	£105	19075	£28	18875	£8		£19	20373	77	19,890	34
Total Parcels and Misc Traffic and Receipts	27377	£1498	27347	£1571	27988	£2005		£1988	27858	1806	28,605	1,833
TOTAL COACHING RECEIPTS		£10326		£10397		£10477		£11157		£13704		£13,674

GOODS TRAFFIC	FORWARDED TONS	RECEIVED TONS	FORWARDED TONS	RECEIVED TONS	FORWARDED TONS	RECEIVED TONS	FORWARDED TONS	RECEIVED TONS	FORWARDED TONS	RECEIVED TONS	FORWARDED TONS	RECEIVED TONS
Coal and Coke											10,837	
Other Minerals (Classes 1 to 6)									651	485	705	230
General Merchandise (Classes 7 to 21)									55	3632	361	2,207
Total Tonnage									706	14,503	1,086	13,274

	TONNAGE Forwarded and Received	Wagons		TONNAGE	Wagons		TONNAGE	Wagons		TONNAGE	Wagons		TONNAGE	Wagons
Total Goods Tonnage Forwarded and Received									5007 / 6,254	2	14,360	6

	NUMBER		NUMBER		NUMBER		NUMBER		NUMBER		NUMBER	
Live Stock Forwarded and Received												
Other Coaching Traffic (items not shown separately above)	Gallons		Gallons		Gallons		Gallons		Gallons		Gallons	
Forwarded Milk (Included in Parcels and Misc. Forwarded above) — Cans												
Tanks												
No.												
Non-Railborne (Not included above)												
Other Goods Traffic (items not shown above) — TONS												
Loco, Coal and Free Hauled (Totals)	F.H.		F.H.		F.H.		F.H.		Loco F.H. 151 46 wagons		Loco F.H. 196 500	
Total Other Tonnages (i.e., Domestic, Point, to Point and Toll)												
Non-Railborne	FORWARDED	RECEIVED	FORWARDED	RECEIVED	FORWARDED	RECEIVED	FORWARDED	RECEIVED	FORWARDED	RECEIVED	FORWARDED	RECEIVED
Permitted Tonnage												
Total Number of Invoices									148		214	
Total Number of Invoice Entries									1836		1,622	

BRITISH RAILWAYS
WESTERN REGION

STATEMENT OF TRAFFIC DEALT WITH AT STATIONS

481A

STATION (Halt or Platform) MARLOW

DISTRICT LONDON

Joint with Region

Names of other Stations, etc., Traffic and Receipts from which are included below

SUPERVISED BY STATION MASTER AT or Names of Stations, Halts, Platforms, supervised

YEAR	1959		19		19		19		19		19	
Number of Staff Regularly Employed :—												
Clerical and Supervisory ...	3											
Wages ...	3											
TOTAL ...	6											
COACHING TRAFFIC	NUMBER	RECEIPTS	NUMBER	RECEIPTS	NUMBER	RECEIPTS	NUMBER	RECEIPTS	NUMBER	RECEIPTS	NUMBER	RECEIPTS
Passengers Booked by Rail, including Excess Fares Collected	52773	£ 7255		£		£		£		£		£
Season Tickets ...	903	£ 5064		£		£		£		£		£
Platform Tickets ...	—	£	—	£	—	£	—	£	—	£	—	£
Seat Registration ...	—	£	—	£	—	£	—	£	—	£	—	£
Cab Rents ...	—	£	—	£	—	£	—	£	—	£	—	£
Car Parking ...	—	£	—	£	—	£	—	£	—	£	—	£
Lavatories ...	—	£	—	£	—	£	—	£	—	£	—	£
Other Receipts ...	—	£ 60	—	£	—	£	—	£	—	£	—	£
Total Passenger and Various Receipts ...	—	£ 12379	—	£	—	£	—	£	—	£	—	£
Parcels & Misc. Forwarded ...	10707	£ 2407		£		£		£		£		£
Parcels & Misc. Received ...	20055	£ 25		£		£		£		£		£
Total Parcels and Misc Traffic and Receipts ...	30762	£ 2432		£		£		£		£		£
TOTAL COACHING RECEIPTS ...	—	£ 14811	—	£	—	£	—	£	—	£	—	£
GOODS TRAFFIC	FORWARDED TONS	RECEIVED TONS	FORWARDED TONS	RECEIVED TONS	FORWARDED TONS	RECEIVED TONS	FORWARDED TONS	RECEIVED TONS	FORWARDED TONS	RECEIVED TONS	FORWARDED TONS	RECEIVED TONS
Coal and Coke ...	-	8929										
Other Minerals (Classes 1 to 6) ...	644	-										
General Merchandise (Classes 7 to 21) ...	213	3464										
Total Tonnage ...	857	12509										
Total Goods Tonnage Forwarded and Received	TONNAGE 13366		TONNAGE		TONNAGE		TONNAGE		TONNAGE		TONNAGE	
Live Stock Forwarded and Received ...	Wagons		Wagons		Wagons		Wagons		Wagons		Wagons	
Other Coaching Traffic (Items not shown separately above)	NUMBER		NUMBER		NUMBER		NUMBER		NUMBER		NUMBER	
Forwarded Milk (Included in Parcels and Misc. Forwarded above) ...	Gallons		Gallons		Gallons		Gallons		Gallons		Gallons	
	Cans	Cases	Cans	Cases	Cans	Cases	Cans	Cases	Cans	Cases	Cans	Cases
	Tanks	£	Tanks	£	Tanks	£	Tank	£	Tanks	£	Tanks	£
Non-Railborne (Not included above) ...	No.	£	No.	£	No.	£	No.	£	No.	£	No.	£
Other Goods Traffic (Items not shown above) ...	TONS	TONS	TONS	TONS	TONS	TONS	TONS	TONS	TONS	TONS	TONS	TONS
Loco. Coal and Free Hauled (Totals) ...	Loco. 155	F.H. 34	Loco.	F.H.	Loco.	F.H.	Loco.	F.H.	Loco.	F.H.	Loco.	F.H.
Total Other Tonnages (i.e., Domestic, Point to Point and Tolls) ...												
Non-Railborne ...												
	FORWARDED	RECEIVED	FORWARDED	RECEIVED	FORWARDED	RECEIVED	FORWARDED	RECEIVED	FORWARDED	RECEIVED	FORWARDED	RECEIVED
Permitted Tonnage ...												
Total Number of Invoices ...	309	1616										
Total Number of Invoice Entries ...												

Appendix 3 — LOCOMOTIVES ALLOCATED TO MARLOW

LOCOMOTIVES RECORDED ON MARLOW BRANCH SERVICES PRIOR TO 1902

Year	Number	Class
1895	565	'517' 0—4—2T
	981	'Metro' 2—4—0T
	1156	'517' 0—4—2T
1896	1195	Standard Goods 0—6—0
1897	535	'517' 0—4—2T

LOCOS ALLOCATED TO MARLOW

Year	Number	Class
1902	617	'Metro' 2—4—0T
	620	" "
	972	" "
	3585	" "
1903	4	'Metro' 2—4—0T
	616	" "
	620	" "
	981	" "
	1411	" "
	1460	" "
	3583	" "
1904	464	'Metro' 2—4—0T
	467	" "
	619	" "
	967	" "
	976	" "
	981	" "
	982	" "
	986	" "
	1419	" "
	3582	" "
1905	5	'Metro' 2—4—0T
	6	" "
	463	" "
	619	" "
	967	" "
	976	" "
	981	" "
	982	" "
	1423	'517' 0—4—2T
	3563	'Metro' 2—4—0T
1906	5	'Metro' 2—4—0T
	6	" "
	458	" "
	463	" "
	466	" "
	467	" "
	623	" "
	981	" "
	3568	" "
1907	6	'Metro' 2—4—0T
	458	" "
	467	" "
	623	" "
1908	5	'Metro' 2—4—0T
	456	" "
	458	" "
	623	" "
	1408	" "

Year	Number	Class
	3564	" "
	3570	" "
	3583	" "
1909	5	'Metro' 2—4—0T
	456	" "
	615	" "
	3582	" "
	3591	" "
	3594	" "
	3599	" "
1910	5	'Metro' 2—4—0T
	456	" "
	613	" "
	1417	" "
	1454	" "
	3582	" "
	3594	" "
	3597	" "
1911	5	'Metro' 2—4—0T
	1415	" "
	1454	" "
	3569	" "
1912	5	'Metro' 2—4—0T
	1406	" "
	1454	" "
	3585	" "
1913	1454	'Metro' 2—4—0T
	3561	" "
	3563	" "
	3566	" "
	3581	" "
	3595	" "
1914	1417	'Metro' 2—4—0T
	3562	" "
	3563	" "
	3581	" "
	3582	" "
	3584	" "
	3587	" "
	3596	" "
1915	1404	'Metro' 2—4—0T
	1408	" "
	1417	" "
	3500	" "
	3562	" "
	3581	" "
	3584	" "
1916	1404	'Metro' 2—4—0T
	1411	" "
	3561	" "
	3563	" "
	3569	" "
	3581	" "
	3584	" "
	3587	" "
1917	1408	'Metro' 2—4—0T
	1411	" "
	1417	" "
	3563	" "
	3569	" "
	3582	" "

Year	Number	Class
	3596	" "
	3599	" "
1918	1403	'Metro' 2—4—0T
	1408	" "
	1418	" "
	3594	" "
	3596	" "
1919	1418	'Metro' 2—4—0T
	3564	" "
	3566	" "
	3581	" "
	3582	" "
	3587	" "
	3594	" "
1920	1409	'Metro' 2—4—0T
	3566	" "
	3581	" "
	3582	" "
	3584	" "
	3587	" "
	3594	" "
	3596	" "
1921	1403	'Metro' 2—4—0T
	1418	" "
	3566	" "
	3581	" "
	3587	" "
	3596	" "
1922	1409	'Metro' 2—4—0T
	1418	" "
	3561	" "
	3563	" "
	3565	" "
	3566	" "
	3569	" "
	3596	" "
1923	1408	'Metro' 2—4—0T
	1409	" "
	1418	" "
	3561	" "
	3563	" "
	3564	" "
	3565	" "
	3581	" "
	3594	" "
1924	1403	'Metro' 2—4—0T
	1408	" "
	3561	" "
	3581	" "
	3594	" "
	3596	" "
1925	616	'Metro' 2—4—0T
	1403	" "
	3563	" "
	3569	" "
	3596	" "
1926	616	'Metro' 2—4—0T
	1403	" "
	3563	" "
	3565	" "

Year	Number	Class	Year	Number	Class	Year	Number	Class
1927	616	'Metro' 2—4—0T	1934	3568	'Metro' 2—4—0T	1940	4837	'48XX' 0—4—2T
	986	,, ,,		3583	,, ,,		4842	,, ,,
	1406	,, ,,		3592	,, ,,		4862	,, ,,
	1408	,, ,,	1935	2026	'2021' 0—6—0ST	1941	4837	'48XX' 0—4—2T
	3561	,, ,,		3568	'Metro' 2—4—0T		4842	,, ,,
	3563	,, ,,		3583	,, ,,	1942	4837	'48XX' 0—4—2T
1928	459	'Metro' 2—4—0T		3592	,, ,,		4842	,, ,,
	616	,, ,,		4827	'48XX' 0—4—2T	1943	4837	'48XX' 0—4—2T
	1407	,, ,,		4838	,, ,,		4842	,, ,,
	3594	,, ,,		4847	,, ,,	1944	4837	'48XX' 0—4—2T
	3599	,, ,,	1936	4807	'48XX' 0—4—2T		4842	,, ,,
1929	972	'Metro' 2—4—0T		4809	,, ,,		4844	,, ,,
	1497	,, ,,		4838	,, ,,	1945	4807	'48XX' 0—4—2T
	3596	,, ,,		4842	,, ,,		4837	,, ,,
1930	1403	'Metro' 2—4—0T		4847	,, ,,		4842	,, ,,
	3564	,, ,,		4862	,, ,,	1946	1437	'48XX' 0—4—2T
	3588	,, ,,	1937	4807	'48XX' 0—4—2T		1442	,, ,,
	3589	,, ,,		4809	,, ,,	1947	1437	'48XX' 0—4—2T
	3595	,, ,,		4817	,, ,,		1441	,, ,,
1931	1404	'Metro' 2—4—0T		4842	,, ,,		1442	,, ,,
	3583	,, ,,		4847	,, ,,		1446	,, ,,
	3588	,, ,,		4862	,, ,,		2112	'2021' 0—6—0PT
	3589	,, ,,	1938	4807	'48XX' 0—4—2T		3562	'Metro' 2—4—0T
	3595	,, ,,		4809	,, ,,		5421	'54XX' 0—6—0PT
	3598	,, ,,		4817	,, ,,	1948	1437	'48XX' 0—4—2T
1932	1404	'Metro' 2—4—0T		4837	,, ,,		1442	,, ,,
	2744	'2721' 0—6—0PT		4842	,, ,,			
	3563	'Metro' 2—4—0T		4862	,, ,,			
	3589	,, ,,	1939	4842	'48XX' 0—4—2T			
1933	*Details not available*			4862	,, ,,			

Cty. Mrs. E. Hobbs

Appendix 4 — ARCHITECTURAL DRAWINGS AND TRACK PLANS

BOURNE END TRAIN SHED
This drawing is based on a tantalizing official plan which provides some idea of the early arrangement of the Marlow bay platform.

The earliest known plan of Bourne End station taken from 25 inch Ordnance Survey for 1876.

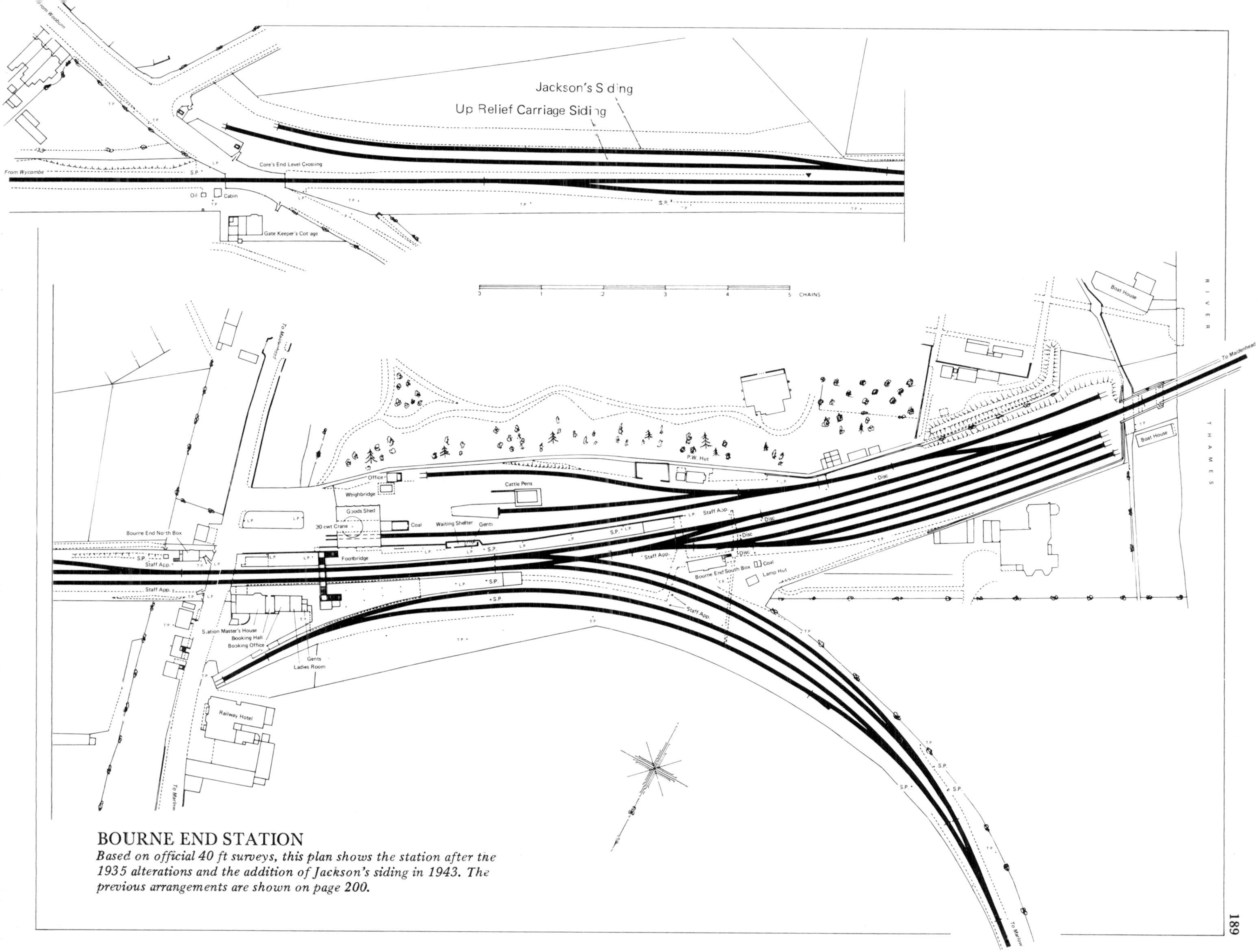

RIVER   THAMES

Boat House

Boat House

Jackson's Siding

Up Relief Carriage Siding

5 CHAINS

To Maidenhead

To Marlow

Coo's End Level Crossing

Gate Keeper's Cottage

Cabin

Oil

From Wooburn

From Wycombe

Jackson's Siding

P.W. Hut

Cattle Pens

Waiting Shelter Gents

Coal

Office

Weighbridge

Goods Shed

30 cwt Crane

Footbridge

Coal

Lamp Hut

Bourne End South Box

Staff App.

Staff App.

Station Master's House

Booking Hall

Booking Office

Gents

Ladies Room

Railway Hotel

Bourne End North Box

Staff App.

Staff App.

To Maidenhead

To Marlow

BOURNE END STATION

Based on official 40 ft surveys, this plan shows the station after the 1935 alterations and the addition of Jackson's siding in 1943. The previous arrangements are shown on page 200.

C. W. R. Marlow Branch.
Reconstruction of Viaduct over Bourne En

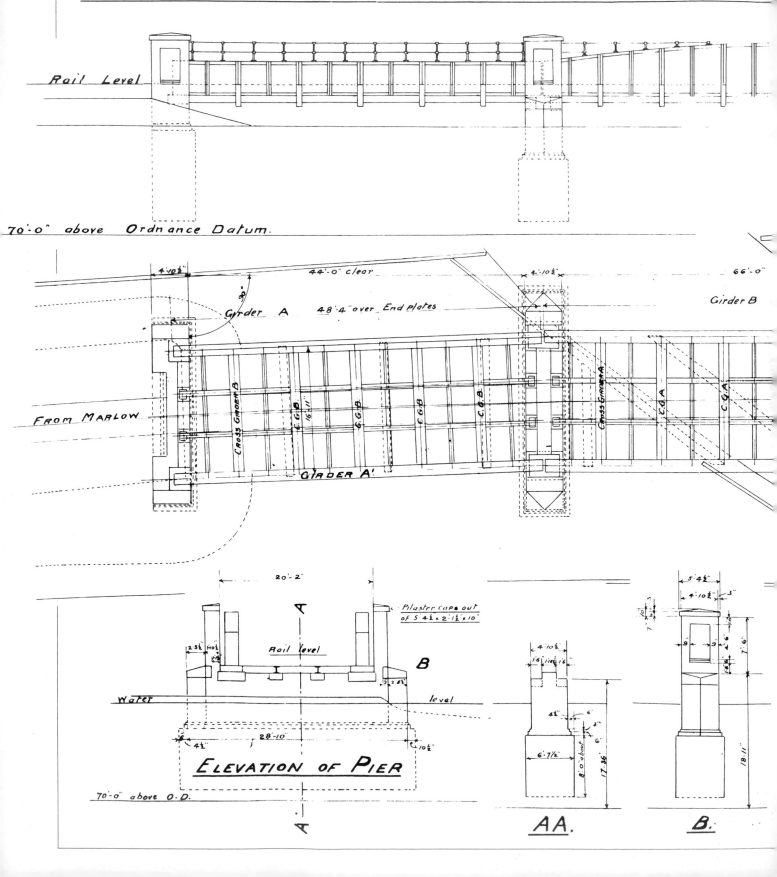

Rail Level

70'-0" above Ordnance Datum.

4'-10½"   44'-0" clear   4'-10½"   66'-0"

Girder A   48'-4" over End plates   Girder B

FROM MARLOW

Cross Girder B   E.G.B 16'-11"   E.G.B.   E.G.B   E.G.B   Cross Girder A   C.G.A   C.G.A

GIRDER A'

20'-2"

Pilaster Caps out of 5'4½" × 2'1½" × 10"

2'3½"   Rail level   B

Water   level

28'-10"   C 10½"

4½"

ELEVATION OF PIER

70'-0" above O.D.

A   A'

5'4½"
4'-10½"

4'-10½"   7'-6"
1'6" 1'10" 1'6"   18'-11"
6'-7½"   17'-36"

AA.   **B.**

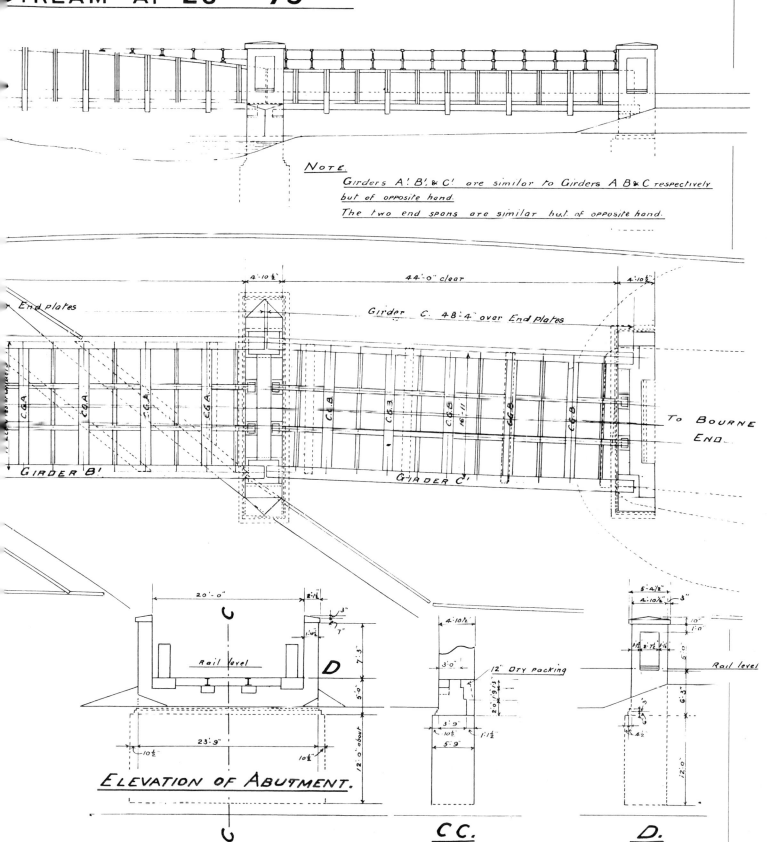

NOTE.

Girders A'. B'. & C' are similar to Girders A B & C respectively but of opposite hand.

The two end spans are similar but of opposite hand.

4'-10½"   44'-0" clear   4'-10½"

Girder C. 48'-4" over End plates

End plates

C.G.A.   C.G.A.   C.G.A.   C.G.A.   C.G.B.   C.G.B   C.G.B   C.G.B   C.G.B

16'-11"

GIRDER 'B'   GIRDER C'   To BOURNE END

ELEVATION OF ABUTMENT.

20'-0"   2'-1"

Rail level

C   D

7'-3"

5'-0"

23'-9"   12'-0" about

10½"   10½"

CC.

4'-10½"

3'-0"   12" Dry packing

20'-9½"

3'-9"   1'-1½"

10½"

5'-9"

D.

5'-4½"

4'-10½"   3"

Rail level

6'-3"

12'-0"

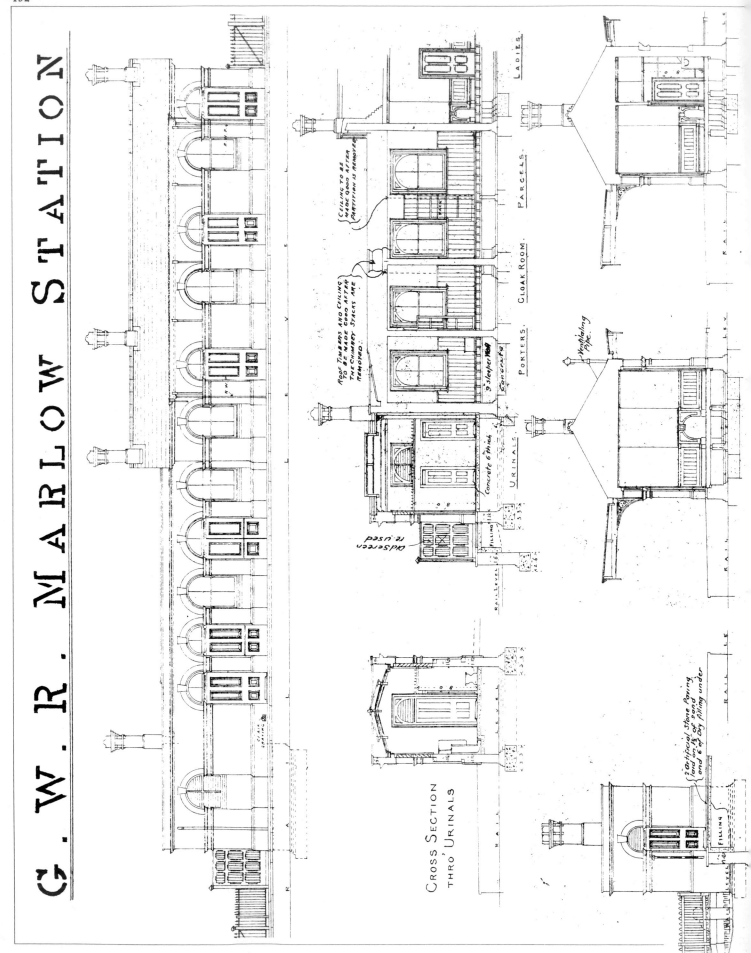

G. W. R. MARLOW STATION

CROSS SECTION THRO' URINALS

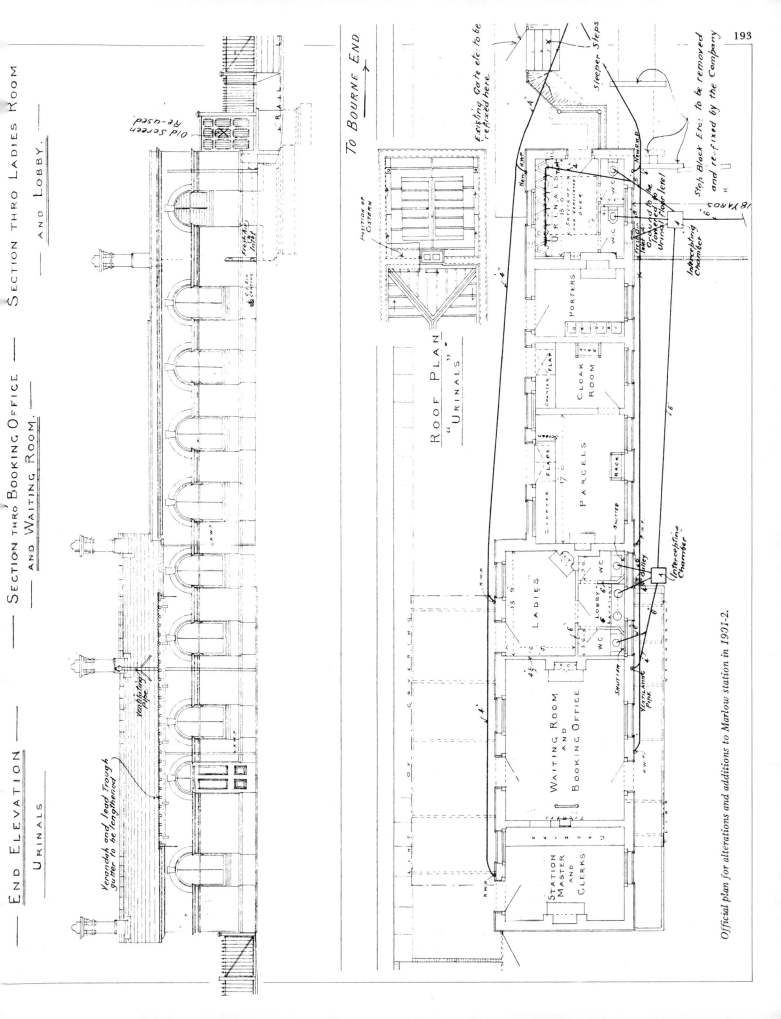

— END ELEVATION —

— Urinals —

— SECTION thro' BOOKING OFFICE —

and WAITING ROOM.

— SECTION thro LADIES ROOM —

— and LOBBY. —

Old Screen Re-used.

Fresh Air Inlet

Verandah and lead Trough gutter to be lengthened

Ventilating Pipe

TO BOURNE END

Existing Gate etc. to be re-fixed here

Sleeper Steps

Stop Block Etc: to be removed and re-fixed by the Company

18 YARDS 9

New RWP

URINALS 13.0

Skylight & Ventilator over

W.C

W.C W.C

Ground to be lowered to Urinal floor level

Intercepting Chamber

POSITION OF CISTERN

ROOF PLAN

"URINALS"

PORTERS

CLOAK ROOM

PARCELS 17.6

SHUTTER FLAPS

COUNTER FLAP

RACK

SHUTTER

RWP

LADIES 13.9

WC LOBBY WC

Galley

Intercepting Chamber

WAITING ROOM AND BOOKING OFFICE

SHUTTER

Ventilating Pipe

STATION MASTER AND CLERKS

RWP

LINE OF COVERING

VERANDAH

Official plan for alterations and additions to Marlow station in 1901-2.

194

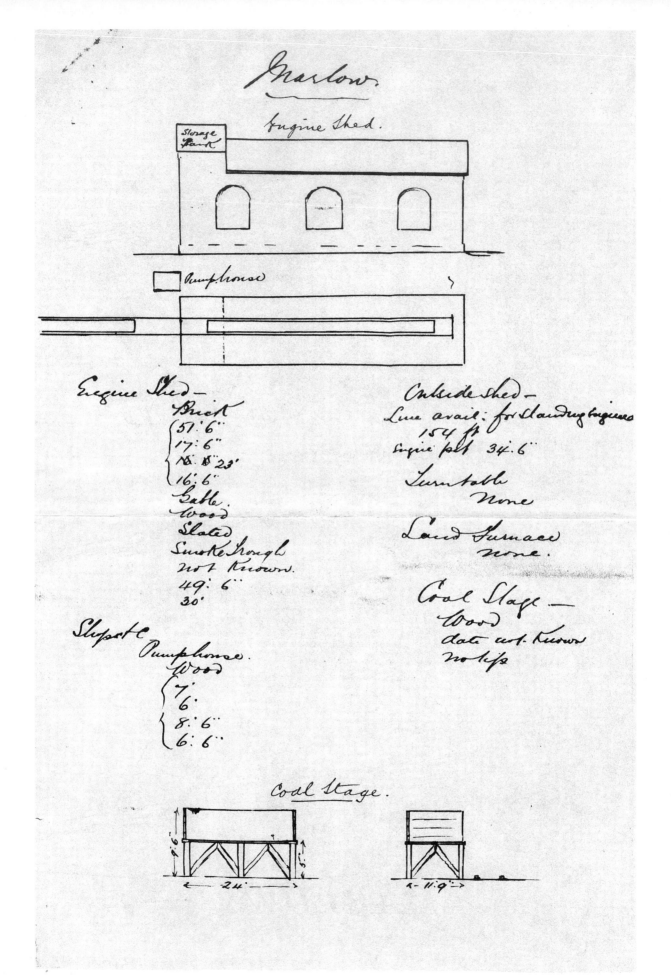

Reproduction of official sketch of 1901.

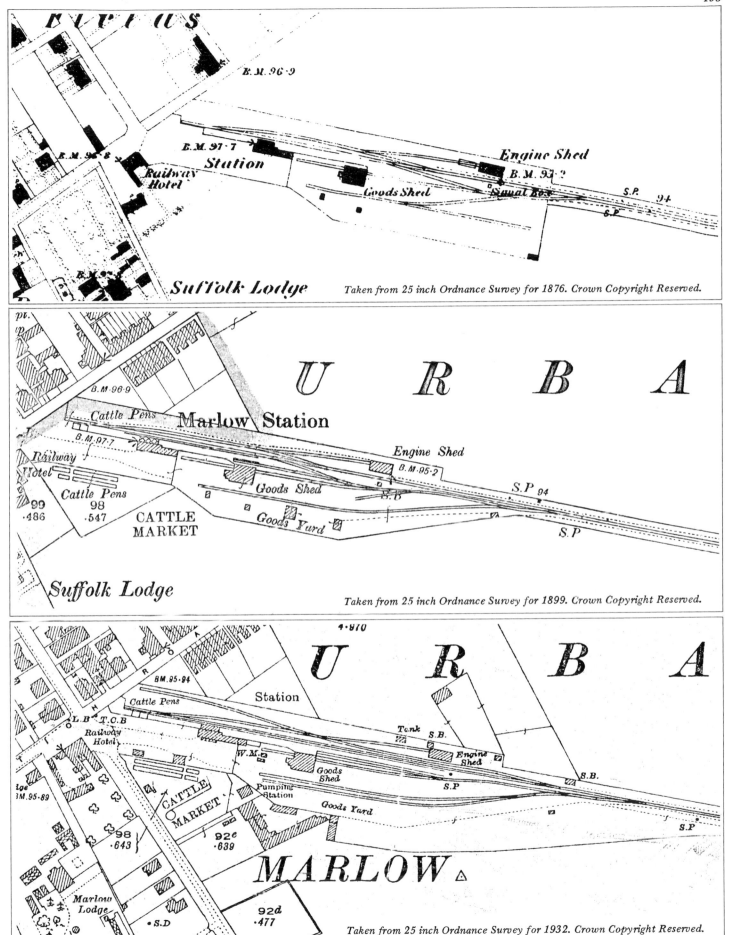

Taken from 25 inch Ordnance Survey for 1876. Crown Copyright Reserved.

Taken from 25 inch Ordnance Survey for 1899. Crown Copyright Reserved.

Taken from 25 inch Ordnance Survey for 1932. Crown Copyright Reserved.

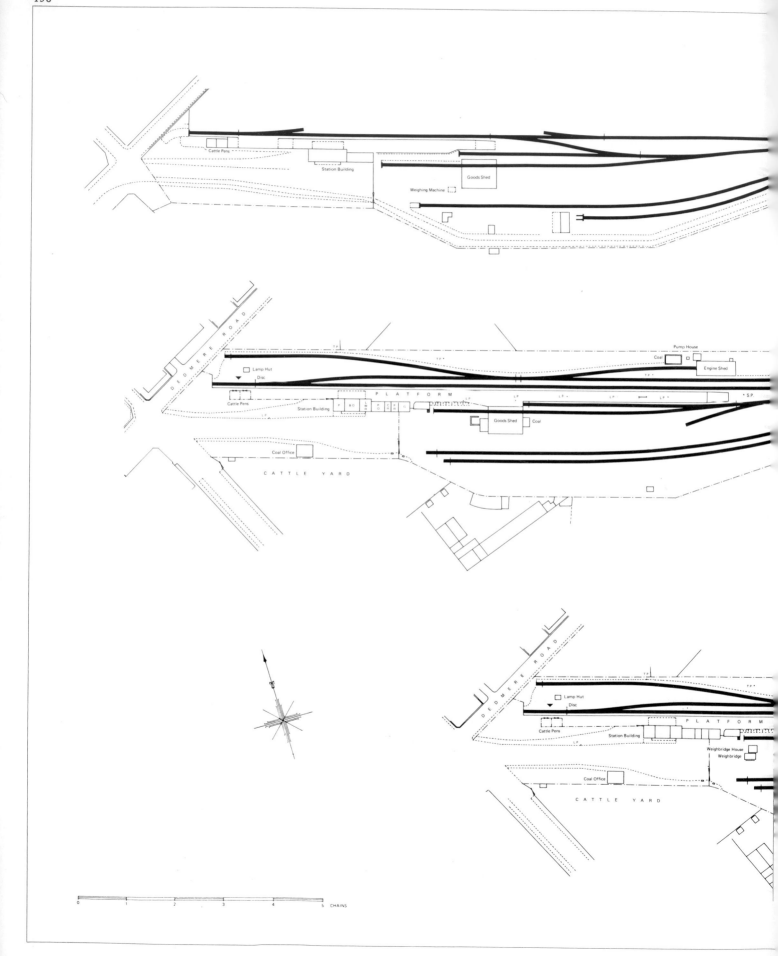

Cattle Pens

Station Building

Goods Shed

Weighing Machine

D E D M E R E   R O A D

Pump House

Coal

Engine Shed

Lamp Hut

Disc

Cattle Pens

P L A T F O R M

LP

LP

LP

LP

LP

LP

S.P.

Station Building

Goods Shed

Coal

Coal Office

C A T T L E   Y A R D

D E D M E R E   R O A D

Lamp Hut

Disc

Cattle Pens

P L A T F O R M

Station Building

Weighbridge House

Weighbridge

Coal Office

C A T T L E   Y A R D

0   1   2   3   4   5   CHAINS

MARLOW STATION

Extract of 1900 track plan included in official agreement to allow O. P. Wethered to pass 'along the company's roadway' along the edge of the yard from Station Road to the occupation crossing for 'cartage of hay and occasionally driving to and from the meadows in the tenant's occupation on the south side of the company's line'. The run-round loop, engine shed, signal box and the mysterious spur siding not featured on this plan are shown on the 1899 OS map on the previous page.

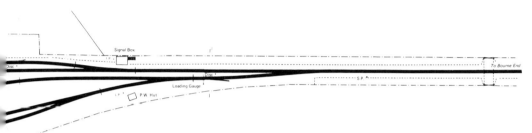

1912 track plan based on official 40 ft survey, showing signal box with steps facing Bourne End. Without photographic evidence it is difficult to establish whether this was (a) a proposal not carried out (b) the original position of steps fitted to the box illustrated elsewhere (c) a signal box preceding that known.

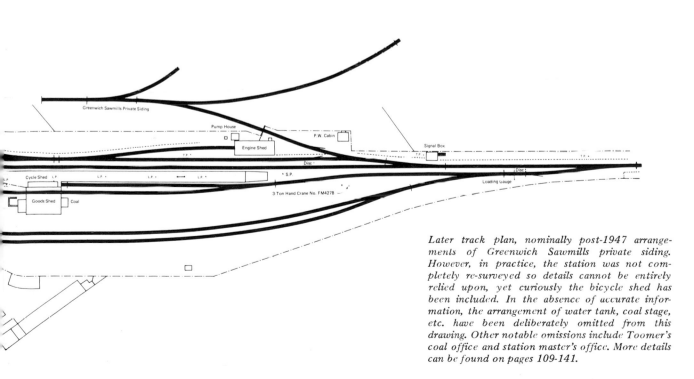

Later track plan, nominally post-1947 arrangements of Greenwich Sawmills private siding. However, in practice, the station was not completely re-surveyed so details cannot be entirely relied upon, yet curiously the bicycle shed has been included. In the absence of accurate information, the arrangement of water tank, coal stage, etc. have been deliberately omitted from this drawing. Other notable omissions include Toomer's coal office and station master's office. More details can be found on pages 109-141.

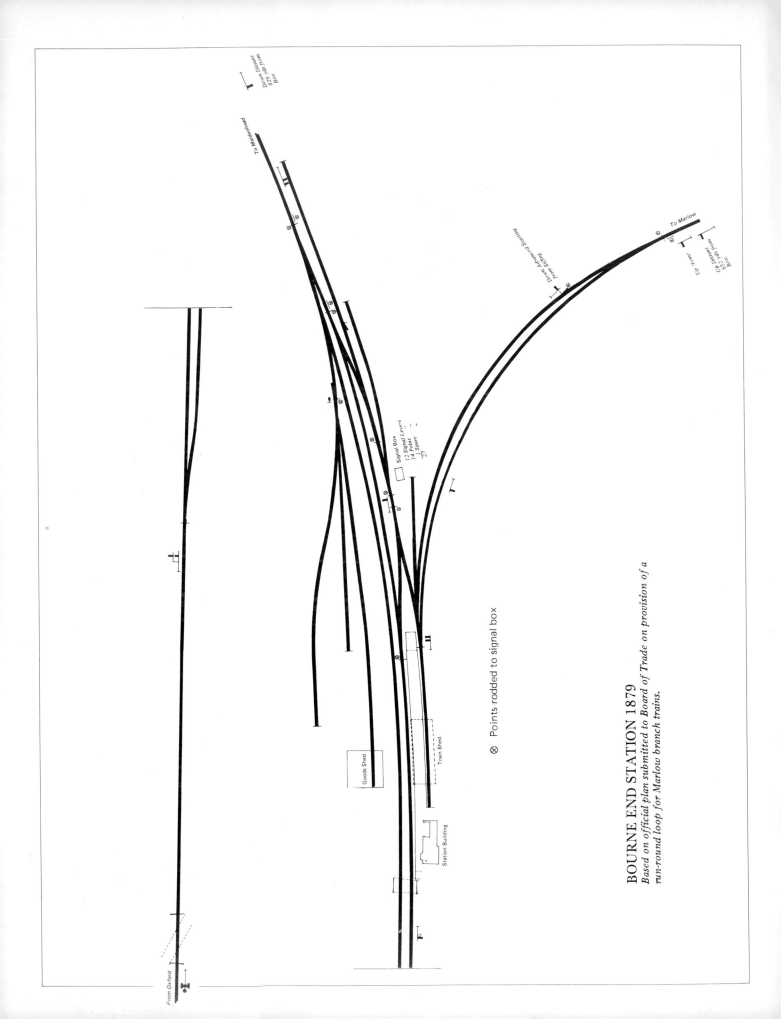

Down Distant
829 Yds from
Box

To Maidenhead

To Marlow

Up Home

Up Distant
852 Yds from
Box

Down Advanced Starting
from Sig'ling

Signal Box
12 Signal Levers
14 Point   "
1 Spare   "
27

Goods Shed

Train Shed

Station Building

⊗   Points rodded to signal box

From Oxford

BOURNE END STATION 1879

*Based on official plan submitted to Board of Trade on provision of a
run-round loop for Marlow branch trains.*

Appendix 5 — SIGNALLING

by Mike Christensen

When the Wycombe Railway was opened to traffic from Maidenhead to High Wycombe (as a broad gauge line) on 1st August 1854, the art of railway signalling was in its infancy, and the minimum standards of the inspecting officers who had been appointed under the General Regulation of Railways Act of 1840 were only in their formative stages. The fourteen-page list of requirements issued by the Board of Trade after the Regulation of Railways Act of 1889, was a long way off. The essentials of safe working were, however, already laid down, and writing from 18 Duke Street, Westminster on 28th July 1854, Brunel replied to a question posed by Captain Tyler of the Board of Trade saying that the Wycombe Railway would be worked by the GWR 'with those precautions which have hitherto highly successfully been adopted on single lines', namely 'the working of only one engine on the line at any one time'. The precise layout of the point levers at Marlow Road is not known, but contemporary GWR practice would have been to provide individual levers adjacent to the points. The photograph on page 9 shows that some equipment was worked remotely by rods — the rodding can be seen at the foot of the platform face. So far as is known, the only signals were disc and crossbar signals beside the gates of the level crossings at the station and Cores End, a road crossing 14 chains north of the station.

On 29th April 1858 Captain (later Sir) Douglas Galton sent a circular letter to seventy-nine railway companies with an accompanying statement setting out the latest requirements of the officers of the Board of Trade. By 1868 this simple list had grown to four sections covering six closely printed pages. Initially these requirements applied to additions and alterations to layouts made after they were circularised. New requirements did not have retrospective effect until the Board of Trade was given powers under the 1889 Act to enforce the provision of continuous brakes on passenger trains, and block working and the interlocking of points and signals on passenger lines. Only then did the Board of Trade have the authority to demand (though gentle persuasion was usually sufficient) the upgrading of lines which had been opened and approved for use by passenger trains to old standards which were later deemed to be inadequate. Amongst the 1868 requirements was B.21:

'The signal-handles and the levers of the switches at junctions should be brought together under cover upon a properly constructed stage, with glass sides enclosing the apparatus. They should be so arranged that while the signals are at danger the points shall be free to move; that a signalman shall be unable to lower a signal for the approach of a train until after he has set the points in the proper direction for it to pass; that it shall not be possible for him to exhibit at the same moment any two signals that can lead to a collision between two trains, and that after having lowered his signals to allow a train to pass he shall not be able so to turn his points in the wrong direction as to cause or admit of a collision between any two trains. Every signalman should be able to see the arms and the lamps of his main as well as his distant-signals, and the working of his points.'

No signal box had been put up at Marlow Road when the Wycombe Railway was built, so when the GWR — which had absorbed the nominally independent Wycombe Railway on 1st February 1867 — made preparations for the junction with the new Great Marlow Railway in 1873, extensive signalling work was needed in addition to simply laying in the branch points. In his letter to the BoT on 27th May 1873, Grierson, the General Manager of the GWR, stated that 'a proper signalbox is now being erected and all the levers will be concentrated and worked from the cabin in about a month's time.' When Colonel Yolland inspected the interlocking in June, he found a few minor changes were necessary (see his report, p. 13) but these were quickly done and when he wrote on 28th June after another visit to the line, he reported that 'the points and signals have been properly interlocked'. The signalling

arrangements at Marlow were acceptable but a cabin over the levers had not been provided in accordance with the requirements, and Yolland insisted that a signal cabin be erected to cover them. The company had to give an undertaking as to how the single line would be worked, and on 25th June the Great Marlow Railway Co. wrote from Marlow (though not on headed notepaper nor under seal), 'We hereby undertake that the traffic on the Great Marlow Railway between Marlow Road Station and Great Marlow shall be worked by one engine only in steam, or by two or more engines coupled together and forming part of one train, at one and the same time.' The undertaking was signed by Wethered as Chairman and Batting as Secretary, and countersigned by the Engineer of the GWR — 'I concur with the above on behalf of the Great Western Railway'.

The very basic arrangements made for the Great Marlow Railway quite quickly proved inadequate, and by the end of the decade a BoT inspector was back looking at new facilities. This time it was Lt. Col. Rich. On 28th March 1879 Rich reported on his inspection at Great Marlow and Bourne End. At Great Marlow the expansion of siding facilities meant that the connection from the sidings to the running line had been moved 60 yards further from the station and the signal had been correspondingly shifted. The company advising the BoT that the work was ready for inspection, stated that 'the new connection is worked in precisely the same plan as the old one that was approved at the opening of the line in 1873 and that it works exceedingly well' but that was not enough to get the work approved. In the interval since 1873 the BoT had added to its list of requirements, and now expected that facing points be secured by locking bolts as well as lifting bars (the function of which was to prevent the points being moved when a vehicle was closely on the approach side in a facing direction). So Rich insisted that a bolt be fitted to the new points in addition to the lifting bar already installed. Rich apparently felt that he could not *require* that the other two facing points at the station (which had not been altered and were therefore not 'new work') be similarly altered, but he recommended that this would be desirable. It is not clear if this recommendation was carried out, but probably not. The letter from the Marlow Company dated 2nd April 1879 simply stated that the company had written to the GWR Engineer's Office at Reading asking that *a* lock be fixed as *required*.

At Bourne End the long overdue provision of a run-round loop for Marlow branch trains had been attended to. 'An old siding has been extended to form a siding loop on which the empty passenger trains may be placed so that the engine may run round the train. The siding used for this purpose is too short for some of the trains.' The signalling at Bourne End now reflected the transition from old signalling principles to new (see the plan opposite). At the north end of the station the points were not (so far as the plans show) rodded to the box, but they were apparently interlocked with the signal by a plunger lock effected off the signal wire. For trains from Wycombe, Cores End level crossing was protected by a disc and crossbar signal worked (like the 'slot' control on the starting signal towards Wycombe at the end of the station) by the crossing keeper. At the Marlow end of the new loop siding the signals were described by Rich as 'satisfactory'. The facing point was locked with the signal and secured with lifting bar and locking bolt; the siding had a safety switch (trap point) interlocked with the signals. The difference in standards between the old and the new was considerable. For all the new work the requirements had been strictly adhered to, so Rich was obliged to pass the work for use. He added, however, that many of the existing works fell below the current standards. In addition to the fact that the platforms were too short and that clocks were required in the signal box and on the platform, there were two specific matters to do with signalling. Rich said that all the sidings should be controlled with safety points and all facing points should be secured with lifting bars and locking bolts. If this work was done, the frame in the signal box may have been altered. When Rich

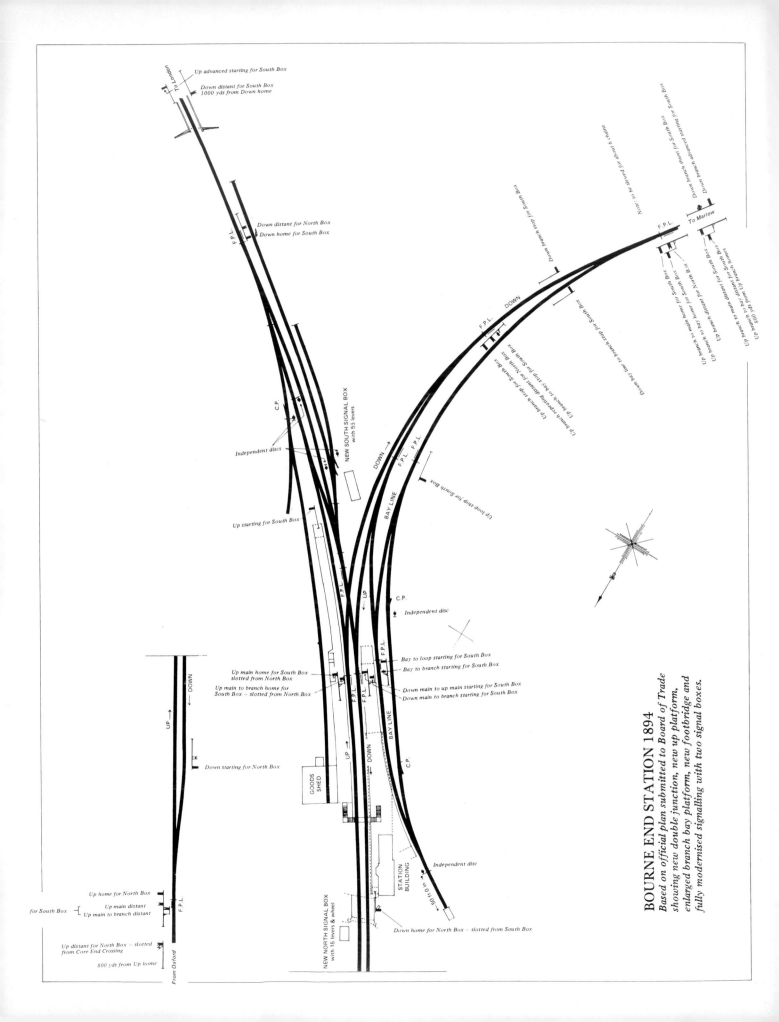

BOURNE END STATION 1894

*Based on official plan submitted to Board of Trade
showing new double junction, new up platform,
enlarged branch bay platform, new footbridge and
fully modernised signalling with two signal boxes.*

To London

Up advanced starting for South Box

Down distant for South Box
1000 yds from Down home

F.P.L.

Down distant for North Box
Down home for South Box

C.P.

Independent discs

NEW SOUTH SIGNAL BOX
with 55 levers

Up starting for South Box

DOWN

BAY LINE

UP

F.P.L.

C.P.

Independent disc

Bay to loop starting for South Box
Bay to branch starting for South Box

Up main home for South Box
slotted from North Box

Down main to up main starting for South Box
Down main to branch starting for South Box

Up main to branch home for
South Box – slotted from North Box

F.P.L.   F.P.L.

DOWN

UP

DOWN

BAY LINE

C.P.

GOODS
SHED

Down starting for North Box

STATION
BUILDING

Independent disc

50 to 10 in

Down home for North Box – slotted from South Box

NEW NORTH SIGNAL BOX
with 15 levers & wheel

Up home for North Box

for South Box   Up main distant
Up main to branch distant

F.P.L.

Up distant for North Box – slotted
from Core End Crossing

800 yds from Up home

From Oxford

Note: to be placed for about 6 chains

Down branch stop for South Box

F.P.L.

DOWN

Up loop stop for South Box

Up branch repeating distant for South Box
Up branch repeating distant for North Box

F.P.L.   F.P.L.

To Marlow

Down branch shunt for South Box
Down branch advanced starting for South Box

F.P.L.

Up branch to main home for South Box
Up branch to bay home for North Box
Up branch distant for South Box
Up branch to main distant for South Box
Up branch to bay distant for South Box
Up branch from Up branch homes
Up branch 800 yds from Up branch home

Down bay line to branch stop for South Box

saw it, the frame consisted of 27 levers of which one was spare, 12 worked signals and 14 worked points. A formal return to the BoT by the GWR in 1880 stated that Bourne End was the only station on the Wycombe Railway that was 'fully interlocked' — the others were only 'partially interlocked'.

The 'One Engine in Steam' system of operating the branch was very restrictive, and especially unsuitable for a line with heavy traffic at certain seasons of the year. In the 1880s the GWR extended block working (which ensures a space interval between following trains) to its single lines, and generally adopted Train Staff and Ticket working where Train Staff only or One Engine in Steam had been used before. Grierson wrote to the BoT on 20th February 1885 asking what undertakings had so far been given to the Board in respect of no less than 44 lines now worked by the GWR, not all of which had been owned by the company at the time that the original undertakings had been given. As the change to block working progressed, new undertakings were given. Amongst those made by the GWR in a letter dated 5th January 1887 was one in relation to the line from Maidenhead to Kennington Junction (Oxford) which was now to be worked on the train staff and ticket system in conjunction with the block telegraph. Under this system, the driver of each train to pass in one direction on the single line was shown the staff by the person in charge, and if another train was to follow, he was handed a paper ticket authorising him to proceed on to the single line. The driver of the last train in any group was handed the staff, and only when the staff had been carried by him through the section could a reverse flow of trains commence. Security against meeting a train travelling in the opposite direction on the single line was assured by the train staff. Security against running into the back of the preceding train was provided by the block telegraph system.

On 9th November 1886 Grierson wrote to the BoT asking what undertaking the Great Marlow Railway had given as to the working of its single line, and he was sent a copy of the 'One Engine in Steam' undertaking given in 1873. On 3rd July 1888 the Assistant Secretary of the GWR, writing from Paddington, sent a letter from the GWR, as the company working the Great Marlow Railway, 'hereby undertaking that the single line of railway between Bourne End and Great Marlow shall be worked by the Train Staff and Ticket system in conjunction with the block telegraph'. The undertaking was signed by Gooch as Chairman and Higgins as Secretary. The type of block instrument used is not known for certain. On some single lines, for example the Abingdon branch, the GWR standard Spagnoletti 'Disc Block' was used. The papers for the Great Marlow Railway, however, consistently refer to an 'interlocking block' and the fuss made by the Board of the Marlow company (see p. 24) suggests that one of the patent systems available in the 1880s was used. It is possible that the system was true 'lock and block' with the starting signals locked until released by the block instruments (though the plans available do not show any such locking). Such control of the starting signal at the opposite end of the section was already in use on the GWR at Ledbury (installed in 1885). The GWR electrical wiring diagram books refer to an 'Electric Locking System, New Pattern 1894', and the Marlow branch may well have had instruments to the earlier pattern. It is tempting to conclude that the GWR saw a way of trying out new equipment at another company's expense.

In the aftermath of the terrible accident at Armagh in 1889, the BoT sought to enforce a minimum standard on all railways as regards the interlocking of points and signals, the adoption of block working, and the use of continuous brakes on passenger trains (this latter having serious implications for the working of mixed goods and passenger trains.) The Great Marlow Railway had little to do to enable it to comply with the new standards, but nonetheless was served with a formal order requiring compliance — the order was dated 28th November 1890. In the correspondence about the use of block working, the Great Marlow Railway Co. told the BoT that it was probably that it and the GWR would 'make joint application to the BoT to allow the Train Staff system to be adopted on our line during the greater part of the year on the undertaking to have

only one engine in steam, while the interlocking block system shall be adopted in the busier months'. In effect, block working would be abandoned during the quieter months, with the saving of the costs of a man at Marlow employed to work the instruments. No such application appears ever to have been made.

The layout at Bourne End, with only one platform, was quite inadequate for the traffic, and did not allow two passenger trains to cross or be on the main line at the same time. As a result of an order served by the BoT in 1890 under the provisions of the 1889 Act, the GWR decided in 1891 upon a programme of improving the signalling at all the stations between Maidenhead and Wyombe, and on 12th June 1893 the GWR sought provisional sanction from the BoT for a completely modernised layout providing two platforms, a double junction on to the branch, and fully modernised signalling. The new signal boxes were ordered from the signal works in May 1892 (North box) and June (South box). The North signal box was built adjacent to the troublesome level crossing, with a wheel to work the gates directly from the box, and control over the wicket gates for pedestrians. The box had a frame of fifteen levers, of which two were spare. A new signal box was also provided at the south end of the station, for the old box dating from 1873 could not have accommodated the 'double twist' pattern frame of 55 levers (of which 3 were spare) now required to work the expanded layout. The work was ready for inspection by 5th December 1894. When Colonel Yorke inspected for the BoT in January 1895, he noted that the 'whole station has been resignalled and interlocked to modern requirements' and he only recommended some minor changes to the interlocking at the South signal box (9 and 30 to be interlocked, also 7 and 8). The crossing loop had an effective length of 1,052 feet between fouling points, and double line absolute block working was used between the North and South boxes. 'Wrong direction' movements were allowed out of the down platform, so that up trains for Maidenhead or Marlow could leave from the platform in which they arrived. The GWR must have been pleased that it had gone to the expense of modern level crossing controls — they enabled it to ride out the storm of protest raised some short while after by local worthies about the delays to road traffic at the crossing. The crossing loop formed during this remodelling, however, proved to be too short, and in 1907 (ready for inspection by 2nd October) the loop was lengthened at the north end. The plan for the work done shows that by this time all the distant signals at Bourne End had been made unworkable (fixed), as was by now standard GWR practice, and the splitting distant signal on the up line for the South box applying trains on to the Marlow branch, had been removed. Cores End level crossing, which had a disc and crossbar signal to protect the gates from the time that the line opened, was equipped with a new set of protecting signals during the 1894 resignalling. These appear, however, to have been removed during the 1907 work, and the crossing brought under the protection of the signals worked from the North box. Certainly by 1933 the lever frame at Cores End did not work any signals; the levers merely provided a means of interlocking the level crossing gates with the signals worked from North box (see the 1935 diagram of the North box).

On 30th March 1878 a patent was awarded to Edward Tyer, a contractor supplying electrical signalling instruments, for what was to prove to be the first practical instrument for controlling the traffic on single lines which avoided the problem inherent in the staff and ticket system — the fact that a train could not proceed if, because of some unforeseen circumstance, the staff was at the opposite end of the single line section to that at which the train was standing. Tyer's instrument provided for a number of 'Train Staff Tablets' to be held in two instruments, one at each end of the section of single line. The instruments were electrically interlocked so that a tablet could only be taken out if no other tablet had been withdrawn and was still out — only one tablet could be obtained (at whichever end of the section) at any one time, and the essential safety of the train staff system was maintained. The first design by Tyer had a number of defects. Some were minor and were soon corrected, but there was one serious drawback. Once a tablet

The interior of the prototype key token instrument. The builder's model steam locomotives are lined up on the shelf at the back of the room.   *Cty. Public Records Office*

had been taken out of an instrument, it could not be put back into that instrument. It had to be taken through the section to the instrument at the other end. If the train could not go forward, perhaps because the engine had failed, there was a serious problem. This caused the officers of the London and North Western Railway, which conducted trials with Tyer's Tablet instruments, to reject the system and to devise one which worked on somewhat different principles. Metal train staffs were used instead of the disc-shaped tablets of the Tyer's system, and the new apparatus became known as the Electric Train Staff (ETS). The officers of the BoT inspected the ETS at Bedford on the LNWR in July 1888 and after some modifications had been made, gave approval to the system in November of 1889. There was then some debate as to whether the ETS system constituted block working as required under the 1889 Regulation of Railways Act. This was finally settled at a meeting held on 22nd July 1890 'between the Inspecting Officers of the Board of Trade and the General Managers of the Principal Railway Companies'. It was agreed that the ETS was a block system, and it was adopted by the GWR as its standard. Inevitably, the busier lines were fitted up first, and quiet branch lines took second place to the West of England main line and the busy mineral lines in South Wales. The ETS was installed on the Wycombe Railway in 1893 but it was not until 6th March 1901 that the directors authorised the installation of the ETS on the Marlow branch, in place of Train Staff and Ticket and the contentious block telegraph. The papers record that the sum of £124 was authorised to the 'Telegraph Dept for substituting Electric Train Staff Apparatus between Marlow and Bourne End for the existing Lock and Block System'. The work was completed on 9th June.

The introduction of the ETS was concurrent with other improvements. On 6th March 1901 the directors authorised the spending of £1,891 on new work at Marlow and a further £211 for 'Locking and signalling to bring signalling arrangements up to date'. The work at Marlow was completed by 20th March 1902 but not inspected by Colonel Yorke for the BoT until January 1903. The scheme had involved extending the platform, lengthening the loop, altering the sidings in consequence, and the erection of new signals. 'A new signal box has been built containing 16 levers all of which are in use.' Yorke added that 'The interlocking is correct'. He noted that on Regatta days the siding behind the platform was used for passenger trains but that since 'special precautions' were taken for their safety 'the occasional use of this bay line for passenger traffic need hardly be objected to.' Other companies might not have got away with it, but the inspecting officers showed on a number of occasions that they considered the officers of the GWR to be responsible people who could be trusted to make proper arrangements.

The Electric Staff apparatus on the Marlow line was only seven years old when in 1908 the GWR decided to adopt Tyer's No. 7 tablet instruments (a vast improvement on the earlier versions, and easier than staff instruments to maintain) as the standard for all new work. So tablet instruments were never used at Marlow. The line was, however, to have a pioneering role in the development of the next type of single line instrument.

On 4th December 1912 the Signal Engineer's Office of the GWR at Reading wrote to the BoT, referring to the Board's 'note on requirements' of 1905 which stated that the BoT would require to approve any new types of tablet or staff instrument before they were brought into use. The GWR asked whether the BoT wished to inspect a new key token instrument before it was used. The instrument had been devised at Reading and, being cheaper and simpler than the staff or tablet, it had been approved by the General Manager of the GWR. A pair of instruments had been set up at Paddington and were available for inspection there. A patent for the apparatus had been applied for on 14th October by A. T. Blackall and C. M. Jacobs, who were respectively the Signal Engineer of the GWR and his Electrical Assistant. Colonel Yorke inspected the apparatus for the BoT and suggested a 'small mechanical improvement' which the GWR (naturally) adopted. On 13th February 1913 the BoT wrote approving the use of the instruments provided that they conformed to the usual conditions applying to staff and tablet instruments. The remainder of 1913 was apparently spent on developing the machine, in particular providing a larger magazine capable of holding a greater number of tokens. The first pair of the new Electric Key Token (EKT) instruments was brought into use in January 1914 — between Bourne End South and Marlow (the second section to get key tokens was St. Blazey Bridge to Luxulyan, brought into use on 19th October the same year). The appearance of the instrument was now largely as it was to remain throughout the rest of the life of the GWR, and the Key Token is still standard single line instrument of British Rail. The form of the token itself, however, had not evolved to its final shape. Like the staffs it replaced, the token incorporated a separate key for unlocking ground frames. It was cheaper and more convenient to do this than to change the locks already fitted to ground frames, and it was a few years before it became standard to use the configurated end of the token which fitted into the instrument to actuate the ground frame locks as well.

The maintenance schedule kept by the GWR contains an entry for 29th May 1919 — 'Marlow — renewal of signalbox, age unknown, estimate £480'. Precisely what work was done is unknown. The signal box which survived until 1954 was of a style which predated 1919, but would be appropriate to one erected in 1902, and had the same number of levers as that noted by the inspecting officer in 1902 (16 levers). It seems strange that the GWR Engineer did not know the age of a signal box put up only seventeen years before, and that such a relatively new structure should require renewal.

The prototype key token instruments set up on a bench at Paddington station for examination by the Inspecting Officer of the Board of Trade. The limited capacity of the magazine for storing the tokens (see the drawing on p. 205) was the notable difference between the prototype and the production version.
Cty. Public Records Office (PRO Ref. MT6/2148/2)

For signalling maintenance purposes, the Marlow branch was covered by the linemen from High Wycombe. The signal fitter, who was responsible for points and signals, was required to check the apparatus once a fortnight. The telegraph lineman, who looked after the block apparatus, telephones, token and staff instruments, was scheduled to visit once a month.

The GWR used a system of classifying signal boxes, and thus setting the rate of pay for the men in any particular box, by reference to a 'Marks' score. The principal Marks Agreement was finalised on 20th March 1920. Marks were given for each train signalled through or terminating/starting, the number of times levers were moved, level crossing gates swung, bell code signals received and sent, and so on. The number of marks would be adjusted by fixed percentages for a number of factors, such as the power to regulate (change the order of the running of trains), and the resultant overall figure divided by the hours over which the activity took place, to give an average figure of marks per hour. No allowance was given specifically for the equipment with which a box was fitted out (this did not feature in the marks system until a revision in 1972).

The marks were taken at Bourne End on 11th and 12th February 1920, and on 6th May the signalmen were issued with notices placing both the North and South signal boxes in Class 4, with a standard rate of pay of 55/- per week. This compared with a rate of 29/- under the previous (but by now out of date) classification, but the signalmen at the South box were receiving pay at the rate of 64/-. The marks averaged over 24 hours were: North box 94, South box 147. Cores End crossing was in Class 5 (30-74 marks), as was Marlow with only 64 marks. The signalmen at the South box were incensed at being put in the same class as those at the North box, and wrote to their station master to protest.

South Box
Bourne End

Classification of Signal Boxes

Dear Sir,

We have today received our notices informing us that this box is placed in class 4, standard rate of pay 55/- per week.

We are also informed that the North Box at this station is on the same grade and we beg to submit that, in view of the much heavier work and responsibilities of this Box, the classification is unfair and we appeal for the post to be regraded.

We give below a comparison of the two boxes.

	South Box	North Box
Pre-war rate	29/-	24/-
" " hours of duty	8	10
Lever frame	55	15
Operating		
Signals	25	4
Points	13	1
Lock-bars	9	1
Gates	—	5
Spare	8	4
Gate wheel	—	1
Instruments		
	Double line to North	Double line to South
	E.T. Staff Cookham	E.T. Staff Wooburn Green
	E. Token Marlow	—

The production token instrument, with only one token in the magazine. In operation there would be several more, usually thirty to a pair of machines. The Annett's key on the handle of the token was discontinued after a few years.

GWR Magazine (August 1914)

The simplicity of the token instrument, and the ease of access to its components for maintenance purposes, are evident from this view taken of a partly constructed machine with its back panel removed. The ease with which the contacts could be serviced and the locking mechanism checked, was much appreciated by linemen used to the train staff instruments, in which access to the 'innards' was really very poor. *GWR Magazine*

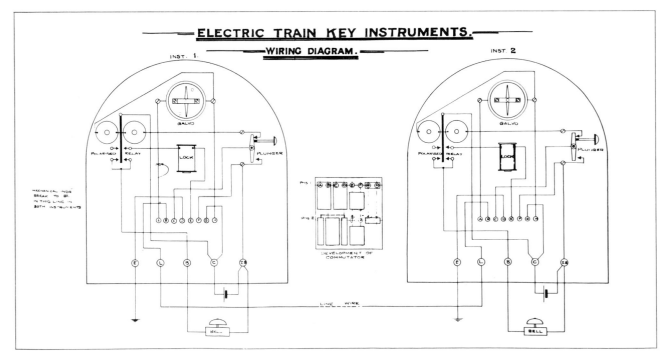

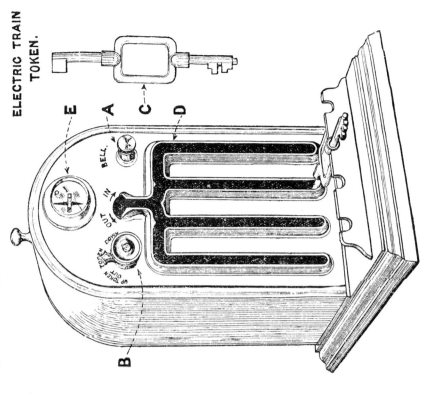

ELECTRIC TRAIN TOKEN.

DESCRIPTION OF APPARATUS.

The apparatus consists essentially of:—

A plunger (A). For transmitting bell signals to the distant station or for sending a current to release a Token.

A pointer (B). For indicating to the distant station when a Token has been withdrawn, and for indicating to each Signalman the state of the block section at any time. A switch operated by this pointer also works the keyless disc at an intermediate level crossing where such a disc is provided.

A number of Tokens (C).

A magazine with four slots for receiving Tokens (D).

An indicator (E). For indicating all outgoing and incoming signals sent on the plunger from either end.

Each instrument is provided with a separate bell.

To work a single line between stations "A" and "B" on this system requires an instrument at "A" and another at "B" and the single line between the two stations is called a "Token Section."

The two instruments for the section are furnished with a number of train Tokens. Only one of these Tokens can be out of the instruments at any time, except when taken out by the Telegraph Lineman as shewn in clauses 35 and 36 of the Electric Tablet or Staff Block Regulations appearing on page 53 of the General Appendix. A Token can be replaced in either instrument at any time without any communication being made with the opposite end of the section. The Tokens for each block section controlled from any one signal box, differ essentially, as do also the Token instruments fixed in the box, so that a signalman who has more than one set of Tokens to deal with, cannot by mistake place a Token in the wrong instrument.

OUTLINE OF WORKING.

Let "A" and "B" represent two Token stations.

"A" sends "call attention."

"B" returns "call attention."

"A" sends "Is line clear."

"B" returns "Line Clear," and when pressing in plunger for the last time keeps it in and watches the needle of indicator until it has returned to the upright position, when he releases the plunger.

"A" takes out Token, which act will cause bell of his instrument to ring once, which must NOT be understood as a signal coming from "B."

"A" turns pointer to "Up Token Out" or "Down Token Out" as the case may be, pressing it hard down for a moment. "B" turns pointer to "Up Token Out" or "Down Token Out" as the case may be.

"A" sends "Train entering section."

"B" returns "Train entering section."

"B" on arrival of train places Token in instrument and sends "Train out of section" and turns pointer switch to "Token In."

"A" returns "Train out of section" and turns pointer switch to "Token In."

The apparatus will now be in the normal position and ready for the passage of another train over the section. When taking out a Token from the instrument it is necessary that it should be lifted from the magazine to the aperture in the centre at the top and pressed therein in a similar manner to a key being used in an ordinary lock, and when in this position must be turned to the left, or in an anti-clockwise direction until the movement is checked, when it can be withdrawn.

In placing a Token in the instrument it must be pressed into the aperture in the centre and turned to the right or in a clockwise direction and then lowered into either of the columns of the magazine.

NOTE.—A Token must not be left in the aperture at the top but must in all cases be taken out of the instrument, or lowered into the magazine as the case may be.

The diagram shewn below represents the Electric Token instrument, when it is in its normal position, that is, when there is no train in the section, and also shows an Electric Token:—

South Box	North Box
Controlling switch for regulating crossing arrangements Bourne End & Loudwater — page 73 appendix to No. 1.	—
Various Junction Box	—
44 trains booked from & to Marlow daily	—
Whole of yard shunting and exchange sidings	—

This comparison will show at a glance the additional work which we have to perform, and a consideration of the facts that we have the whole of the Junction work and the regulating of the crossing of trains, will make it clear that our responsibilities are far heavier.

We feel convinced that a review of the case will satisfy you that we are justified in making this appeal for the regrading of our post — which, as it now stands, is obviously most unfair.

We are
Yours Truly
R. G. Green
T. Small
Mr. Taylor   Signalmen
Station Master

The men had something of a case, for Class 4 covered the band 75-149 and Class 3 the range 150 to 224, so at 147 they were only just below the threshold for Class 3. The point was conceded, and the South box upgraded to Class 3 (60/-).

After a few years the signalmen felt that recent increases in traffic justified a further uplift.

Bourne End South Box
27—5—27

Application for re-grading from present rate 60/- to 65/-
Dear Sir,

We the undersigned Signalmen of this box after careful consideration and observation of the work generally, on the different turns of duty, now feel justified in making this application for an increase of 5/- per week.

It is difficult to compare the work here one week with another, even when closely watched, the tail traffic for one instance fluctuates so much that any one not seeing the work done would hardly credit that it was so.

Then again taking 'Goods Traffic', the winters of 1925 & 1926 with the extra traffic also the special trains for Thomas & Greens siding, the work done here and the various methods of dealing with same, the lack of proper, and the insufficient accommodation, owing to our cramped up position, makes present day working not only harder but entails more responsibility.

It is when one takes a look at various diagrams, and lever work incurred, and compares work done, that it becomes obvious that we honestly earn another 10d per day.

We should appreciate any remarks from you regarding this application, being certain they will at least be just.

We are
Yours Truly
Signalman — R. G. Green
„   A. E. Ginger
To Mr. Taylor
Station Master

The marks were duly taken again on 16th June 1927, but only came to 149.9, so the application was turned down flat. The men clearly felt cheated about the date that the marks had been taken, and wrote in protest.

Bourne End
South Box
30.1.28.

Re-classification South Box
Dear Sir,

In May last we made an application as above and the movements were taken on June 15th 1927 after the holiday period when there were only 25 wagons in up & down sidings inclusive & traffic for Thomas Siding practically nil.

We have during the Autumn again got back to our usual routine full up & overflowing thereby causing the unavoidable delays to other trains, & the extra lever work & verbal communications added, as mentioned in that application & the same facts are as true today as then. Would you be good enough to mention the tonnage dealt with for Thomas siding during the last 2 or 3 months when making your remarks on this application as it only seems fair to us that we should be given some allowance for the shunting of this firm's traffic, "no small item". We do not know how we came out for the number of marks for June 15th but under the circumstances bad enough no doubt.

We know we have no right of appeal for 12 months, but neither do we stand on ceremony when there is work to do whatever its nature.

We do not ask for movements to be taken again as we are quite aware of the unfairness of this method & more so at station Junctions.

We do hope that after due consideration we shall take up our old position in regard to rate i.e. as to Wycombe South & Maidenhead Middle for we are quite sure we have not gone down in 12 months from our own countings.

Was the controlling switch for regulating trains as per page Appendix No. 1 taken into account also the fact that the South Box Signalman is in charge & responsible from 8.20 p.m. to 8.0 a.m. for arranging traffic & regulating generally, the staff acting on his instruction, also goods guards during the night.

We do not ask you to recommend this application as you have only been here about 5 months, but we do ask you to give any remarks you think fit on the reasonableness of this application & your experience.

We are
Yours Truly
Signalman Green
„   Ginger
(3rd post vacant)
To Mr. James
Station Master
Bourne End.

Exceptionally, the marks were taken again, on 28th February 1928, although less than a year had elapsed since they had last been taken. The men kept their own chronicle of events and wrote:

Bourne End
South Box
25—2—28

Dear Sir,

The lever movements of this Box were as promised carried out on 23—2—28, thanks to yourself & Mr. Compfield. I attach hereto a paper showing a few particulars and to emphasise the fact mentioned in our last letter re Thomas & Greens traffic.

Also the question of controlling switch which in our opinion makes the North Box here & Wooburn Green, 'posts which actually work under our instructions' and we would like to know what value in marks this is to us, we know of its value to company.

Now we want full consideration to be given for the 160 yards for staff running normal working, with the up & down steps that tries one's boots to the extent of 3 new pairs per year, we cannot use old boots for Box owing to going in & out all weathers.

We think that this information now will to some extent help Mr. Compfield when he deals with the record he will soon have for the 23rd and to our mind the positive proof of the unfairness of the Lever Movement system. We hope that we may obtain the extra 1¼d per hour and that more use   might well soon be made of this line, it may result in some of the now bad times being made good.

Will you please send on early.

We are
Yours Truly
Signalmen R. Green. A. E. Ginger
Mr. James
Station Master

The marks came out at 163, marginally higher than the previous June and thus partly justifying the signalmen's complaint about the timing of the taking of the marks, but still way below the level needed to get upgrading to Class 2. In 1930 the men applied for the

Record for 3 weeks of 5 Goods Trains
arr & dep Bourne End,
From January 9th to 28th 1928.

January	arr pm	Dep		TRAIN	arr pm	Dep	Date January
TRAIN 9th	1·54	4·46		11·42 Am	4·16	4·52	9
1·0 pm 10	1·41	4·45	Level	Oxford 10	4·14	4·53	10
TAPLOW 11	2·26	6·13	Movements	11	4·32	4·54	11
2·20 S.O. 12	2·39	6·13	taken on	12	4·17	5·0	12
13	2·27	4·44	June 15 1927	13	4·7	4·45	13
14	2·52	5·52	Times	15/6/27 14	4·13	4·58	14
16	1·51	4·43	arr Dep	arr Dep 16	5·7	5·35	16
17	2·??	4·42	2·18 4·4?	17	4·2	11·36	17
18	1·42	5·14		18	5·4	5·32	18
19	1·43	4·40		4·31 - 4·47 19	4·27	4·46	19
20	1·49	5·19	February	20	4·18	6·4	20
21	2·52	7·22	23rd 1928	23·2·28 21	4·36	4·54	21
23	2·32	4·44	2·56 4·4?	4·17 - 5·1 23	4·34	4·52	23
24	2·28	6·12		24	5·12	6·24	24
25	2·15	4·42		BLOCK ON 25	3·45	4·0	25
26	2·23	4·47		RIBBONS 26	4·34	4·50	26
27	2·24	4·43		27	4·10	4·43	27
28	2·53	5·53		28	5·3	5·31	28

Return	arr pm	Dep		Return	arr pm	Dep	th
9	11·20	11·55		4·52 pm	6·16	7·3	9
8·27 pm 10	11·17	11·40	June 15th	10	6·12	7·26	10
11	10·15	10·48	1927	TAPLOW 11	6·10	6·58	11
Loudwater 12	11·29	1·58	arr - DEP	12	6·54	7·57	12
13	9·8	9·43		15·6·27 13	7·1	7·52	13
14	10·14	1·0	8·44 8·58	arr Dep 14	7·33	8·10	14
16	11·23	11·46		6·11 6·50 16	7·3	7·58	16
17	11·21	11·35	Feb 23rd 1928	17	6·10	6·53	17
18	11·17	11·43		18	7·35	8·29	18
19	9·23	9·57	8·57 - 9·13	23·2·28 19	6·13	7·3	19
20	11·21	11·56		20	8·22	7·56	20
21	10·54	11·1?		6·11 6·53 21	6·57	8·32	21
23	11·22	11·56		23	6·56	8·0	23
24	11·54	12·25		24	8·50	9·48	24
25	9·16	10·?		25	6·48	7·1	25
26	11·22	11·58		26	6·57	8·20	26
27	9·19	9·57		27	6·54	8·14	27
28	1·14	11·52		28	8·4	8·37	28

Branch Goods 7·14 Am Bourne End to Marlow

Departure times dates as above.

Jan 9th 10 11 12 13 14 16 17 18 19 20 21 23 24 25 26 27 28
7·15 6·37 6·57 6·57 6·54 6·52 7·35 7·33 7·? 7·? 7·35 7·35 7·0 7·3 6·55 7·14 6·58 7·12

Level Movements

June 15th 1927.   February 23rd 1928.
6·31 Am Dep.   6·56 Dep.

Thomas & Green's Siding

Wagons Inwards	Oct 1st 1927	Wagons Outwards
1865	Jan'y To 28th 1928 12·0 Noon	1848 Total 3713

Remarks:
From October 1st to January 28th the 11·42 Am Oxford
carried out its own work 25 days out of the 103.
This meant that Engine of 1·0 Taplow done the work & this
Box had to handle the traffic 3 times over.

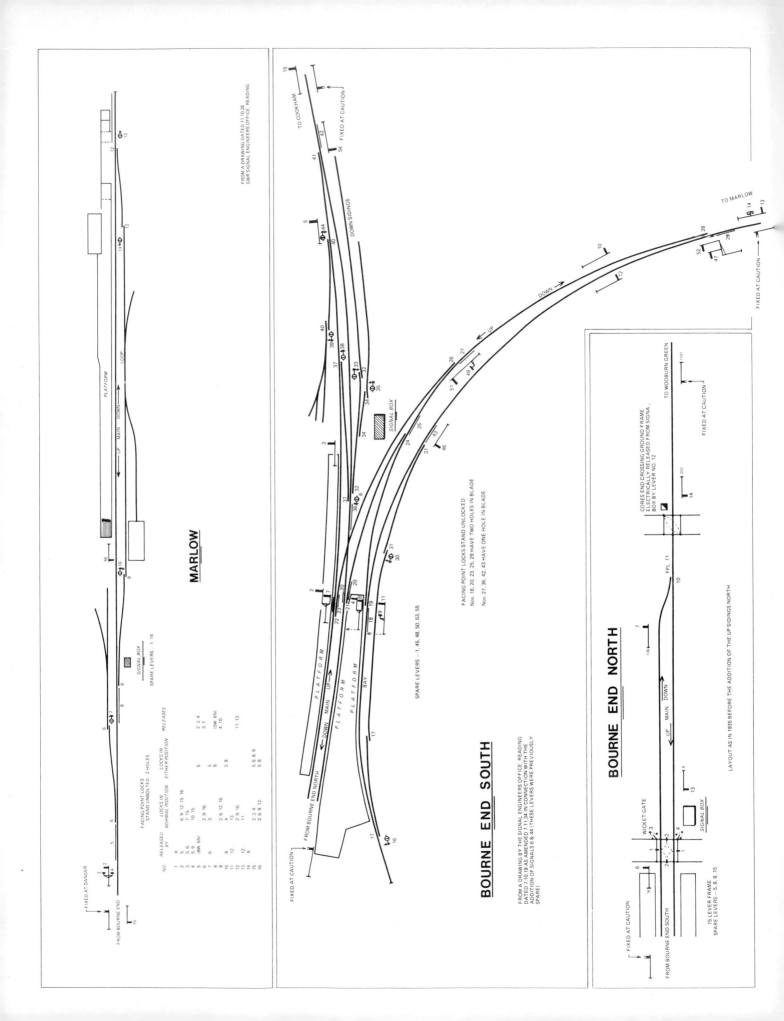

MARLOW

FIXED AT DANGER

FROM BOURNE END

PLATFORM

UP MAIN DOWN

LOOP

SIGNAL BOX

SPARE LEVERS – 1. 14

FACING POINT LOCKS
STAND UNBOLTED 2 HOLES

NO.	RELEASED BY	LOCKS IN NORMAL POSITION	LOCKS IN EITHER POSITION	RELEASES
1	X	6 9 12 15 16		
2	5 6	7 15		2 3 4
3	5 9	10 15		3 7
4	(8W 6N)			
5	6	2 9 16	6	(5W 6N)
6		3	5	
7			9	
8		2 6 12 16	5 8	4 10
9	9	4		
10	12	13		
11		2 9 16		11 13
12	12	11		
13	X			
14		2 3 4		5 6 8 9
15		2 6 9 12		5 8
16				

FROM A DRAWING DATED 11.10.26
GWR SIGNAL ENGINEERS OFFICE. READING

BOURNE END SOUTH

FIXED AT CAUTION

FROM BOURNE END NORTH

TO COOKHAM

FIXED AT CAUTION

DOWN SIDINGS

SIGNAL BOX

DOWN MAIN UP

PLATFORM

PLATFORM

BAY

DOWN

UP

SPARE LEVERS – 1. 45. 48. 50. 53. 55

FACING POINT LOCKS STAND UNLOCKED
Nos. 18, 20, 23, 25, 29 HAVE TWO HOLES IN BLADE
Nos. 27, 36, 42, 43 HAVE ONE HOLE IN BLADE

FROM A DRAWING BY THE SIGNAL ENGINEERS OFFICE. READING
DATED 7.10.19 AS AMENDED 7.11.34 IN CONNECTION WITH THE
ADDITION OF SIGNALS 6 & 44 (THESE LEVERS WERE PREVIOUSLY
SPARE)

BOURNE END NORTH

FIXED AT CAUTION

FROM BOURNE END SOUTH

WICKET GATE

SIGNAL BOX

15 LEVER FRAME
SPARE LEVERS – 5. 8. 9. 15

TO WOOBURN GREEN

TO MARLOW

FIXED AT CAUTION

CORES END CROSSING GROUND FRAME
ELECTRICALLY RELEASED FROM SIGNA-
BOX BY LEVER NO. 12

FPL 11

UP MAIN DOWN

FIXED AT CAUTION

LAYOUT AS IN 1935 BEFORE THE ADDITION OF THE UP SIDINGS NORTH

This photo was taken before the signalling modifications in the bay line in the mid-1930s and shows the bay to loop starting signal with a bay to branch starting miniature arm bracket beneath (see page 200) as well as the up and down platform bracket signals in their 1894 form. *C. L. Mowat*

marks to be taken yet again, and this was done on 9th May. It was noted that the distances from the box to the staff catching apparatus was 36 yards for the branch, 37 yards to the up line and 16 to the down line — all rather less than the figure of 160 yards mentioned by the signalmen in their letter of 25th February 1928. The marks this time came to only 158, and the men gave up the battle.

The layout at Bourne End after the remodelling in 1894 allowed 'wrong direction' movements southwards out of the down platform, but not into the down platform from the High Wycombe direction, nor into the up platform from Marlow or Maidenhead. In the mid 1930s work progressed on the installation of the 'Up Sidings North' east of the line on the Wycombe side of the North signal box 'for H.M. Government'. Access to these sidings was from the up platform line, but in the down direction and required the provision of a signal to protect the level crossing during shunting. The opportunity was taken to improve operational flexibility by making the up platform bi-directional (though this did not include allowing trains to run into this platform directly from Maidenhead). At the North signal box the signal protecting the gates from shunting moves in the up platform — somewhat cumbersomely called the 'Up line down inner home' — was made in the form of a bracket. The lower bracketed arm read into the sidings, the main arm applying along the up line towards High Wycombe. Another new signal was installed between the sidings and the up line to act as the starting signal towards High Wycombe and also to protect the gates at Cores End level crossing from 'wrong direction' movements. Changes were also made at Bourne End South signal box. The little used connection from the branch to the bay adjacent to the signal box (points 19 and 24) were taken out of use in January 1935, and the trackwork remodelled to give a slightly longer run-round loop, albeit at the expense of losing the ability to run round a train in the bay without the engine going out on to the branch running line. A new signal (44) was also provided to permit movements from the Marlow branch to the up platform.

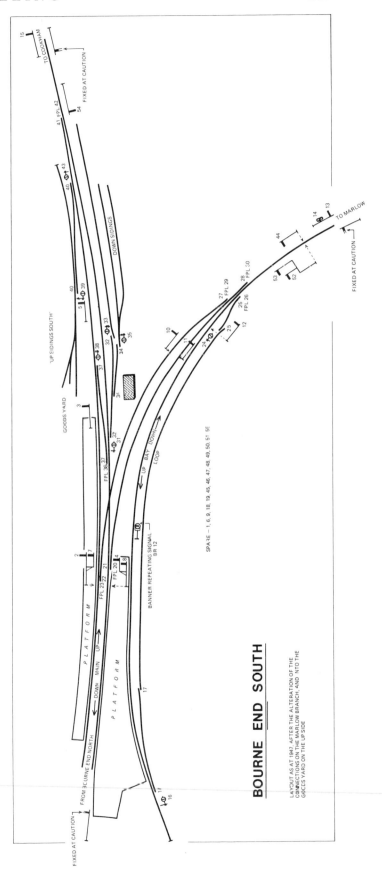

BOURNE END SOUTH

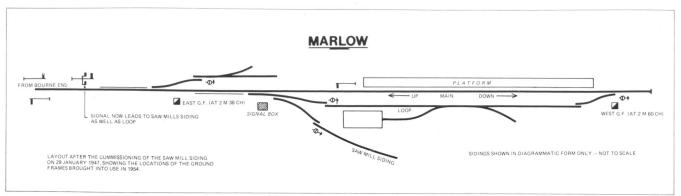

MARLOW

FROM BOURNE END

SIGNAL NOW LEADS TO SAW MILLS SIDING
AS WELL AS LOOP

EAST G.F. (AT 2 M 38 CH)

SIGNAL BOX

PLATFORM

← UP   MAIN   DOWN →

LOOP

WEST G.F. (AT 2 M 60 CH)

SAW MILL SIDING

LAYOUT AFTER THE COMMISSIONING OF THE SAW MILL SIDING
ON 29 JANUARY 1947, SHOWING THE LOCATIONS OF THE GROUND
FRAMES BROUGHT INTO USE IN 1954.

SIDINGS SHOWN IN DIAGRAMMATIC FORM ONLY – NOT TO SCALE

Marlow saw an extension of facilities in 1947, when on 29th January a new connection to the sawmill siding was commissioned and minor changes to the signalling and locking were made. It was not long, however, before the management undertook a careful scrutiny of the costs of signalling on this two-mile long branch line. Marlow signal box, which was open from 5.20 a.m. to 11.30 p.m. in both 1938 and 1945 (on two turns, hence the extensive and expensive overtime the signalmen enjoyed), was reduced to being 'open as required' by 1953. More drastic changes were to come the following year. On 26th September 1954 the signal box at Marlow was closed. The points forming the release crossover were connected up to a new one-lever ground frame, the West G.F. Another frame, the East G.F., was provided to work the loop and yard points at the London end of the station. The key token instruments were taken out of use, and the line reverted to working by one engine in steam, with a train staff.

At Bourne End the inexorable process of making 'economies' ran parallel to that at Marlow. Bourne End South signal box was closed, and the layout drastically altered and simplified. The bay run-round line was removed, and the double junction on to the branch abolished, leaving just a single connection from the branch to the down platform line. The crossing loop was shortened at its

Having cleared the loop points, the crew of 0–6–0PT No. 9653 are about to collect the single line token in the course of running round the train in 1951. Beside the signal box is the horn of the token setting-down apparatus. To enable the fireman to see to put the hoop of the token carrier over the horn in the dark, the tip of the horn is painted white, and illuminated by the lamp on the separate post by the door to the locking room of the box. The momentum of the token carrier was killed by a rope net mesh stretched on a frame behind the horn, but by 1951 the years of impact had taken their toll, and the net had been cut so badly that it had a substantial hole in it.

J. H. Venn

southern end, cut back to the end of the up platform, and the up to down trailing crossover that had been adjacent to the South box was removed. A new two-lever ground frame, Bourne End South GF, was installed to control the points giving access to the goods yard. The simplified layout was all placed under the control of the North signal box, which was the box that had to be retained because it was adjacent to and controlled the level crossing. The North box had, however, been the less important of the two at Bourne End, and the frame was far too small to control the whole layout, simplified though it had been. The box was therefore extended at the Wycombe end so that it could take a new frame of 44 levers at 4 inch centres, fitted with vertical tappet 5-bar locking. The change-over was planned for the weekend of 28th to 30th January 1956. Services were suspended for a few days, and buses substituted. It was one of those occasions when everything seemed to go wrong. On the Saturday night when the work began, torrential rain made progress virtually impossible. Holes prepared for the new signals filled with water so quickly that it was not possible to erect the posts. Then, as wet coats were being dried in the mess van stabled in the South sidings, a Tilley lamp fell on them and set part of the van ablaze. The local fire brigade turned out, but the mess van had been made unusable, and the men had to shelter in the station. By Monday morning the station is said to have taken on the appearance of a battlefield.

The new layout at last gave Bourne End full bi-directional working on both sides of the passing loop. Indeed this was essential, in view of the fact that there was now no connection from the up platform on to the Marlow branch. The additional signals provided allowed trains to run from Maidenhead to the up platform, and from the High Wycombe direction onto the down line.

When the new 'centralised' signal box was brought into use, the question of the grading of the box came up again. The box was provisionally put into Class 3. The marks were taken on 6th March 1956 and came out at 162, so the provisional grading was confirmed, and the box formally upgraded from Class 4 (its grade since 1920) to Class 3.

During the 1956 remodelling of Bourne End, the bracket signal allowing up trains to depart from the down platform was fitted up with centre-balanced signal arms, in an attempt to improve the sighting of the signal. This arrangement did not last long, and on 11th December 1960 the signal was completely renewed. At the same time the up line down inner home signal (signals 9 and 15) was renewed, but in the form of a straight post with a disc signal attached in place of the bracket signal.

The 1960s saw a continuation of the process of modernisation, with a mixture of reduction in layouts and the upgrading of equipment. In April 1965 Cores End level crossing was equipped with lifting barriers in place of crossing gates. The crossing beside the North box was similarly converted on 26th November 1967. The days of roadside freight trains, however, had passed, and the goods yard points and the associated Bourne End South ground frame were abolished on 14th January the following year.

At Marlow, the loop line was remodelled over a period from 28th February to 20th March 1966, though the yard was closed to sundry goods traffic from 18th July of that year.

The layout at the East frame was changed yet again with the opening of the new station at Marlow in July 1967, but this proved to be another short-lived investment, for the sidings controlled by the ground frame were taken out of use on 26th July 1970 (the private siding agreement with J. Davies was terminated on 14th March).

At Bourne End even more drastic changes were made. The line northwards was closed as a through route to Wycombe on 4th May 1970 and the line was severed at Cores End crossing. Further alterations to the signalling followed in the mid summer of 1971 and the layout reduced to that of a 'basic railway' on 22nd August of that year. Bourne End signal box and all its signalling were taken out of use. A new 5-lever ground frame (with levers at 4 inch centres and 5-bar horizontal tappet locking) provided. Just two new signals

This timber-posted home signal at Marlow replaced an earlier version with smaller centre pivot arms bracketed from the main post, which performed the same functions and dated from the 1901 improvements. The signal shown had the date 1928 stamped into the post.

J. F. Russell-Smith

On the closure of Bourne End South signal box in January 1956, the up direction signal gantry was changed to the form shown here, with centre-balanced arms on the running signals. A standard ground disc signal was added between the two running signals, to signal movements from the down platform into the down sidings.The very clear 'off' indication given by the centre-balanced arms of signals 38 (shown off) and 36, is apparent in this view of No. 6115 waiting in the down platform at Bourne End with a train for Maidenhead making the cross-platform connection with the Marlow Donkey which had just arrived in the bay propelled by No. 1448, on 26th April 1959. Note the wooden boxing attached to the lower part of the post to conduct the signal operating wires to sub-platform level without the risk of injury to (or interference from) passengers.

Nick Lera

The signal bracket at the Marlow end of the down platform was renewed on 11th December 1960 by a tubular post bracket, on which the running arms were set slightly higher than on its predecessor. The sighting was, from the driver's point of view, made worse by this change, but not materially so. The signalman could not see the signal arms clearly because of the intervening footbridge, and electrical repeaters showing the position of the arms were provided in the signal box — the rectangular boxes just above the spindles of the signal arms contained the necessary electrical contacts. This picture was taken on 26th March 1961.

Roy Patterson

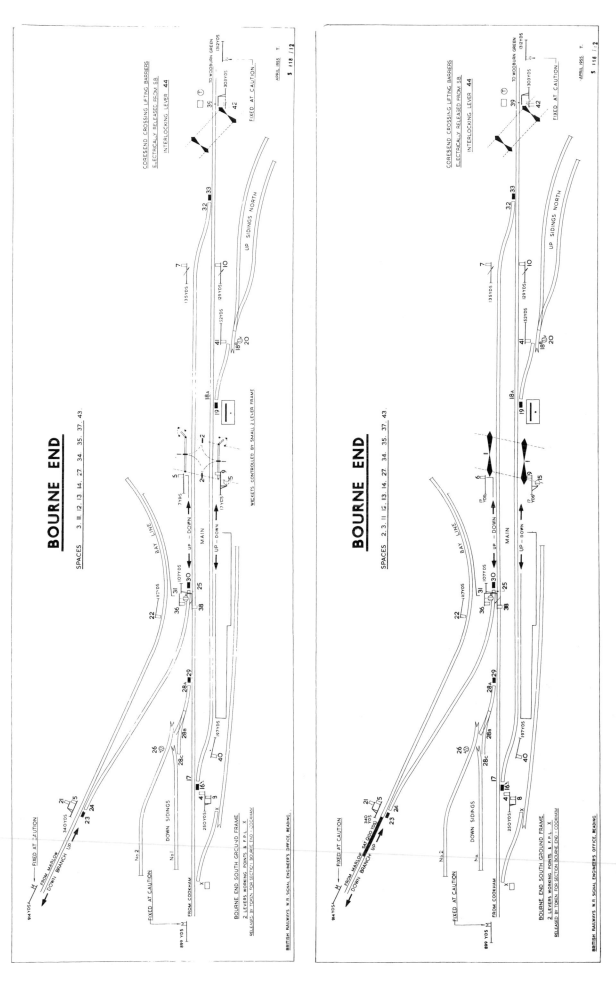

Facsimile copies of diagrams from Bourne End signal box. *Upper:* the layout from 21st April 1965, after the installation of lifting barriers at Cores End level crossing. Signal 9/15 is in the form put up on 11th December 1960, in place of the bracket signal shown in the photographs. The arrow on the posts of signals 7, 10, 38 and 40 indicated that the levers for these signals could only be pulled when a token for the section of single line ahead had been obtained by the signalman to give to the train crew. *Lower:* the layout from 26th November 1967 (installation of lifting barriers at the station level crossing and track circuit 5AT on the branch) until 14th January 1968 (when the Up Sidings North and South, together with Bourne End South ground frame, were taken out of use).

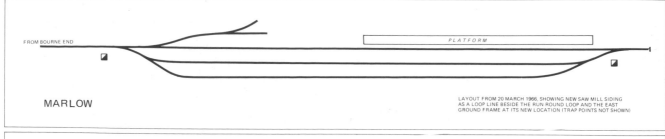

FROM BOURNE END

PLATFORM

MARLOW

LAYOUT FROM 20 MARCH 1966, SHOWING NEW SAW MILL SIDING
AS A LOOP LINE BESIDE THE RUN ROUND LOOP AND THE EAST
GROUND FRAME AT ITS NEW LOCATION (TRAP POINTS NOT SHOWN)

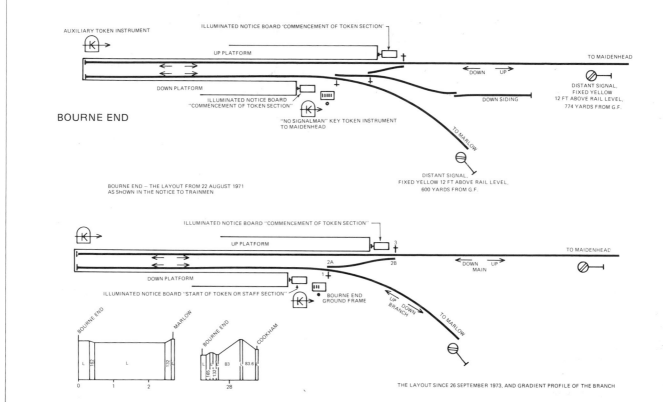

AUXILIARY TOKEN INSTRUMENT

ILLUMINATED NOTICE BOARD 'COMMENCEMENT OF TOKEN SECTION'

UP PLATFORM

TO MAIDENHEAD

DOWN   UP

DOWN PLATFORM

ILLUMINATED NOTICE BOARD
"COMMENCEMENT OF TOKEN SECTION"

DOWN SIDING

DISTANT SIGNAL,
FIXED YELLOW
12 FT ABOVE RAIL LEVEL,
774 YARDS FROM G.F.

BOURNE END

"NO SIGNALMAN" KEY TOKEN INSTRUMENT
TO MAIDENHEAD

TO MARLOW

DISTANT SIGNAL,
FIXED YELLOW 12 FT ABOVE RAIL LEVEL,
600 YARDS FROM G.F.

BOURNE END — THE LAYOUT FROM 22 AUGUST 1971
AS SHOWN IN THE NOTICE TO TRAINMEN

ILLUMINATED NOTICE BOARD "COMMENCEMENT OF TOKEN SECTION"

UP PLATFORM

TO MAIDENHEAD

2A   2B

DOWN   UP
MAIN

DOWN PLATFORM

ILLUMINATED NOTICE BOARD "START OF TOKEN OR STAFF SECTION"

1

BOURNE END
GROUND FRAME

UP   DOWN
BRANCH

TO MARLOW

BOURNE END   MARLOW   BOURNE END   COOKHAM

L   162   L   132   165 132   83   83.6

0   1   2   28

THE LAYOUT SINCE 26 SEPTEMBER 1973, AND GRADIENT PROFILE OF THE BRANCH

were installed — fixed colour light distants on each approaching line, to act as landmarks and warn of the approach to the buffer stops. Two lines were left into the station, into what had been the up and down platforms. A simple crossover between the two lines, and one lead into the down siding, were the only connections left. The existing Maidenhead-Cookham and Cookham-Bourne End token sections were abolished and a new token section ('B' configuration) worked by the 'no signalman' method brought into use between Maidenhead and Bourne End ground frame. An auxiliary key token instrument for this section was provided at the town end of the up platform at Bourne End. The ground frame points to the former down platform are released by both a token and the Marlow branch train staff. The last remaining down siding did not last long. It was taken out of use on 19th December of the same year, and levers 4 and 5 in the ground frame made spare.

Maidenhead signal box was abolished on 21st October 1974. Key token working on the line to Bourne End was retained, but now controlled from Slough panel signal box. A token instrument was provided on the platform at Maidenhead in place of the one in the signal box.

Although the Bourne End to Marlow line is now but a shadow of its former glories, the signalling arrangements are of interest because of the manner in which the line is worked, with two single line

The Marlow branch train staff, photographed in the lock at the Bourne End ground frame in 1984.

M. R. L. Instone

sections at Bourne End, and a junction between them not under the control of fixed signals. Before a train can leave Maidenhead, a token must be obtained, this action releasing one of the starting signals leading on to the branch. If a train is to proceed to Marlow, it must use the crossover at Bourne End. The points lever in the ground frame (lever No. 2) is usually left pulled over, with levers 1 and 3 normal, locking the points, so that trains normally use the down platform.

Before lever 2 can be moved, both the key token for the section from Maidenhead, and the train staff for the section from Marlow, must be inserted in locks on the frame, and lock levers No. 3 (released by the key token) and No. 1 (released by the train staff and lever No. 3 pulled over) pulled over to the 'reverse' position. When a train for Marlow has passed into the down platform, the point lever in the ground frame is restored to normal, the train staff is taken by the driver so that his train can proceed to Marlow, and the key token is placed in the instrument beside the ground frame to clear the Maidenhead-Bourne End section, which now has no train in it. Trains from Maidenhead can then work independently into Bourne End up platform until the Marlow train requires to return to Maidenhead. There are track circuit controls in the platforms at Bourne End to ensure that a key token cannot be released at Maidenhead if the platform to which the points are set at Bourne End is occupied, and the lie of the points cannot then be changed until the train carrying the token is at Bourne End.

Bourne End ground frame in 1984. Although the notice to train crew, and other BR papers, consistently refer to this as a ground frame for five levers, there are clearly spaces for six!

M. R. L. Instone

MAJOR SIGNALLING ALTERATIONS AT MARLOW FROM 1954

26/9/54 (week commencing): Marlow signal box and all associated signalling taken out of use. Two new ground frames commissioned. Marlow East G.F., a three-lever frame working the down facing points and facing point locks giving access to the down sidings, loop and sawmill sidings; released by key on a new wooden train staff. Marlow West G.F., a one-lever frame working the connection from the platform line to the loop. Frame situated beside the line adjacent to the platform end of the connection. Lever released by key on the train staff.

28/2/66: Marlow East G.F. repositioned 95 yards nearer to Bourne End. The facing connection into the loop and sawmill sidings taken out of use and the corresponding lever in the frame bolted.

20/3/66: New facing point in the single line, adjacent to the repositioned East G.F., brought into use, together with a new sawmills siding. The sawmills siding now lies alongside the loop line, which has been extended to the G.F. The sawmill siding has a stabling capacity of 300 feet, with handworked connections to the loop line at both ends.

10/7/67: Trains now commence to use a new platform via a new crossover at 2 miles 35 chains to new buffer stops at 2 miles 54 chains. The new platform is 220 ft long. The former platform and buildings taken out of use.

26/7/70: All remaining sidings formally taken out of use.

MAJOR SIGNALLING ALTERATIONS AT BOURNE END FROM 1955

11/12/55: Connection from the Bay to the Bay Loop siding removed.

18/12/55: The new 44-lever frame in the North signal box tested. The double junction on to the branch removed, and a new connection provided from the down main to the down branch.

28-30/1/56: South signal box abolished and loop shortened at London end. New ground frame provided to work the points giving access to the Up Sidings South.

1/56: Signals 36 and 38 renewed with centre pivot arms.

3/56: Wicket gate locking removed at Cores End level crossing.

6/12/58 (week commencing): Up branch home signal bracket renewed and reduced in height to 26 feet.

11/12/60: New up main down direction inner home signal (9, 15), and down main up direction starting (36, 38) bracket signal brought into use.

4/5/63: Up distant signal renewed, reduced in height to 18 feet.

29/3/65: Illuminated permanent speed restriction boards on the Marlow branch replaced by standard signs.

10-16/4/65: Double half lifting barriers and flashing road signs installed at Cores End level crossing in connection with road alterations and widening.

26/11/67: Level crossing gates at the station superseded by double half lifting barriers, closing to the road only, with flashing road lights. A new track circuit installed on the Marlow branch in rear of the up home signal bracket – 5AT.

14/1/68: The connections to the Up Sidings North and Up Sidings South spiked and clipped out of use. Bourne End South ground frame taken out of use.

30/3/68: Connection to No. 2 Down Siding removed.

9-15/5/70: Maidenhead to High Wycombe line closed beyond Cores End level crossing. Barriers at Cores End recovered. The up line from Cores End to 41 signal retained as a shunt spur, 41 signal being renewed 50 yards nearer the box with a 3 ft arm in place of the 4 ft arm. Signals 7, 10, 39, 42 and up fixed distant abolished and 32 points taken out of use. A new disc signal provided at the foot of signal 9 for shunt movements across the level crossing on to the shunt spur (former up line).

13/6/71: Stop blocks installed on the station side of the level crossing adjacent to the signal box. The shunt spur taken out of use, and signal 6, 9 and the disc at the foot of signal 9 taken away. The Marlow bay line taken out of use, points clipped, and the Up Branch to Bay and Bay Line Starting signals removed.

27/6/71: Barriers and road lights at the redundant road crossing taken away.

22/8/71: Bourne End signal box abolished and new layout controlled from Bourne End Ground Frame into use.

19/12/71: Down Siding recovered and point leading thereto replaced by plain line.

26/9/73: Ground frame connections rearranged so that both ends of the crossover are now worked by one lever. The notice board on the down platform changed to read 'Start of token or staff section'.

STATION	YEAR	Supervisory and Wages (all Grades) No.	Paybill Expenses £	TOTAL RECEIPTS £	Tickets issued No.	Season Tickets No.	Passenger Receipts including S.T. etc. £	Parcels Number No.	Parcels Receipts £	Total £	Coal and Coke "Charged" Fwd Tons	Other Minerals Fwd Tons	General Merchandise Fwd Tons	Coal and Coke "Charged" Recd Tons	Other Minerals Recd Tons	General Merchandise Recd Tons	Coal and Coke "Not Charged" (Fwd and Recd) Tons	Total Goods Tonnage Tons	Total Receipts (excluding "Not Charged" Coal and Coke) £	Livestock (Fwd and Recd) Wagons	Total Cartec Tonnage (Included in Total Goods Tonnage) Tons
Marlow Branch. Marlow.. ..	1903	14	829	20,633	61,149	*	5,389	35,129	1,952	7,341	21	102	9,603	2,393	2,080	13,486	10,305	37,990	13,292	305	7,580
	1913	14	930	17,367	56,558	276	5,630	48,818	1,917	7,547	—	116	3,448	1,866	2,994	9,584	12,100	30,108	9,820	432	3,958
	1923	14	2,369	22,747	71,719	834	10,889	34,868	2,131	13,020	90	134	915	713	1,731	4,760	13,121	21,464	9,727	480	2,170
	1929	14	2,250	19,513	51,140	1,434	8,231	32,673	1,731	9,962	9	189	870	2,871	2,891	4,073	12,540	23,443	9,551	390	2,169
	1930	14	2,273	20,046	41,213	1,419	6,736	32,995	1,847	8,583	8	57	801	3,299	5,225	5,001	11,920	26,311	11,463	278	2,135
	1931	14	2,360	17,003	34,925	1,421	5,830	29,511	1,741	7,571	—	30	589	2,320	6,168	3,654	11,601	24,362	9,432	174	1,995
	1932	14	2,365	14,328	31,114	1,394	5,281	27,700	1,567	6,848	—	44	524	2,399	3,266	3,126	11,139	20,498	7,480	116	1,764
	1933	14	2,153	12,781	30,745	1,488	5,198	25,893	1,215	6,413	—	112	523	1,595	2,717	2,618	11,280	18,845	6,368	84	1,727
	1934	14	2,263	16,005	35,098	1,612	5,690	27,830	1,432	7,122	11	75	570	2,712	6,547	2,547	9,581	22,043·	8,883	46	1,987
	1935	13	2,093	12,986	36,968	1,294	5,494	29,799	707	6,201	13	114	450	1,517	3,822	2,228	10,154	18,298	6,785	123	1,928
	1936	13	1,929	13,267	34,389	1,266	5,672	31,018	720	6,392	—	284	458	1,771	3,991	2,347	11,658	20,509	6,875	46	2,131
	1937	13	1,996	12,953	36,769	1,376	5,790	30,369	647	6,437	21	406	428	2,400	2,540	2,157	10,405	18,357	6,516	27	2,140
	1938	13	2,106	11,284	35,252	1,214	5,476	29,352	530	6,006	—	154	363	1,329	858	2,226	10,962	15,892	5,278	13	2,115
Bourne End..	1903	15	898	16,192	69,791	*	4,094	23,520	1,340	5,434	37	5,278	5,545	9,107	3,219	8,788	6,325	38,299	10,758	48	1,832
	1913	18	1,190	15,084	68,811	419	4,360	32,061	1,112	5,472	28	714	5,852	4,826	2,701	9,510	14,628	38,259	9,612	22	2,493
	1923	21	3,428	26,079	74,074	808	8,766	23,216	1,294	10,060	—	29	5,228	739	2,625	10,551	19,776	38,948	16,019	38	2,261
	1929	21	3,053	28,040	62,927	1,649	7,049	21,124	1,267	8,316	97	72	7,271	974	4,847	12,554	22,101	47,916	19,724	5	5,652
	1930	21	3,121	25,702	61,904	1,653	6,498	18,474	1,113	7,611	11	164	7,005	803	4,635	12,306	23,354	48,278	18,091	5	5,509
	1931	21	3,376	23,789	58,285	1,670	6,095	18,969	1,182	7,277	8	96	6,628	851	3,496	11,122	23,639	45,840	16,512	7	6,620
	1932	21	3,096	20,684	51,375	1,669	5,753	19,242	1,143	6,896	—	31	5,936	687	2,733	8,209	22,354	39,950	13,788	1	6,679
	1933	21	3,358	21,747	47,790	1,509	5,461	19,206	1,064	6,525	56	31	5,480	620	3,808	9,915	25,960	45,870	15,222	4	8,666
	1934	21	3,404	23,613	46,263	1,464	5,359	19,342	1,066	6,425	7	149	5,573	658	4,101	11,617	27,963	50,068	17,188	2	9,705
	1935	21	3,671	22,275	47,328	1,585	5,817	17,132	679	6,496	8	59	5,516	805	3,459	10,437	31,906	52,190	15,779	4	9,180
	1936	22	3,734	22,825	46,454	1,569	5,970	18,629	843	6,813	—	93	5,803	1,108	3,552	9,707	31,994	52,257	16,012	2	10,250
	1937	22	3,700	25,103	49,456	1,749	6,273	18,543	722	6,995	—	51	6,487	844	4,018	12,051	36,648	60,099	18,108	1	14,463
	1938	22	3,447	22,184	49,231	1,527	5,790	18,111	789	6,579	29	63	5,478	929	3,223	8,786	32,535	51,043	15,605	—	10,840

ACKNOWLEDGEMENTS

The journey through the winding avenues of research to produce this volume has been an unexpectedly long and pleasurable one, often full of surprises. Along the way we have met with much kindness, sometimes overwhelming, and we are pleased to have made many friends, in particular James and Hilda Venn. They have made us more than welcome on countless visits and fed and watered us between many tales about bull terriers and, of course (although less often!) the Marlow branch. James has been a wonderful guide, pointing us in many new directions and allowing unrestricted access to his material. This book would certainly have been the poorer without his help and trust. Bernard Wheeler, whose father was Marlow's last station master, now works at Bourne End station. He has also been extremely kind and provided no end of contacts. Bourne End historian Brian Wheals put up with numerous intrusions and gave not only his time and knowledge but also generous access to his large photograph collection. The descendants of Owen Peel Wethered and Peter Borgnis — Anthony Wethered and Cedric H. C. Borgnis — have given us support and encouragement, the former additionally writing the foreword. We owe a special thanks to Judy Gascoyne who kindly loaned her diary, thereby offering an unusually personal window on the wartime period, and Mrs. E. Hobbs who was good enough to trust us with some valuable pictures of her late husband and Marlow signal box. Mike Christensen gave up many evenings to produce a signalling appendix at extremely short notice (again!) and John Norris was good enough to check the early chapters.

Richard Rigby and Reginald Stephenson, both formerly of Greenwich Sawmills, have also been very kind and overwhelmed us with material. Mr. Rigby, in particular, has given up hours to our cause and we owe him special thanks.

We would also like to record our sincere thanks to the following: M. Anderson, A. Attewell, Mrs. Bailey, T. Bailey, K. Binks, Sean Bolan, J. Boot, A. Brooks, S. Brooks, A. Brown, Mrs. E. Brown, G. Bunce, Mrs. M. Burger, H. Burgess, 'Jock' Cairns, Roger Carpenter, the Carr family, Cyril Chalk, C. Chapman, Glenys Church, S. Clark, David Collins, John Copsey, Ian Coulson, E. Course, C. J. Crew, S. C. Crook, L. Crozier, Reg. Daniells, Mr. & Mrs. D. Davis, J. J. Davis, Colin Dawson, Mrs. Dean, G. Dean, R. Denison, J. Denton, L. Doughty, M. Downing, Mr. & Mrs. R. Emmett, M. Esau, J. M. Faulkner, Mrs. F. Funnell, S. Fletcher, C. Gammon, David Gardner, E. E. Garrett, Mrs. E. Genery, H. Goddard, R. Goodearl, Dr. R. Gulliver (for permitting the use of E. L. Mowat photographs), M. Hajwa, A. Hall-Patch, C. P. Hampshire, A. C. Harold, Chris Hawkins, D. Hill, J. Hinton, Mrs. C. Hollis, R. House, R. How, K. B. Humphrey, D. Hyde, M. R. L. Instone, D. James, D. L. James, S. C. Jenkins, Monica Jones, R. Judge, F. Keeley, Mrs. V. Keen, J. E. Kite, G. Knight, Lenny Lean, Mr. & Mrs. W. Lee, D. Leggett, Lens of Sutton, N. M. Lera, B. W. Leslie, M. Lidgley, K. Lovett, F. Lunnon, Mrs. Maddocks, E. R. Martin, J. Martin, Klaus Marx, Mr. & Mrs. K. Maslin, M. McIntyre Ure, J. Mead, J. H. Meredith, R. Miles, W. Mitchell, J. Moore, Ivor Morgan, John Norris, Fred Nottingham, R. Oakton, Mrs. Owen, M. Pardoe, G. Parsons, R. Patterson, Mr. & Mrs. P. Peyman, Douglas Quarterman, R. C. Riley, R. F. Roberts, Mrs. D. Robertson, J. H. Russell, J. F. Russell-Smith, T. Saint, G. Saunders, J. Scrace, Miss B. Serls, Mr. & Mrs. G. Shaw, A. E. Smith, D. & J. Smith, Joan Staton, A. P. Stringer, Len Stroud, W. Tame, Mrs. M. Taylor, O. G. Trill, Mrs. J. Turner, Mike Walker, B. Ware, Major S. Weaver, Peter Webber, Alan Wheeler, R. F. ('Joe') Whitelock, M. F. Yarwood, Aerofilms, Institution of Civil Engineers (W. Morris, Archivist), House of Lords Record Office, British Library, Aylesbury Record Office and Museum, Bucks Free Press, Maidenhead Advertiser, Hammer Film Productions Ltd., British Film Institute, Public Records Office, Kew, British Railways, The Railway Club, Guildhall Library, Bishopsgate Institute Library, Reading, High Wycombe and Marlow Libraries, David & Charles for use of the L & GRP photographs, Officer Commanding Grenadier Guards, and Pendon Museum.